PRAISE FOR

"Sandra Worsham has written a candid and memorable narrative of her life in Flannery O'Connor's home town of Milledgeville, Georgia: coming out as a lesbian, converting to Catholicism, and finding a life partner. Her struggles with family, church, and self constitute a compelling story that will resonate with many readers, especially those confronting issues of sexual identity and faith." **Sarah Gordon**, author of *Flannery O'Connor: The Obedient Imagination, A Literary Guide to Flannery O'Connor's Georgia, and Distances*

"In *Going to Wings*, Sandra Worsham combines a southern raconteur's charm and candor with a social anthropologist's objective awareness to tell the story of a woman's second coming-of-age as a lesbian in a deeply conservative southern town. The result is a memoir both engaging and socially significant."
--**Peter Selgin**, author of *Drowning Lessons*, winner of the Flannery O'Connor Award for Short Fiction, and *The Inventors*, a memoir.

"Sandra Worsham loves women and she loves Catholicism. The result of loving both is a dramatic struggle well worth following. Worsham tells her story--one of stunning losses and successes--with admirable style and wit, with charming innocence, and with honesty. I gobbled up this book with delight." --**Bruce Gentry**, Professor of English, Georgia College & State University, Editor of the *Flannery O'Connor Review*, and author of *Flannery O'Connor's Religion of the Grotesque*.

"'Years later I realized I had committed a murder for I had buried a part of myself.' So says Sandra Worsham in a tender and entertaining memoir about love, family, sexuality, and faith in God. This is a story about growing into life and accepting death, about standing up for yourself while not putting others down, about finding yourself by giving yourself away. I laughed and I cried. I couldn't put this book down." --**Sister Jeannine Gramick, SL,** Co-founder of New Ways Ministry, a Catholic organization working for justice and reconciliation of LGBT Catholics with the wider Church, Author of *Building Bridges: Gay and Lesbian Reality and the Catholic Church*, 2006 Laureate of the International Mother Teresa Awards for her role as a human rights activist

GOING TO WINGS

Other Works by Sandra Worsham

Essential Ingredients: Recipes for Teaching Writing
ASCD, 2001

Going to Wings

Sandra Worsham

For Erin,
Sandra Worsham

Third Lung Press

2017

Published by Third Lung Press, Hickory, NC 28601

Edited and Layout Robert Canipe

Cover Design by Letha Hawkins

Photography by Joe DeGrandis

ISBN-13: 9781548828103

"The secret of life is to find out who you are and then be it."

E.A. Robinson

DEDICATION

For Linda Worsham Waller,
My Sister and Hero

For Elizabeth "Teeny" Horne,
My Friend and Mentor

And Especially for Letha Hawkins,
My Love and My Happy Ending

CONTENTS

I.

CHAPTER ONE: THE TELLING

1975

I didn't have the courage to say the words out loud. Instead, I wrote a letter that was in my purse on the car seat beside me. It was written on notebook paper that I had folded and refolded so many times since yesterday that it had become as soft as a baby's diaper. Whispering to myself in the car, I moved my lips as I read the words again, my heart pounding as I imagined Mama in her house, looking forward to my visit, unsuspecting what it would bring.

"Dear Mama,

I hope you understand what a hard letter this is for me to write. I hate even to mention this name because I know how much you hate to hear it. But, Mama, I have been in touch with Ellen again. Four years ago when Harvill discovered our relationship and forced me to tell you about it, I know I promised to break it off and not to see her again. I told you both that I would be a good wife and maybe a mother. I was afraid you and Harvill were going to put me into the State Hospital to try to cure me of what you thought was my sickness."

As I read the words I had written in my straight-up-and-down handwriting, I realized that this was much worse than the day I told Harvill I wanted a divorce. I continued to read, pretending that I was Mama, holding the letter in front of her.

"Ellen and I want to be together. We want to buy a house here in Milledgeville and be happy and teach English and have a normal life. I have prayed about this, and it feels right to me. I want you to understand and give me your blessing. I love you, Sandra"

I tried to imagine Mama paying attention to my feelings and trying to understand. After all, she was my mother. She was the only one who would care if I bumped my funny bone or if I got a splinter. At the edge of the yard was the mimosa tree I climbed as a child. Daddy had propped a short ladder against the trunk so that I could reach the first juncture. From there I could climb higher into the tree. I never learned to shinny up the trunk like a boy, but once there, I could pull myself up and settle into the lap of the tree, where I wallowed: I put my cheek against the trunk; I stripped the fan-shaped leaves and breathed in their fresh green scent; I buried my nose in the tickly peach-scented blossoms. From my vantage point, I watched our neighborhood below- -Roy and Howard Pounds tumbling in the grass two houses over, the Negro maids walking to their jobs cleaning houses, and Sallie, my childhood best friend walking up the street to bully me once again. Mama had rescued me one day when I fell out of the tree and lost my breath. She was always somewhere close and watching, ready to come to me. She had taught me how to defend myself against Sallie, how to grab the sensitive skin under her arm and pinch hard. I had gone one step further, balled up my fist, and punched her in the mouth. Mama had been proud of me.

I folded the letter, put it back into my purse, and got out of the car, slamming the door behind me. I walked across the spring clover to the front stoop. The French door was open, and the black screen was hooked. I put my nose against the metallic-smelling metal and peered inside. Mama wasn't in the living room in her pink velour chair.

"Mama!" I called as I pressed the buzzer and looked down the shiny wooden hallway that led to my sister Linda's old room and then out the window, where I saw Mama's silhouette in the swing on the back porch, moving back and forth. She was facing the neighbor's backyard, her arms folded across her chest, her feet crossed at the ankles. She often sat there in the late afternoon and thought about how much she missed Daddy, since he had died young at fifty-seven. She had told me that Daddy was the only one she could talk to about many things. I feared that this afternoon would be something she needed Daddy for, except for one thing: she wouldn't want him to know.

A paved walkway ran around the side of the house leading to the back porch. As I got to the gate, I heard the swing chain creaking rhythmically. At the top of the steps outside the screen door, the string mop hung on a nail. As a child, I made this mop my friend. Propping the stick against a chair, the string end hanging down like damp, pungent hair, I separated the strands. In my hands the mop became a girl with long hair and a slender body.

Seeing me stump around the backyard with the mop, Daddy sawed a square face in his wood shop and nailed it up close under the hair. With a magic marker he drew on eyes, nose, and mouth, and then he nailed a stick across her chest for arms. On the stick body, Mama hung a green-and-white checkered dress with a sash. Dressed up this way by my parents, my friend looked disguised, ready to go to a Halloween party. She didn't look like the friend I saw in her, a girl whose essence I felt more than just a face with features or body with flesh.

Passing the mop, no longer with its face, I pulled open the screen door and stepped onto the porch. I sat down in the rocking chair beside the swing. The grass in the backyard was dappled in patches of shade and sun. The swing set where I used to hang by my knees was rusted, the wooden seat rotten and hanging loose on one end.

"How was your day?" I asked Mama.

"Well, I did two washes and made a lemon Jello cake and took it to Mrs. Layfield from my Sunday School class," she said. "She's shut in with a broken leg. I'm glad you came by," she said. "I was hoping you would."

I was rocking big in the chair, my feet tapping the concrete floor. Out of the corner of my eye, I saw a flash of myself as a child wearing red shorts at the swing set, my hands on the bar overhead, my feet lifted up off the swing, my hands gripping the bar tighter, the moving swing coming back and striking the top of my right foot, creating a bleeding gash, Mama rushing out the door to me. She had asked me many times not to begin a sentence with, Mama, I have something to tell you. A sentence that began that way always meant bad news. Instead, I said, "Mama, I have something I want to talk to you about. It's hard for me to explain, so I wrote it down." I took the soft paper out of my purse, unfolded it, and handed it to her.

She took the paper from my hand. The swing stopped moving as she began to read. Resting my elbows on my knees, I leaned forward, watching as her eyes moved back and forth across the lines. She had read only half, when the paper slipped from her fingers and drifted to the gray concrete like a wounded bird. She put her face into her hands, shaking her head from side to side. When she looked up, her face was distorted and her eyes wet. "I can't stay in Milledgeville if you do this," she said. "I'm going to have to move." Then she looked down and twisted her hands in her lap. "There were women like that when I was in nurses' training," she said. "Everybody talked about them. They were looked down on. The other nurses were disgusted. Do you know what those women *do*?"

The apartment I went to that day after the Telling was the one I had moved into after my divorce. At the back sliding glass door facing the street, I had set up TV trays and filled them with blooming African violets, a flower that I seemed to understand. They bloomed in many colors—pink, purple, white, red, lavender. I knew how to break off a leaf from the older plants and root it, the new baby leaves sprouting beside the mother. I knew to cut off the mother when the fuzzy baby green leaves reached the size of my thumbnail. I knew how to wean violets; yet, I had never learned how to wean myself.

In the seventh grade I had loved Mrs. Matthews. I waited for the times when she called me to her desk, when I sat beside her and smelled her perfume, her soft powdered cheek and her red lipstick close to me. When she directed the class in an oral reading of Rudyard Kipling's "If," I was enthralled as I followed the rise and fall of her delicate arms, the closed eyes and the look on her face of being lost in the poetry. I was a seventh grade girl wearing an ugly permanent wave and cat-eye glasses, totally in love with my teacher. When, at the end of the year, she moved away, I was heartbroken. I lay across my bed and sobbed as Mama stood in the doorway and said, "What's the matter with you? She's your teacher; she's not your mother." I dreamed about Mrs. Matthews for years; each time when I awoke, I cried with disappointment that we were not together again, merged as one, the way we had been in my dream. It became a dream within a dream, so that I thought, "This time's for real. This time it isn't a dream."

That night in my apartment I began to throw up. I took off my teacher clothes and threw them into the corner of the room. While it was still light outside, I put on a red tee shirt and crawled into bed. I sweated; I tossed from side to side; I ran to the bathroom and leaned my head into the toilet, again and again, my knees digging into the floor. Guilt was a black shadow with webbed bat wings that enveloped me, its fingers twining around my neck and choking off my breath. I wretched with dry heaves, and my tongue was dust.

I reached into the bedside table and took out my King James Bible. I turned on the lamp and let the Bible fall open. It opened to Psalm 139. A Bible would naturally fall open to the Psalms, I had learned in the Baptist Church, because the Psalms were exactly in the middle. As I read, I began to cry, harder and harder, heavy sobs that came from deep inside, that hurt my chest as they came. I heard my voice wail, a sound that seemed to come from somewhere else.

O Lord, thou hast searched me and known me...Whither shall I go from thy spirit...Thou hast covered me in my mother's womb...My substance was not hid from thee, when I was made in secret...thine eyes did see my substance...Search me, O God, and know my heart.

All night I pulled God to me and pushed him away. I begged him to take away the horrible feeling of shame and sorrow. I saw my mother's anguished face, and again and again I felt the words, I am Wrong, I am Wrong, I am Wrong. By morning I had promised God that I would never kiss another woman. I hung my head and cried with grief for the loss of the soft lips and smooth cheeks that I would miss. I would take back my words to my mother. I would break Ellen's heart, as well as my own. I would change myself; I would not be one of those women that my mother despised. I would make the choking feeling of guilt go away forever. It was 1975, and I was twenty-eight-years old. For the rest of my mother's life, she and I never mentioned that subject again. My life was divided into two parts, before and after the Telling.

II.

CHAPTER TWO: BLANK SPACES

"I love you as certain dark things are loved, secretly, between the shadow and the soul."
— Stephanie Perkins, *Anna and the French Kiss*

O n July 20, 1969, the day the astronauts first stepped on the moon, I married Harvill Holsenbeck at the First Baptist Church in Milledgeville, Georgia. I did not know that, three weeks earlier, the Stonewall riots had occurred in New York City, or that they had anything to do with me.

The Baptist Church was across the street from Memory Hill Cemetery, where my Daddy was buried on Father's Day in 1966, when I was nineteen and my sister, Linda, was fifteen. Liberty Street connected the Georgia College & State University campus to the gates of the cemetery. Local history states that the college sat on the former location of a state prison, and that the street was named "Liberty" because the only way to escape the prison was death. When I heard that story, I imagined the thin white souls of the convicts flying above the street towards the cemetery, a sound like dissonant violins leading them to freedom. The old cemetery had shaded paths with low-hanging Spanish moss. On one end beside a path was the grave of Flannery O'Connor, always covered with coins and slips of paper containing poems or prayers left there by pilgrims. At the back end of the cemetery were the unmarked graves of slaves containing chains buried into the cement slabs. Local folklore had it that one chain meant born a slave and lived a free man; two chains meant born and lived a slave but died a free man; and three chains meant born, lived, and died a slave. Halfway through the cemetery, between the slave graves and Flannery O'Connor's, was my family's plot. I never thought that Daddy would be buried there and not giving me away on my wedding day.

Daddy had gone for weeks with unbearable dizziness, having to stay home from the barbershop where he worked. He could hardly bear for us to walk beside his bed as he lay there, the windows open on the hot summer days. Even a breeze blowing out the sheer white curtains made his head swim and the room float in circles around him. The doctors sent him to Augusta to the Medical College in an effort to find out what was wrong. Home from Georgia Southern for the summer after my freshman year, I rode in the backseat of our pink '57 Chevrolet station wagon where Daddy lay stretched out for the ride. I sat on the hump in the middle, a bucket containing ice water beside me on the floor, the ice rattling and the water sloshing as Mama drove over the bumpy roads. Again and again, I submerged a face cloth into the water, squeezed it, and wiped Daddy's face and his bald head. With each movement the car made, sweat broke out on his forehead and his upper lip. His eyes fluttered, and he moaned. Although my Daddy, the Baptist Deacon, would never have said it, I knew that this was the trip from hell for him.

Finally settled in the hospital room, he suffered for days as the white uniformed staff put him on elevators to go up and down for various tests, rolling him on a gurney down the hall. It was after one of those tests that he had a massive heart attack, a Code Blue causing doctors and staff to rush to his room, to no avail. He was gone. Several days before he died, he had said to Harvill, "Take care of Sandra for me." Now Daddy's brother, my Uncle Roy, was going to walk me down the aisle and say in response to the preacher's question, "Who gives her away, " "Her mother and I." Such a strange custom that seems to me now. A bride is never her own person but is given from her father and mother to her husband.

Earlier on that hot day of my wedding, I had fixed Mama's hair as she sat on a straight chair in front of me in her living room. Standing behind her, I could see our reflection in the mirror over the television set. Her hair was rolled on pink foam curlers, and as I took the curlers out one by one, her silver hair curled around my finger. I looked at the two of us, my head above her head, her hair as silver as mine is now, my then dark hair brown and cut short. As I brushed out Mama's hair, I looked around the room, trying to memorize the way it looked that day. A newspaper lay across the piano bench where my sister Linda and I sang "Whispering Hope," Mama and Daddy's favorite hymn. Linda sang soprano, and I sang alto, and Daddy said we sounded like the gospel singers on the radio. Behind me was Daddy's recliner where he sat and watched "Gunsmoke" on TV and drew rabbits and horses on a paper pad. In the middle of the room was where Daddy sometimes set up his amplifier and played his steel guitar, using the slide to make the Hawaiian sounds that he liked. The name of his band was "Harvey Worsham and the Hawaiian Stringsters." Mama always sat in her chair beside the sofa where she often watched Billy Graham on TV. Sitting with Mama in the living room while she watched Billy Graham made me feel guilty, as if I had something to hide.

"Tonight might not turn out like you think," Mama said to me, looking at me in the mirror. "You might feel like you want to get up and take a bath."

I moved to the side so that she would not be able to see my reflection. Oh Lord, I thought. Surely she is not going to bring this up now. "Don't worry, Mama," I said. "I'll figure it out."

Harvill and I had had sex before marriage. It happened while we were students together at Georgia Southern in Statesboro. In high school we had parked at Clover Hill where all the kids went to make out in their cars. We kissed and hugged and petted on top of our clothes, but I always drew the line at anything further. But in college all the other girls in the dorm were talking about who had done it and who hadn't, and it seemed to me that it might be time.

One night Harvill and I parked beside the lake near my dorm. It was a dark, isolated place, and we had been making out when I let Harvill put his fingers inside my underpants. It's strange to me now that I don't remember more, but the only thing I remember about that night is the feeling I had. All the other girls had described how exciting their first time had been, how they had thrown their heads back and moaned. But all I felt was a tender broken feeling, something mixed with rawness and guilt. I was dry, and Harvill's fingers were fumbling. I thought there was something wrong with me that I didn't lose myself and moan, that I really didn't feel anything at all. But once we had had sex, I believed that I had no choice but to marry Harvill. To marry someone else would mean that I would commit adultery. The Baptist Church had no confession with which to wipe the slate clean.

Years later people would ask me what I saw in Harvill or why I ever married at all. People who asked that didn't understand how it was to grow up in a small town in the deep South right smack dab in the middle of the Bible Belt, where the first two of the Ten Baptist Commandments were 1) Don't drink, dance, or gamble and 2) Don't have sex before marriage. But it would also be shameful not to marry at all. Betsy Lerner, in *The Bridge Ladies*, writes, "Marriage was essential for our mothers. They feared for us going forward in life without the same protection they believed came with marrying a Jewish man." But I believed that not marrying meant that no man would have you. You would be an Old Maid. I didn't think it really mattered who I married as long as I married. I lay on the bed in my dorm room and turned the pages of *Brides Magazine*, imagining the wedding, the goal.

The worse shame, I believed, would be to get pregnant before marriage. It never occurred to me back then that there could be a shame worse than that—the unspeakable one. The word *lesbian* would have been the equivalent of the word *whore* or *murderer*, something dark and sordid, something that meant you were rotten to the core, something that meant you should throw yourself in front of a train rather than ruin your family. I am not exaggerating; I speak the Truth as it was in my town. Today rumors emerge about the close relationships Flannery O'Connor had with the women she wrote letters to—"A" and Maryatt Lee from her collected letters, *The Habit of Being*, edited by Sally Fitzgerald. But Flannery would never have entertained such thoughts, for to do so would have made her soul unacceptable to the Father. It never once occurred to me that I had a choice not to marry. From the toy stoves and child-sized vacuum cleaners to the baby dolls from Santa Claus, marriage and family was the goal to be reached. Any man would do as long as he was acceptable to my parents. Harvill's mother and mine had been in nurses' training together and were friends.

At the church on my wedding day we got dressed in the same room where I had dressed for my baptism at age nine. I got baptized because Preacher Hughston came into our Sunday School class and said it was time, and because Judy Brown did. The white gowns made from sheets still hung in the closet in that room. I could still smell the chlorine wafting up from the baptismal pool and remembered the feeling of my head going backwards down into the clear blue, the sound of the water splashing as I rose to new life.

My wedding day was the second time that I had walked down that aisle in a white dress. The last time was when I did what most Baptist girls do, became a member of Girls' Auxiliary, the G.A.'s, and completed my forward steps—first Maiden, then Lady-in-Waiting, and then Princess. When I was crowned Queen, I walked down that aisle to "Pomp and Circumstance" at the G.A. Coronation. That night, instead of my white bouquet, I carried the Bible between my palms, left hand on bottom, right hand on top. Once on stage, I recited the words to Proverbs 31:10-31: "Who can find a virtuous woman, for her price is far above rubies. The heart of her husband doth safely trust in her..."

As I walked down the aisle to "Here Comes the Bride" on Uncle Roy's arm, Harvill stood at the front of the church, his dark eyes serious as always. The organist had tried to talk me out of the "Wedding March" because he said it was from an opera in which the marriage didn't last. But to change the music would have changed my dream of myself, walking down the aisle of that church in my white dress to that music towards my future husband. In the front of the church Harvill looked like a statue of a little boy. I had promised him that I would not break up with him the way that three girls before me had. I thought that I was the one who would make him happy.

The moment in the wedding that I remember more than any other is the lighting of the unity candle, the two candles burning on each side of an unlit candle. We stood at the candelabra and each lifted the lit candle on our side. We then lit the center candle together, symbolizing the part in the Bible that says, "A man shall leave his parents and cling to his wife." But when Harvill blew out his own single candle, he accidentally blew out the Unity candle as well, which he then re-lit it with a cigarette lighter from his pocket.

As we drove out of town toward Jekyll Island for our honeymoon, I looked down at my hand on the seat between us, the wedding ring on my finger, and I felt strangely sad, as if something was ending instead of beginning.

I had packed in my suitcase the white negligee I bought for our first night as a married couple. As I bathed slowly in the bathroom, Harvill waited for me in the bedroom of the Buccaneer Hotel. When I opened the bathroom door and stepped out, instead of looking up at me, as I had imagined, he was sitting on the edge of the bed smoking a cigarette, watching the small black-and-white television set in the room. The smoke from his cigarette curled in the air in front of his face. I sat on the bed beside him and looked at the television screen. The astronauts were stepping on the moon for the first time, and we heard the words, "One small step for man. One giant leap for mankind."

I had planned my wedding day, but I had never planned beyond that. The goal was the wedding, and I don't think it had occurred to me that after the wedding, I had to be married. In September, 1969, I started teaching at Jones County High School in Gray, Georgia. I taught eighth grade reading— boys who squirted one another with the chalkboard cleaner and girls who polished their fingernails and put on lipstick at their desks. I wore love beads around my neck, and on my bulletin board was an American flag with a peace sign emblazoned on the star field. The principal, an old fart with a bald head and a sour disposition, didn't like me. He said I didn't plan.

But I did. I used Simon and Garfunkel to teach poetry. I gave the students the words, and then I played the album as they followed along: from "Dangling Conversation," "And you read your Emily Dickinson, and I my Robert Frost, and we mark our place with the bookmarkers, and measure what we've lost." Then students wrote stories about the losses they had had in their lives. They read E.A. Robinson's "Richard Cory" as I played the Simon and Garfunkel version in class: "And I worked in his factory, and I cursed the life I'm living and I cursed my poverty, and I wished that I could be Richard Cory." Then the students wrote about someone they wished they could change places with.

At home I tried to learn to be domestic, to fit into the role I had imagined for myself, to become the woman on TV happily vacuuming, but my head was always somewhere else. Harvill and I bought a copper-colored double-wide trailer and put it on Holsenbeck land down the hill from his parents. One of the rooms in the house I claimed for mine and put my books and my records and guitar in it. During the afternoons before Harvill got home from his job as a Social Worker at the Family and Children's Services, I went to my room and smoked and sang Joan Baez songs on my guitar, sad ballads about love and loss. Then I played Peter, Paul, and Mary and wrote in my journal. I experimented with ways to make housecleaning more interesting to me: dusting on Monday, vacuuming on Tuesday, cleaning the bathrooms on Wednesday, the kitchen on Thursday. It seemed useless to me, to be mopping or wiping counters when I could be reading or writing.

One night when we were watching television in the living room, the doorbell rang. Because of his Social Anxiety Disorder (SAD,) Harvill got up and went to the bathroom as he always did when company came. I turned on the porch light and opened the door. Standing there was a young man wearing a suit and holding a big briefcase. "Good evening, Ma'am," he said, nodding his head. The porch light flashed in his slick black hair. I was irritated that a salesman would come to the door after dark. If I lived alone, this would have frightened me. "I'm sorry to bother you," he said, "but this is my last day in Milledgeville, and your neighbor down the street suggested that you might be interested in what I have to offer before I leave town. Mrs. April Foster? She says you might be interested." I barely knew Mrs. Foster, and I was irritated that he was dropping names.

"Come in," I said to him. "What are you selling?" I asked as I motioned for him to sit down on the red-flowered chair that went with the sofa. "Harvill, come on," I called out. "A man is here selling something."

The man had opened up his case and held up a picture of the Gerber baby. "Do you know who this is?" he asked as I sat down and crossed my leg.

"It's the Gerber baby," I said.

The toilet flushed, the bathroom door opened, and Harvill came into the room, nodded to the man, and sat down beside me on the sofa.

"Do you know who this is?" the man turned to Harvill and asked again. Harvill looked at him and wouldn't answer.

"I told you the Gerber baby, so go ahead," I said.

The man was selling photographs of the first eight years of our children's lives. "But I'm not pregnant," I said to him. "We haven't even thought about starting a family yet."

"Don't you want a family?" the man asked.

It was true that I did imagine mine and Harvill's future with children—babies like the dolls I still had, children with Harvill's dark eyes. The man took out an album and showed page after page of children, holding puppies, tossing a ball, sitting with arms folded, lying in a crib playing with feet, sitting in a highchair; then pages of family pictures, groups of three, four, five and larger pictures with children and grandparents across generations. I looked at the photographs and at Harvill, and I could begin to imagine how our lives would be as we filled in the blanks in the family tree. Harvill sat and listened but wouldn't express an opinion.

"What do you think?" I asked him.

"Whatever you want," he said, shrugging, then drawing on his cigarette and putting it out in the ashtray. We ended up buying all the pictures. But the album stayed on the shelf in the laundry room, along with all the paperwork that went with it, while I continued to take my birth control pills.

In the evening when I came home from teaching all day, I wanted to write; I did not want to have sex. I always had other things I wanted to do more. But every day, it seemed, Harvill tried. I began to feel that I didn't fit into the role I was trying to play. I became my mop friend, dressed up in a green checkered dress with a sash, a wooden plank on my face with drawn-on features.

I looked in the newspaper ads and found a meeting of the National Organization for Women. It was being held in one of the older historic homes downtown. One night I told Harvill that I was going to the meeting. He shrugged and said, "Whatever!" At the meeting were about twenty women sitting in folding chairs, chatting noisily. At one point in the meeting I stood and asked if any of the other women there besides me were tired of being maids. I told them that I didn't understand why, when my husband and I both worked, it was my job to do the cooking and cleaning. When I had finished, the women applauded. On my way home I decided what I was going to do.

The next day I made a list of household chores. I included mowing the yard, because that was the only job that Harvill took responsibility for. This was my list: (1) dust, (2) vacuum, (3) clean the bathrooms, (4) clean the kitchen, (5) cook, (6) do the laundry, (7) empty the trash, and (8) cut the grass. A total of eight chores. After supper we were sitting at the dining room table smoking cigarettes. "Harvill, I have something I need to talk to you about," I said, putting my cigarette out in the ashtray. "I'm having a hard time understanding why it is my job to do all the household chores, even though I work outside the home the same way that you do." I realized as I heard myself say "work outside the home" that I sounded as if I were quoting from a book or a magazine, as if I had rehearsed my words ahead of time.

Harvill laughed.

"I would really appreciate it if you would help me with some of these," I said, and I laid the paper with my list on the table in front of him. "These are the things that have to be done, and I need some help. I can't do it all." As I said this, I was thinking to myself that those were not *my* chores and he shouldn't see it as helping *me*, but I didn't go that far. "In fact," I said, "I would appreciate it if you would choose four."

Harvill put out his cigarette and jumped up, almost turning his chair over. He got a beer out of the refrigerator, turned to me and said, "That's bullshit." Then he walked back to the table, picked up the list, and threw it into the trash. "That's what I think of your Women's Liberation meeting," he said, as he slammed out the back door. I threw the dirty dishes into the sink and walked through the living room. I imagined myself picking up my car keys and purse and getting in my car and driving somewhere. But I didn't know where to go. The next morning when Harvill went to the kitchen to have his cereal, the supper dishes were still in the sink, and I had already left to drive to school.

My classroom was halfway down a dusty hall that jutted out from the main building and had a separate entrance. In the mornings I parked in the lot outside my hall and went straight to my room without having to go by the main office. My room was on the left. Also on the left four rooms farther down was another English teacher that I had met named Ellen who was married to a science teacher named Ray, whose classroom was in another part of the building. Sometimes during lunch and after school I sat in the faculty lounge near the office and smoked with Ellen and Ray. And sometimes Ray wasn't in there, and Ellen and I talked alone.

She was intense, one of those people who catch your eye and then you can't look away. She seemed to have an aura around her that I didn't know how to describe. I wanted to be where she was, and I found myself trying to be in the lounge when I knew that she would be there. During lunch I could hear her coming down the hall. She wore tall Aigner boots with heels that assertively pounded the wooden hallway. As she passed my room, she threw up her hand and said "Hey." I often picked up my purse and hurried after her, feeling inside for my cigarette case.

One day when I entered, she was alone sitting at one end of the green sofa, using the large orange ceramic ashtray on the coffee table in front of her. I sat down at the other end of the sofa. I already had my green-and-brown felt case in my hand, and I opened it and took out my pack of Salems, clicked my green Bic lighter, lit my cigarette, and took a big drag. "Oh, that's good," I said. "I've been wanting that all day." She wore a wide leather watchband. She was smoking Winstons. Her hair was brown, straight and wispy, falling to her shoulders. She pushed it behind her ears and with her thumb and forefinger took a fleck of tobacco from her tongue and flipped it into the air. Her leg was crossed, and the toe of her boot almost touched my leg.

It was the week after the Christmas holiday, and I was disappointed about the way Christmas had turned out. Christmas was a time I looked forward to all year. When I was a child, Christmas night made me sad because it meant I had to wait a whole year for Christmas to come again. Getting married and moving out of my childhood home did not change this feeling. Christmas morning meant going over to Mama's house early. My sister Linda and her husband were there, and we followed the same script we had followed for years: Mama met us at the door wearing her apron. Everyone put presents under the tree, and we went to the kitchen for coffee and doughnuts. Then we went to the living room, and Linda and I sang Christmas carols at the piano. After we sang, Mama recited the Christmas story: "And there were in the same country shepherds abiding in the field keeping watch over their flocks by night. And lo…" She recited it the way she recited "Hiawatha" and "Abu Ben Adhem" and all the other poems she had learned in the one-room schoolhouse where she grew up in Dublin, Georgia. She stared into space and said the words as if she were reading them from her mind. After the reciting of the Christmas story, we began to open presents, one by one. "Who is going to play Santa Claus?" Mama said, and one of us began to pass out the presents. As soon as everyone had presents around their feet, Mama said, "All right, who's going to go first?" and we began, one at the time opening presents, taking turns. It lasted a long time, and it was the moment I looked forward to all year.

But that Christmas as Harvill and I were getting dressed to go to Mama's, he asked, "How long do we have to stay?" and he was grumpy driving over. It put a damper on my day. And during the opening of the presents, he shook his foot and bit his fingernails, acting nervous. I could see Mama looking at him and wondering what was wrong with him, and I was embarrassed.

"Did you have a good holiday?" Ellen asked, stubbing out her cigarette. I rolled my cigarette ash into a point in the ashtray.

"It was ok," I said, shrugging. "Sometimes my husband can be a real asshole."

She laughed. "Tell me about it," she said. I couldn't tell if what she had said was an expression, like "Girl, I know what you mean," or if she was really asking me to tell her. But when I looked up at her, she was looking at me and waiting, as if she really wanted to know.

"Well, let's say that marriage isn't turning out the way I thought it would."

She looked over her shoulder, being sure we were alone. "Imagine how it would be if you had to work with him all day and then go home with him at night too."

"I would hate that," I said. My hand was resting on the top of my brown leather purse between us, and I was looking out the window when I felt her hand on top of mine. She didn't leave it there but a moment, in a comforting way of making connection, but it surprised me, and I looked at her. She was gazing at me, and I swallowed hard and looked away. Out the window students were climbing onto buses, the bright colors of their clothes making a wash as I turned my head back to her.

I put my cigarette case back in my purse, took out my car keys, and stood to leave. "Speaking of which," I said, "now I've got to go fix supper. Why is it that cooking supper is always my job, even though we both work?"

She quietly looked up at me, and as I left, her eyes burned into my back. Something had changed, and the world became off-balance. As I walked across the parking lot to my car, I wondered why I became self-conscious around her, why her direct gaze made me so discombobulated. All she did was put her hand on mine the way somebody at church might touch your shoulder. Nothing was strange about that gesture, but as I drove home, I held the steering wheel with my knee and lay my left hand in my lap on top of my right, bringing back the moment.

The next morning before classes started, Ellen came into my classroom. I heard her boots on the wood floor before I saw her and felt my heart start to race. When she came into my room, wearing a chartreus sweater with a brown scarf and leather jacket, I was straightening the desks. She walked over to me and put her purse down on one of the desks. Her head tilted forward, she looked at me with that unsettling gaze.

"You ok?" she asked, her voice soft and intimate, and I felt a sensation between my legs and drew in my breath. I couldn't return her gaze, and I turned, walked to my desk, and began to straighten a stack of books. She walked towards me and said, "Ray and I were wondering if you and Harvill could come to our house for dinner Friday night?"

Before I even answered, I knew that we were going. Harvill was going to hate it, the way he always hated having to go anywhere, but I didn't care.

On the way to Ellen's and Ray's house on Friday night, as I expected, Harvill was grumpy. As we waited at a stoplight, he gunned the motor with his right foot and held the brake with his left. When the light changed, the car lunged forward.

Ellen and Ray lived at Lake Sinclair in a green single-wide trailer in a stand of woods. We pulled into their yard and parked in the shade of a tall pine tree. Nearby, the lake shone like silver. Two concrete block steps led up to their door. When Ellen opened the door, she was wearing a blue apron tied around her waist. Harvill stood behind me.

"Come in," she said. Then she looked at Harvill, "Ray's in the back yard grilling the steaks. Go on out and introduce yourself." As Harvill went out the back door, he took his cigarettes out of his shirt pocket.

In the kitchen Ellen made us Tom Collins with gin and mix from a tall green bottle. She stood at the sink tearing lettuce into bowls. "Can I help?" I asked.

She gave me three cucumbers. "You can peel and slice these," she said.

As I prepared the cucumbers, she stood beside me with the lettuce. In the oven, potatoes baked. I peeled the cucumbers, letting the peels fall into the garbage disposal side of the sink. Ellen brought several bottles of dressing out of the refrigerator and then picked up her drink and leaned against the counter facing me. The smoky aroma of the steaks wafted into the house.

Ellen leaned forward, clicked her glass to mine, and said, "To new friendships."

"To new friendships," I said.

"Let's go sit in here," she said. I sat down on the sofa in the living room, and she went to the record player and put on an album of classical guitar. I was feeling warm and woozy from the drink, all my senses heightened.

"So, how are you?" she asked me. But before I could answer, Ray and Harvill came in the door, Ray holding a plate with the steaming steaks.

Throughout dinner, Ray asked Harvill questions about his job as a social worker. Harvill's face was red, and he was shaking his leg under the table. He and Ray had been drinking beer, and Harvill was more talkative than usual, talking about Welfare and Food Stamps and sounding like a racist. Embarrassed, I looked at Ellen across the table, trying to make eye contact with her so that my eyes could say, You see what I have to put up with? After dinner, Ellen and I washed the dishes, and Harvill and Ray went outside and smoked. I could see them out the window facing the lake. As Ellen moved back and forth drying dishes and putting away leftovers, she touched me on my arm or my back. By the time Harvill came back in, ready to go, my muscles were so tense and my senses so heightened that I was ready to leave, just to get relief.

I thought about Ellen all weekend, replaying in my mind every part of our evening with them. I asked Harvill how he liked them and if he had had a good time.

He shrugged. "It was all right," he said.

On Monday at school Ellen asked me if I wanted to come home with her for a drink after school. Ray had driven his own car and would be staying late at school to tutor some students. I said yes. I followed behind her from Gray to Milledgeville and then along the road to the lake. She pulled into her yard and parked in the shade, and I parked beside her.

Inside, she went to the kitchen and took out the tall green bottle of Tom Collins mix and poured gin into each ice-filled glass and then the green fizzy mixture. I noticed that she had violets in her window, and I touched the fuzzy leaves softly. "You have to have the right window," she said. "Otherwise, they won't bloom."

We took our drinks and sat in the living room; she put on a Neil Diamond record, and "Sweet Caroline" began to play. "Hands touching hands, reaching out, touching you, touching me." I told her about my private room in our house where I kept books and records and went to be alone. We talked about our favorite books—*Franny and Zooey* and *The Little Prince*. We smoked cigarettes, and much of the time we looked at one another, got embarrassed, blushed, looked down. Out the window I saw a flock of geese land on the water and then waddle up onto the grass. I told her the geese were there, but she didn't answer and just looked at me. When Ray's car pulled into the driveway, I got up to leave. She hugged me goodbye at the door and said, "I'm glad to have a friend." As she said "friend," the back door flew open, and Ray was standing there. We pulled back and he gave us a funny look, then pushed past us and went down the hall.

Over the next several days we passed in the hall and smoked in the faculty lounge where there were also other teachers. Ray was often in there too. Then one Friday Ellen told me that Ray had to be out of town to go visit his mother, and she asked me to come out on Saturday. She said she wanted me to help her go through some books and records she was getting rid of, to see if I wanted any. On Friday night I told Harvill that I was going.

Usually on Saturday Harvill worked in the yard and I worked in the house, either grading papers, or writing, or doing that thing that I hated, cleaning up the house. In the middle of the day we had hamburgers for lunch, the real kind, fat ones made out of hamburger meat that I had shaped into patties. That Saturday I made the patties and the burgers, called Harvill in to eat, and after we finished, I told him that I was going to help Ellen. He went back into the yard to finish cutting back the shrubbery.

As I drove to the lake, I couldn't wait to get there. Mama would have said that I was too attached, and she would have been suspicious. She said that I always did that, that my friends got too tight a hold on me.

As usual, Ellen fixed Tom Collins in tall glasses. She handed mine to me and clicked hers to it, making a high-pitched tinkling sound. "Here," she said, "I've got the record albums on the floor. I'm getting rid of these."

We sat down on the floor and began looking through the albums. She said something funny, and we laughed. Then we looked at each other and laughed again, then smiled. Suddenly we were hugging, feeling close. When we pulled back to change sides, her lips brushed mine, then a quick kiss, then a long kiss. A bright light went off in my head. We kissed some more. I was wet between the legs and throbbing. I was confused. This was not right. But yet, it was. I got up and paced the room. Of course! This is it! I thought. But I did not know what *it* was, and I think that Ellen was as surprised as I. I went to her and hugged her and kissed her again, then walked in circles around the room.

By the time I went home, everything had changed. I couldn't think about anything but Ellen, her soft face against mine, her silky hair hanging over her intense eyes, the feel of her lips on mine.

All we thought about the next week was how we could arrange to be together. We sent folded and stapled notes to each other down the hall by students. I couldn't wait until school was over each day. Thank God, Ray was tutoring late most days. I learned that Ellen played the guitar, and I loved to hear her play "Malagueña." She played it loud and tough, her lips pulled tight, her hair hanging over her eyes, her head bent over the guitar. The sound rose to a frenzy, and I was lost in the sound and in my lust for her. Yes, lust; that was what I was feeling. My underpants were wet and I was so drawn to her that I hurt and throbbed. I should have been worried and puzzled about what was wrong with me, but all I knew was the want and the pleasant hurting.

Each day I moved through the day in the fog and the longing. On the third day after she first played "Malagueña," we both knew that we couldn't stand the intensity any longer. The minute we arrived at her trailer and opened the door, we did not go to the kitchen for drinks, we did not light cigarettes, we began kissing as soon as we got inside the door. She led me down the hall to the bedroom, and we fell across the bed kissing and touching and reaching under our clothes to touch. It seemed like only thirty minutes had passed when suddenly she looked at the clock and said, "Oh shit! Ray," and we tried to straighten ourselves before I left. The bright light of the afternoon shocked me, and as I drove down the road toward the highway, I was lost in the world of Ellen. I barely noticed as Ray passed me on the road. It didn't even seem important that he would wonder why I was there so late.

Harvill was home when I got there, and he was mad that supper wasn't ready, wasn't even started. "Sorry," I said. "I had some students..." and then I turned on the oven and took out a frozen pizza.

The next few months were filled with lust, sneaking around, lying, trying to arrange ways to be together. We got to school early before anyone else and locked ourselves in the faculty bathroom, kissing and touching. When we heard the other teachers begin to come, we straightened ourselves, washed our hands, flushed the toilet, put on lipstick, and went to our classrooms. All day I was filled with more lust than any of the kids with puberty in my classroom.

In the afternoon we stayed late in the same bathroom. One afternoon we heard the janitor rattle the doorknob, and we called out, "Just a minute!" and we gave him time to leave before we came out and went to our cars. We were taking risks. People were going to suspect. We sent students back and forth with folded notes on notebook paper, stapled, love notes, passionate love notes, carried in students' unknowing hands. There never seemed to be a break from the lust. Occasionally we asked ourselves, "What does this mean? Does this mean that we are gay?" We wouldn't dare say the L word, an ugly word. We decided that we were not gay but that this was a fluke, two women who happened to fall in love. We couldn't imagine being that ugly thing, and so we turned it into something else.

One night when Ray was out, I told Harvill that I was going to the grocery story, that I had forgotten a few things. I drove as fast as I could to the lake. As I drove, I imagined the moment when Ellen would open the door and I would fall against her warm body and feel her face, her lips, her breasts, all of her. I looked at my watch when I got there. I had to remember that I told Harvill I had gone to the grocery store; it had to be the right length of time. We drank down two Tom Collins fast. We played "Sweet Caroline" loud and danced in the middle of the room, hands touching hands, holding, clinging.

When I had to leave, I drove toward the highway, my foot pressing the accelerator hard. I was imagining what I would tell Harvill when the shock hit me. I had flown straight into the highway without seeing the stop sign. I slammed on brakes, and the car spun in a circle. My car faced the opposite direction, toward Atlanta. There were no cars coming either way on this always busy highway. I was not dead; I had not killed anyone. Slowly I turned in the road facing south.

When I got into town, I pulled into the Piggly Wiggly parking lot and rushed inside. I bought a loaf of bread and a bag of sugar. I grabbed a few cans of pork and beans. When I got home, I walked in the door calling out, "Sorry! The line was ridiculous. A woman in front of me had food stamps. I thought they'd never finish checking her out. What can they buy with food stamps anyway?" I asked, distracting him.

One Friday night I was lying on the floor in the living room watching Kojak with Harvill. When the commercial came on, Harvill got up to go to the bathroom, and while he was back there, the phone rang, and he answered. When he came back into the living room, I knew that something was wrong. His face was red, and he looked as if he had received bad news. I was afraid somebody had died. He stood in the doorway and looked down at me. I waited and then asked, "What's happened?"

"That was Ray. He said... He said... These are his exact words: 'Your wife's been having sex with my wife.'"

Harvill stared down at me. I took in a deep breath and held it. "He found your disgusting 'love' letters," he said. He looked at me as if I were a piece of dog poop lying on the floor.

"Harvill, I'm sorry," I said, looking up at him. Then I looked down at my hands twisting in my lap and said, almost in a whisper, "I'm in love with her."

"Shit!" he said, lighting a cigarette, flipping the lighter three times to make it light. Then he tossed the lighter onto the table and took a deep drag. "What does this mean? That you're a goddam lesbian?"

I sat there with my head down. "I don't think so," I said.

Harvill paced back and forth above me. I put my hands over my face.

"Well, here's what you're going to do," he yelled down at me. "You're going to call your mother and tell her."

I looked up at him, terrified.

"And if you don't, then I'm going to. Take your choice. And I mean tonight. Right now. This minute."

I called her. It was like the many nights when I was a child lying in my bed worrying. Like the night at age eleven when I was worried because my older cousin Harley had kissed me on the lips, and I was guilty, thinking I had done something wrong, needing forgiveness. I went to her side of the bed and asked her if she could come lie down with me. She came, and I told her that Harley and I had kissed like movie stars. She patted the covers, "Well, if you don't ever do anything any worse than that, I won't worry about you." But I didn't feel forgiven. God wasn't enough. It was only Mama who could make me feel forgiven, who could make everything all right.

Only this time she couldn't. I was an adult, and I was not sorry. I could not give up Ellen. I now knew what love was. People always said, "When you are really in love, you will know it." I had never felt that certainty with Harvill. I didn't know how I was supposed to feel, how other women felt about their husbands. Now that Ellen was in my life, I finally knew the feeling people had described. It was true: when you are in love, you will know it! Harvill wanted Mama to be my punishment. He wanted her to talk some sense into me.

I heard the wheels of Mama's car on the gravel driveway. A serious thing had happened that had to be dealt with, a night of sickness.

Like the night years ago in my childhood when Mama and Daddy got up in the middle of the night to go to Aunt Eva's house because Aunt Eva had been, as Mama said when she leaned down and whispered to me, "drinking whiskey."

The doorbell rang, and Harvill let Mama in. She was carrying a clear plastic grocery sack with her blood pressure instrument in it and her black Bible. In her other hand was her small train case for staying overnight. I was still sitting cross-legged on the floor. As she walked into the living room, Harvill pointed down at me, as if to say, There's the dead cockroach, or Look where somebody threw up.

Mama walked to the dining room table and put down her sack and the suitcase. "Where's the oatmeal?" she asked Harvill. "I'm making oatmeal." Oatmeal meant somebody was sick. I had come down with a shameful illness.

As Harvill went to the kitchen to get the oatmeal out of the cabinet, I got up. I was stiff from being in that position for so long. I went to the dining room table and sat down. Mama was not looking at me but began to look in the cabinet for a boiler. I was six again. I was closed up in a dark room at the back of the house, being punished. I had told Linda to say Smart, Fella, Fella, Smart to Mrs. Silvey, who had come to get Mama to give her her B-12 shot. When the adults told Linda, who was two, to say that phrase, she said Fart, Fella, Fella, Fart, and everybody laughed. Mama was in the back getting the needle ready, and I was alone in the living room with Mrs. Silvey who, I thought, it was my job to entertain. I told Linda to say it. When Mama came into the room, Linda was saying Fart Fella Fella Fart, and Mrs. Silvey was looking mad. Mama sent me to the back room, and I didn't know what I had done wrong. When I learned that I had made Linda say "toot" in front of Mrs. Silvey, I was mortified.

This time I knew what I had done wrong, but I still felt six. I was watching Mama. I knew that behind her still face was a sob. No one was going to understand. Looking at myself through my mother's eyes, I saw the dead cockroach on the floor, the throw-up. Mama sat down next to me at the table and put a bowl of oatmeal and a spoon in front of me.

"Mama, I'm sorry," I said, those words that I had said many times before to her.

She had told me repeatedly, "There are some things that saying 'I'm sorry' won't make all right." I guess this was one of those things. Her face made that sad look, and she put a Kleenex to her mouth and shook her head.

But I continued, "Mama I love her. I can't help it. I really love her."

At those words Mama's back got straight, her mouth became a slit, and she said, "You can't do just anything you want if it hurts other people."

I wanted to say, "Who am I hurting?" but I already knew. She meant Harvill, and she meant herself. She meant Linda and all of our extended family. She meant all of Harvill's family, his parents, his cousins. And she meant anybody else in Milledgeville who would find out about it, the scandal.

They thought I had a mental illness. Down the road was Central State Hospital. I was a sick person with something disgusting, something like leprosy, something with sores that eat away at your body, something that eats you from the inside out. I imagined them putting me into the car and taking me out there to the tall buildings with the bars on the windows. I would be given medicine and be made to talk about my aberration, my love for a woman, something so bad that it made people turn away from me and whisper behind my back. No one would want to be my friend. Thinking about Ellen then made me feel broken and wrong. In the presence of Mama and Harvill, with their knowledge in the room, Ellen transformed from my true love to my shameful secret.

I began to sob, but only partly because of all the people I was hurting. Deep down, my heart was crushed to death because I did not want to lose Ellen. I kept thinking that I would be sitting in the dark, that I would not feel the sunshine on my face. I promised to put an end to it, and for that reason I was the saddest that I had ever been since Daddy died.

Late into the night, Mama went to the guest bedroom, and I could hear her rattling the plastic bag, taking out her blood pressure instrument. I knew that she would sit up in the bed and read her Bible for solace, and then she would lie down flat on her back with her glasses on; she would not sleep. She would lie awake and stare into the darkness, and this would be one of those things that she wouldn't feel free to talk to anybody about but God. She would ache to talk to my Daddy, Harvey, but he was gone and she was alone.

I lay in bed beside Harvill. He was all the way over to the edge as far as he could get. I was an outcast, and I wanted Ellen. I wondered what was happening at her house, how Ray was treating her. The next day I would have to avert my eyes as I passed her in the hall. I would have to close my heart and pretend to myself that all of this never happened. I would hear her boots coming down the hall, and I would touch my cheek as I remembered her soft face against mine, her sweet wet mouth. My arms would ache with wanting to hold her, and I would miss her so badly that I would grieve for my loss. I dreaded how much I would continue to want her.

The rest of that school year I was a zombie, moving through cotton. The world looked gray with no color. Later in my life I would learn what the Catholics say about guarding the eyes and occasions of sin. But I did not know that then, and I found my mind wandering, daydreaming about a day when Ellen and I could fall into each other's arms and be together again. It was worse seeing her every day and not being able to connect eyes, to touch skin. My arms desperately missed her arms.

On the last day of school a student came into my room with a folded, stapled piece of paper. I tore it open eagerly, and inside was a note from Ellen, "Meet me at the restaurant after school." It was a restaurant we had been to before, but this time we had to hide. We parked our cars in separate places in front of the restaurant, she around back and me on the side. She went in first, and I knew where I would probably find her. She was in the restroom. We embraced hungrily and kissed hard and long. The relief of being in her arms again made me cry with joy.

We said, "We will see each other again. We will be together." Then we separated and exited, first her, then me. We didn't make any plans for meeting in the future. We didn't exchange phone numbers or say what we thought our futures held. We trusted fate. I thought she was probably going to divorce Ray, but I didn't know where she would go. I was going to try to make my marriage work. I would try to become a normal person who lived a simple life like other people, someone my mother could be proud of. I wanted to try to have a baby. I wanted to begin to fill in the blank spaces in our pre-paid picture album that was sitting un-used on the shelf.

Harvill's baby pictures were pretty, dark curly hair, big black eyes, and long eyelashes. Our baby would look like that. I stopped taking my birth control pills. After we had sex, I put a pillow under my hips and held my legs in the air, giving every last sperm a fair chance to get there. I liked to roll out the crank window above the bed and feel the breeze blow across me, smell the summer smells, think of the sounds of children playing. I imagined a baby forming inside me, and I began to be excited about the idea. I pictured us at Christmas, a family around the tree, hanging a stocking for our little one. I thought Harvill would be a good father. He was wonderful with animals, tender with them. I'd seen that side of him, and I thought a baby would bring it out. He would be happy, and we could focus on our baby and our family. The shameful past would be in the past, and no one need ever mention it again. But month after month my period continued to come, all throughout the summer.

I resigned from teaching at Jones County High School when I got a job at the newly-founded integration-avoidance school, John Milledge Academy. I tried to get a job at my old Alma Mater, Baldwin High School, but there were no openings. The school superintendent thought that I was too young and that, having grown up in a segregated school system, I would go through culture shock and may not know how to teach the black high school students who were at the newly-integrated public high school for the first time in 1971.

In the fall when I began teaching at John Milledge Academy, I had all the students from grades eight through twelve. I was the only English teacher. I had no books, and the entire curriculum was mine to plan. I had six eighth graders, twelve ninth graders, three tenth graders, six eleventh graders, and ten twelfth graders.

Throughout that year I continued to try to get pregnant. Harvill and I went to the doctor and learned how to do a temperature chart. Each morning I awoke and took my temperature. If there was a slight rise, I was ovulating and we needed to have sex that night. But nothing ever happened, and I got discouraged. Other teachers around me were pregnant and having baby showers, but my womb stayed quiet and barren.

By the end of that year I acquired a job at Baldwin High School from where I had graduated in 1965, and I was glad to take my leave from the white flight mountain.

CHAPTER THREE: THE APPRENTICE

"It is better to live your own destiny imperfectly
than to live an imitation of somebody else's life with perfection."-
--*The Bhagavad Gita*

1971-1972

The experience with Ellen imprinted itself on my brain like a tattoo. It became the significant event that I had to tell any new close friends, or else they wouldn't know me. It was my secret, and it was the most important event in my life so far. To tell someone was a test of our friendship. I didn't tell many people, but with any new friend a moment came when I knew that I was disguising myself and I needed to tell. This is the way I told it, "A while back I had a sexual relationship with a woman." I told it as if it were a fluke, an aberration, a once-in-a-lifetime event. I never used it to define myself as gay or lesbian.

The second important event in my life was my relationship with Mary-Louise Brown, a woman twenty years older than I, who moved to Milledgeville from Manhattan to become the organist/choir director at the Methodist Church. Our friendship was platonic and took the form of mentor-mentee, Pygmalion-like. She saw me as a sweet young thing with potential, and she wanted to teach me about the world outside of Milledgeville, Georgia. Our friendship lasted only two years, but it emblazoned itself on my memory so that now, many years later, it is as fresh to me as it was back then. For years, Mary-Louise Brown has been a shadow in my peripheral vision, a question sitting on my shoulder. At times she has been an albatross or a heavy suitcase; at other times a ghost come back to haunt me. Perhaps Mary-Louise's threat to put a curse on all of us was her way of lingering.

When Harvill and I got married, we decided that we would attend the Methodist Church where he grew up because he didn't want to get baptized by immersion in the Baptist Church. He would be embarrassed to be getting wet up in front of people. But on more and more Sundays, he didn't want to go to church at all, so I went to the Methodist Church alone or with his mother.

One Sunday the minister announced that a new organist had arrived. From the edge of the choir loft, a blond woman entered wearing the green choir robe, her sleeves buttoned up so that they wouldn't interfere with her playing. She stepped down into the organ pit, turned her back to us, and sat down at the organ. When she turned on the switch, air filled the pipes with a swooshing sound. When she began to play, the people stopped whispering to one another. She was playing something big, a piece by someone like Bach or Beethoven. Her yellow head bobbed as her feet moved across the pedal keys. Her fingers traveled rapidly over the keys, and it seemed as if she were playing a concert rather than a Prelude to a Sunday morning service. As the piece came to an end, as she played the last long, rumbling chord, the minister said, "Please welcome Miss Mary-Louise Brown, our new organist, all the way from New York City. And now that you have heard her play the organ, I don't think she needs any further introduction."

While everyone was clapping, something that didn't often happen in church, the woman stood, turned toward the congregation, and said in her New York accent, "We need some more voices in the choir. Please join us Wednesday nights at 7:30." Then, turning slightly and back again, she added, "That is, if you can sing." A smattering of laughter passed through the sanctuary. I decided then that I would go. If Harvill wasn't going to go to church with me, then I would join the choir.

I was late to the first practice, and the choir had already begun warming up, singing a series of scales that sounded like "Keeko, keeko, keeko, kee," lower and then higher and higher up the scale until the men and the altos dropped out and only the sopranos sang. Miss Brown's blonde hair was fixed in a loose permanent wave, something from the beauty parlor. I looked at the others in the choir and back at her, and I thought how different she looked from us. Her hair was too yellow to be natural, and she wore more makeup than most of us. She wore a shiny purple paisley blouse, darker purple skirt, and purple stockings. No one in Milledgeville wore purple stockings. She smiled at the choir condescendingly as she handed out the sheet music. "You are going to learn to sing Latin," she said, "beginning with the Schubert Mass in G."

She sat down at the organ and began drilling the sections on their parts, telling us how to pronounce "Kyrie Eleison" and "Gloria." She may have been making fun of our accents because she said, "Don't say Glow-ree-uh, say Glah-ree-uh, and it will come out right." A few times when we forgot and pronounced something incorrectly or sang a wrong note, she shuddered openly, shaking her head violently and shouting, "Honestly!" clapping her hands together. It was as if her ears couldn't tolerate any offensive sounds. "Listen!" she shouted. "Look at me! How can you know what to do if you do not look?"

Suddenly in the middle of the rehearsal, she stopped everything and said, "Okay! Time for a smoke break!" She swung her legs around and off the organ bench and slipped the black ballerina-type shoes off her purple-stockinged feet and put on some low-heeled pumps. She dug around in her purse and pulled out a package of Vantage cigarettes. Some of the choir members went outside, but I followed Miss Brown into her office. She motioned for me to sit in a chair near her desk. As I took out my cigarette, she leaned over and lit it with a green Bic lighter. She had a long thin nose and sharp features. At first her face was not pretty to me, but the longer I knew her, the more beautiful she became.

"So," she said, blowing the smoke out of the side of her mouth, "Tell me about yourself." I suddenly became shy and didn't know what to say. Miss Brown leaned forward and looked directly at me without saying anything, looking into my eyes, the way Ellen and I had looked at one another in the beginning. I looked around the room, away from her eyes, and exhaled my smoke into the air. Miss Brown grinned slightly, a flirtatious grin, the left side of her mouth turning up, and then looked away. "I don't think I'm ever going to finish unpacking!" she said. "Look at this mess!" She motioned to the piles of music and paper on her desk and in the corners of the room. Her hands looked too small and delicate to be able to make those big sounds on the organ. Her nails were trimmed close, and she held the cigarette between two curved fingers.

"How old are you?" she asked me.

"Twenty-five," I said.

"Oh, a child," she said. "I've got twenty years on you. I could be your mother. And you've got that beautiful premature salt-and-pepper hair!"

I began to talk, rattling off that I taught English at the high school. But I was nervous, and I didn't know what questions to ask her about herself. Before she put out her cigarette and summoned everyone back to practice, she said, "Why don't you stop by the church one day after school? I'll be practicing, and I'd like to talk about reading with you."

Driving home that night, I had the same feeling I used to have when I went to the picture show as a child. After watching a movie, when I walked out of the dark theater onto the bright sidewalk, I had slipped into the skin of the main character, and for several days I would be that character. In my head I talked like her and walked like her, and when I looked in the mirror I was surprised that I didn't look like her. That night driving home, I could hear the Northern accent in my head.

The next day at school Mary-Louise Brown was on my mind throughout the day. We had a fire drill in the middle of "Ozymandius." As I stood outside on the sidewalk with my students, I stared down the street and played the words and music to the Latin piece in my head. Afterwards, back in the classroom, I couldn't get my students to settle down.

After school I drove by the church, and Miss Brown's blue '57 Chevrolet was parked there. I parked my car beside hers, went into the side door of the fellowship hall, and stepped into the cool darkness of the unlit room. My feet tapped across the beige-and-green tiles. As I climbed the stairs to the choir loft, I heard the organ playing, the music growing louder and louder. At the top of the stairs, I stepped into a triangle of light. Miss Brown didn't see me, and I stood waiting to be noticed. She was perspiring, and her hair fell loose across her forehead. Both hands and feet moved rapidly back and forth across the black and white keys, the music making a loud rumble under my feet and in my chest. Taking her hands off the keys and bracing on the bench beside her, she leaned back slightly as her feet in the black organ slippers moved rapidly up and down the pedal keys. Then suddenly she stopped, clapped her hands together, shouted "Damn!" and played again with her feet.

When she saw me out of the corner of her eye, the music stopped, and she said, "Oh!" Then, pointing her finger at me, she said, her voice firm and slightly angry, "Listen, Sweetness and Light, don't ever come up on me like that when I'm playing. You're a darling girl, but I've got to practice. I can't be bothered when I'm practicing."

I stepped backward and drew in my breath, my face flushing hot. After all, she had invited me to come by.

"Oh, never mind," she said, her voice softening. "You people are so sensitive."

"I'm sorry," I said. "I didn't mean to interrupt. Your music is beautiful."

"I'm almost finished for the day anyway," she said. "Listen, step up here a minute. Can you read music?" The title of the large sheet music propped in front of her was "Toccata" by Leon Boellman.

"I took piano lessons when I was a child," I answered, remembering the afternoons at the piano in Mrs. Long's dark house, the times I almost fell asleep at the keyboard, the times I asked, "Can I get a drink of water?" so that Mrs. Long would take me back to her kitchen with the violets in the window and give me ice water from a frosted green glass container out of her refrigerator, and I could wake up to continue our lesson.

"Try this," Miss Brown said. "When I get to the end of this page, turn it for me. I'm beginning here." She pointed to a spot on the page. One line on the large staff seemed to fill the page, and when she nodded her head hard and said, "Now!" and then louder, her voice deeper and commanding, "Now! Now!" I hadn't even realized that she was close to the end of the page.

"I've never seen such a long staff before," I said.

Miss Brown pointed to the pedal line. It seemed that only a few seconds of music took up each page. A page-turner would have to turn the large sheets again and again in one piece. "Try it again," she said, "and this time be faster." I followed the rise of the pedal keys and turned the page as she bowed her head deeply. "That's better," she said. "I'll teach you. I'll need a page-turner for my first recital." Then she said, "Listen, my dear," turning off the organ, its motor winding down to silence, "I'm going home now. Why don't you come over? All right?"

As I followed Miss Brown's car to her apartment on Montgomery Street across from the college, I was confused by this woman's erratic personality. But while I was shocked and frightened by her sudden outbursts, I was also drawn to her when she became charming and flirtatious.

Her apartment was inside a two-story antebellum home with columns, the first door on the left off the entranceway, a brass door-knocker attached to the door. "Come in," she said, holding the door open for me. She motioned for me to sit on a gold loveseat beside a table in the center of the room. As I waited, she went down a hallway, calling behind her, "I'll get us a glass of wine. Is that okay? Would you prefer something else? I think all I have is tap water."

"Wine will be fine," I called after her. In front of me was a round table with an intricate design on top. It looked as if it were made out of tiny woodchips and an iridescent shell. In the corner of the room was a grand piano with the top up, the gold strings inside shining in the afternoon sun that filtered through the sheer curtains. Over the mantelpiece was a large portrait of a red-faced man, bald with a stern expression on his face.

When she came back into the room, Miss Brown was holding a round tray containing two wine glasses, a dark green bottle of Taylor Port, and a small wooden bowl of sunflower seeds. "Do you like my mother-of-pearl table?" she asked. She set the tray on the table and sat down in a red velour chair beside the love seat, crossed her legs, and faced me.

"It's beautiful," I said, leaning forward to touch it.

"I got it abroad," she said, "on a concert tour." She picked up the green bottle and poured the dark wine into the two glasses. "Have some Port," she said, and she picked up one of the glasses and held it out to me. "Cheers," she said, clicking her glass to mine. I put the glass to my lips. The wine was strong and heavy, and it burned my chest as it went down.

"So, Miss Brown," I said, "How did you end up here in the South?" I had planned to say this as I drove over.

"Please," she said, "Call me Mary-Louise." She took a cigarette from her Vantage pack and lit it. "Everybody asks me that. I had to nurse my mother and father for years. First, my mother died and later my father." She motioned to the portrait over the mantel. "He was a tyrant." She took a sip of her wine and continued. "In Manhattan, you don't have time for conversations like this. You're rushing all the time. I wanted to slow down and have fresh air to breathe." She reached into the bowl and took a few sunflower seeds and put them into her palm. "I chose Milledgeville because you have the college and because it's close to Atlanta where I won't be isolated from music and dance and the theatre. And there was an offer here at this church. It's as simple as that," she said, lifting her shoulders in a shrug. She rolled the end of her cigarette in the crystal ashtray on the table, turning the ash into a point. "I have been on concert tours all over the world. But out on the streets in the City, the tall buildings smothered me." She looked up, motioning with her hands.

As she poured two more glasses of wine, I realized that my lips were numb. She was telling me about the children's choir and how she couldn't get them to say "tender." "They all say 'tee-n-der,'" she said, and she asked me to repeat after her "*pen*" and "*pin*." I didn't tell her that in elementary school we were taught that pen and pin were homonyms. We were laughing, and Mary-Louise looked at me with that quiet intense look, that direct gaze. But now I was feeling braver, and I tried to force myself to feel confident, to take charge and not to feel confused or off-balance. The smoky room, the dark red oriental rug on the floor, the seal-point Siamese cat named Thap Thim that kept passing through the room, made me feel as if I were in a big city in a foreign country. I became a real woman in an exotic place, a woman in a movie. The light filtering through the lace curtains lit up dust particles dancing in the air.

"Tell me about your concert tours," I said.

"Later," she said. "Tell me about yourself. Did you grow up in this Methodist Church here?" She leaned forward, her cigarette between her fingers, her elbow resting on her knee.

I told her about growing up in the Baptist Church, about singing in the choir and taking piano lessons, about going to college at Georgia Southern and marrying Harvill.

"My father was a Ramakrishna," Mary-Louise said. When she saw the puzzled look on my face, she added, "Their holy book is the *Bhagavad Gita*. My father believed that we have many chances to get it right here on earth. We move in spirals, around and around, coming back, again and again, until we get it right. Then we reach the center, which is Nirvana." I listened in that same dreamy state that I had in elementary school when the teacher was reading us a book.

"The Southern Baptists are interesting," she said. "Do they really dunk people?" I told her about my baptism at the First Baptist Church.

"You are delightful," she said, her eyes smiling, looking interested and amused, that same flirty lop-sided grin on her face. "Tell me more."

I told her about being in Girls Auxiliary, about memorizing "Who can find a virtuous woman?" and about the booklets that listed the tasks to accomplish to move up through the Forward Steps: Maiden, then Lady-in-Waiting, then Princess and Queen. I told her about marching down the aisle with our Bibles to "Pomp and Circumstance."

She laughed, "Oh my God!" she said. "'Pomp and Circumstance?' You've got to be kidding! And a crown?"

"Yes," I said. "A cardboard one," feeling glad that I had good stories to tell her, my mind rushing forward to others that I could tell.

"What did your mother think of all that folderol?" Mary-Louise asked.

"Oh, she had her own lists of requirements," I said. "Her lists of what not to do. Don't eat too fast. Don't talk too loud. Don't lend anybody your bicycle."

"Why not lend somebody your bicycle?" she asked.

"I think because they might fall and you'd be responsible," I said, and then continued, my ideas coming faster. "And then the Baptist church had rules of its own. The Ten Commandments started with

Don't drink, Don't dance, and Don't gamble. And especially, Don't have sex."

"Oh, sex," said Mary-Louise, clicking her tongue, raising her eyebrow. "That's another story." Then, "What do you believe about religion?" she asked, suddenly serious.

My face became hot. I didn't know how to answer, and I didn't want to sound simple or childish to her. "Well, I believe in God. I believe in Jesus," I said, but I didn't know what else to say.

She picked up the tall bottle and filled my glass for the third time. Then she said, "It's a shame you didn't go to a better college. You could have done much better. You have to aim high," she said. "And it's never too late."

I had never before thought that my college wasn't what you would call "a good one." I had chosen Georgia Southern out of the college handbook. My daddy, who had not gone past the eighth grade himself, had saved his earnings at the barber shop and worked hard to send me to college without having to borrow money. Why was this woman discounting my college? And where did she think I should have gone? It would have to be in Georgia; my family couldn't afford out-of-state tuition. She said that she had graduated from Barnard College in New York City.

Mary-Louise got up and went to her hallway to a bookcase and brought back three books. "Here," she said. "Take these home and read them. I'm going to educate you."

The books she put into my hands that afternoon were *The Idiot* by Fyodor Dostoevsky, *Swann's Way* by Marcel Proust, and a thick heavy book called *The Quest for the Historical Jesus* by Albert Schweitzer. She put her hand on top of the last book. "This one is difficult," she said, "but it will be good for you to try it."

When I left that day, I could hardly see the road to drive. I was tired of trying to hide my ignorance on so many subjects; my cheeks were tired from smiling. The books on the seat beside me were not ones taught in the Teacher Education Program to prepare students to teach high school English. It seemed to me that my brain had been lazy for a long time. I wanted to learn new things, to grow. Mary-Louise even pronounced my name differently. She called me "Saundra," rather than "Sandra" because she said she didn't like the flat A sound in my name. I wanted to become "Saundra," an exotic name meant for people who lived far away from Milledgeville, Georgia. I wanted to be able to discuss important subjects with Mary-Louise Brown without feeling inferior or stupid. When I got home, I didn't start to fix supper. I put the books on the nightstand, lay down across the bed, and went to sleep.

When the phone rang, it was Mama. "Where have you been?" she asked. "I thought you might come by after school. I needed to run to the bank, but I stayed here, thinking you might come. I cooked some chicken wings."

"Hi," I said. "How was your day?"

"What's wrong? You sound funny," Mama said. "Are you sick?"

"No, Mama," I said, realizing that my voice sounded irritated. "I had a tiring day. We had a fire drill, and then the students wouldn't settle down."

"Do you want me to come over?" she asked. "Do you want me to bring the wings? I've been calling all afternoon."

"I went by the church after work," I said, honestly. "Our new organist needs someone to turn the pages for her recital, and we practiced that. Then she asked me over to her apartment, and we've been talking. She's a nice person, and she's a good choir director. You should hear her play that organ."

Mama became silent at the other end of the line. Then she said, "You've been there all this time? What did you talk about for so long?"

"Oh, this and that," I said.

"Have you fixed supper? What are you and Harvill going to eat? Are you sure you don't want me to bring the wings?"

When I hung up the receiver, that same stab of guilt hit me, the feeling that something was not quite right between Mama and me. It was that silence that meant that someone had intruded between the two of us, and she was jealous. And, since my relationship with Ellen, she would always be suspicious of any women friends.

That night, sitting up in bed, I began reading *Swann's Way*. As I read, I could feel myself being drawn into another world, a foreign place, different from my own, a place like the exotic world of Mary-Louise's apartment with the grand piano and the oriental rug and the mother-of-pearl table, a place where I could listen to the Northern accent tell me about important things and faraway places. When I turned out the light, I smiled into the darkness.

Several afternoons a week, I went from school to Mary-Louise's apartment. She had been practicing at the church or rehearsing with the children, and I had been teaching. We were ready for conversation. We smoked and drank Port and talked about books and many other subjects. Because Mary-Louise didn't want anyone dropping in on her, she gave me a code for the door-knocker. Tap the knocker three times fast, then one single, the beginning of Beethoven's *Fifth* Symphony.

"How do you like the Proust?" Mary-Louise asked as she made us a Manhattan to celebrate what she called my "awakening." After I took one sip of the dark, fruity bourbon, my whole body got warm. I had never had a Manhattan before, and I felt sophisticated sitting there on the gold loveseat holding the slender glass with the red liquid and the long-stemmed cherry.

When I got home on those afternoons, when Mama called as she usually did, I made up a meeting at school or a trip to the grocery store. I stopped telling Mama where I had been. In Mary-Louise's apartment, I became that person that Mary-Louise was molding me into. My heart hardened against Mama. At least Mary-Louise's outbursts were not like Mama's silences. It was the silences that were unsettling. As I had with Ellen, I was again lying and hiding, from both Harvill and Mama.

During the school day, I hummed the alto to the Schubert Mass in G. We had learned the Kyrie, the Credo, the Agnus Dei, one after the other, and Mary-Louise taught us to pronounce the Latin words. As I watched my students at their desks writing, I re-played the words in my mind: "Credo in unum Deum, something, something, potentum, et unum sanctum catolicam, et apostolicam ecclesiam."

"How do you like the Schubert?" Mary-Louise asked me.
"I love it," I answered. "It's on my mind all day."

One afternoon after she had fixed us Manhattans, Mary-Louise brought a pad and a pencil over to the mother-of-pearl table and said to me, "I want you to help me plan a party. I want to get a feel for the South. I want to have a party for the Southern Aristocrats here. I need you to help me make the invitation list."

What? I thought. It sounded like a game, something wild and funny, as if Mary-Louise had said she wanted to give a party only for the mentally retarded or only for prisoners.

"Who are they?" she asked me, her pen poised above her pad.

I had no idea who the aristocrats in Milledgeville were. I tried to think of the rich people I knew who lived in the big white mansions around the college, in the historic district, the houses that had not yet been made into apartments but which were still inhabited by single families who had been living in them through several generations. But I didn't know those people. I drank more of my Manhattan. I ate my cherry. I tried to think of the rich people I knew who lived in the subdivision near the mall or up at the lake.

"No, those aren't Aristocrats," Mary-Louise said. "Those are the *nouveau riche*. I want the Southern Aristocracy, capital S, capital A."

"I don't know any," I said, embarrassed.

"Well, of course the Northern Aristocracy will be much older than the Southern." She shrugged and continued. "You may not have any real Aristocracy down here. Who are some of the old families you remember from your childhood? Some of the old 'gentlemanly gentlemen.' Who are some of the people who own businesses here?"

I named Mr. Albert Haygood, who owned Haygood's Funeral Home, and Mr. Roy Fredricks, who started the picture show and also owned several old apartment buildings. I named Jack Maple of Maple Drygoods and Sam Gardner, the President of the oldest bank in town. As I named these people, Mary-Louise wrote the names on her list.

In the cool dim apartment, drinking the Manhattans, talking and laughing with Mary-Louise, I let the time pass. Off and on I thought of the phone ringing at home, of it being Mama, but I decided that I would rather go through my mother's interrogations later than to leave. Through the sheer draperies at the window, I saw that it was getting dark outside. Mary-Louise turned on a floor lamp beside the grand piano, and the light reflected on the gold strings inside.

"I'd better go," I finally said, realizing that my legs were weak and my arms heavy.

"Wait," Mary-Louise said. "I want to do your chart." She went down the hallway and came back with a notepad that had on it a round diagram containing squiggles and symbols that I had not seen before.

"What is that?" I asked. "Astrology?"

"Of course!" she said. "Now, when is your birthday?"

All I knew of astrology was the column in the newspaper. Mary-Louise pointed to first one symbol and then another. She used words such as *ascendancy*, and she said the names of Zodiac signs grouped together, this one controlled by that one, this one's ruling sign. As she wrote on the pad, she began to smile. "How interesting!" she said. "I knew there was something unique about you!" She looked up at me and said, "You, my dear, have Moon in Scorpio!"

I waited for her to explain.

"Moon in Scorpio can make your emotions go crazy," she said. It can make you do something on impulse. I'll have to warn you when it comes."

I blushed. I liked being protected, having something that made me unique.

"Wait! There's more!" she continued, leaning over the page in her lap, drawing marks around the diagram, murmuring softly to herself. "You will have an interesting life," she said, looking up at me. "You will meet some famous people. I'll teach you how they like to be treated."

I was intrigued. What famous people would I meet, and why did they need to be treated differently? I wondered if Mary-Louise was one of the famous people I would meet.

One afternoon she asked me, "Why did you get married? Your husband sounds like a jerk."

I had told her about Harvill's inability to be sociable. "It's what girls are supposed to do," I told her. "I mean, you're given dolls and stoves and refrigerators for Christmas. You look forward to the day when you can be a bride. I didn't want to be an Old Maid."

"Old Maid!" Mary-Louise said, laughing. "You've got to be kidding!" I'm single, and I've never been called an Old Maid! I've had affairs I could tell you about!" she said, drawing on her cigarette, rolling her eyes and clicking her tongue. "You know, a woman can choose to remain single!"

Really? I thought. Can she? It had never once occurred to me that I could actually choose to be a woman alone. Or that I would want to. But then, sitting in Mary-Louise's living room with her, it seemed that I could imagine it, being alone, being independent, making my own decisions without having to consult a man. It did not have to mean that I couldn't find a husband. It would mean that I actually had a choice.

That night I dreamed that I was getting into an elevator, one of those old kinds that had a person operating it. When I stepped inside, I saw that Mary-Louise was the operator. In my dream I felt cozy, as if I were stepping into a comforting place. I walked to the back of the elevator, and Mary-Louise leaned forward and closed the cage-like grating, then the main door. "Going up or down?" she said, looking back at me. I looked at her, and I didn't know what the right answer was. "Hurry up," Mary-Louise said. "You'll have to decide."

She invited Harvill to her party for the Aristocrats. When I told him, he grumbled and complained but eventually agreed to go. I promised him that we wouldn't have to stay long and told him he didn't have to wear a tie, for Harvill hated having to wear a tie. I wore a long cotton dress with tiny purple flowers, a peasant dress, and blew my pixie hair forward in a tousle.

When we parked in front of Mary-Louise's house, Harvill got out, lit a cigarette, and paced in the grass, me standing beside him.

When she came to the door, Mary-Louise was wearing a long green-and-blue caftan with a cloisonné pendant around her neck. "Darling!" she said, taking my arm and pulling me inside. "You look adorable in that dress!" Then looking behind me, she asked, "Where's Harvill? Didn't he come?" I looked behind me, and Harvill had stepped to the side, standing in the hall beside the staircase. Mary-Louise took him by the arm and led him inside. "So wonderful to finally meet you!" she said, her hand on his arm. Harvill grinned nervously.

"What can I get you?" she asked him. "We have wine and mixed drinks."

"Do you have a beer?" Harvill asked.

"Go look in the back of the refrigerator," she said to me. "I think I have one." I went down the hall and when I came back with a brown bottle of Michelob, Mary-Louise was leading Harvill around introducing him to people. I could see that he was already uncomfortable, his hand shaking, his head down, his voice so soft when he spoke to people that they could hardly hear him. I handed him the beer and suggested he sit in the armchair in the corner. Mary-Louise handed me a Manhattan.

"Come help me in the kitchen," she whispered, taking my arm, leading me down the hallway. She took from the refrigerator a large platter containing a pink shrimp salad in a copper mold shaped like a fish. I felt silly and warm, and we giggled as we let the long pink shape slide from its mold onto a bed of lettuce. "Get an olive out of that jar," she said, "for the eye." She put the eye onto the fish. "Isn't that marvelous!" Mary-Louise said, her white cheek and red shiny lipstick close to my face, her perfume making me woozy. Together we arranged crackers around the fish.

She asked me to carry the tray containing the fish, and when I stepped into the room, I felt like a movie star, the guests standing and talking to one another, and me, carrying the tray with the beautiful pink fish. I moved around the room, leaning over to those sitting down, smiling, saying, "Have some shrimp! It's delicious!" When I leaned down to Harvill sitting in his chair, he said to me under his breath, "You look like an idiot!"

Later in the evening, Mary-Louise brought out caviar and was disappointed when I couldn't swallow it and had to spit it onto a napkin. I knew that I had let her down. The room became filled with cigarette smoke. Mary-Louise was moving through the crowd, laughing, flirting, pleased that her party was going well. She held a Manhattan in her left hand and a cigarette in her right. No matter where I was in the room, Mary-Louise's face was in my vision, her face the only one in focus. I was completely under her spell. How could I not be? When she was entertaining, she was charming and enchanting. Everyone in the room was slightly in love with her, her white skin and blonde curls, her red lipstick and the delicate fingers holding the glass containing the red liquid.

Suddenly I realized that Harvill was not in the chair. I stepped into the hallway, and he was standing there, smoking, his face gloomy. "Come on!" he said. "Let's go! You said we didn't have to stay long!"

I went back inside and whispered to Mary-Louise, "I've got to go."

"You really know how to work a room!" she said.

On the way home, Harvill mimicked her, "You really know how to work a room, 'Saun-dra.'"

On one of my afternoon visits, Mary-Louise asked me, "Are you ready to see your first ballet? Rudolph Nureyev is in Swan Lake in Atlanta. I've gotten us tickets."

"How much will it cost?" Mama asked me later on the phone.

"Mary-Louise is paying for it," I answered.

"Of course," Mama said in that tone. Harvill, too, had that tone in his voice when I told him. I knew that they were both remembering Ellen, that they thought I was getting attached to another woman.

The Saturday of the ballet, Mary-Louise picked me up at our double-wide. Harvill had been in the yard all day, sulking. When I heard her car coming down the gravel driveway, I looked at myself once more in the mirror. I wore my green cotton peasant dress with the lace collar up close under my chin. My hair was blown dry and tousled, the way Mary-Louise liked it.

I stood at the top of the driveway, looking around, trying to locate Harvill so that I could tell him I was leaving. He was in the back corner of the yard tossing leaves over the fence into the woods. "Harvill!" I called. "I'm leaving." He didn't say anything and didn't even turn around. "Harvill!" I called again.

Mary-Louise had gotten out of her car and was walking toward me. "He's pouting," I said to her.

"God! How do you stand it!" she said as I was getting into the car. As she backed down the driveway, Harvill came around the side of the house and stood there. I felt sad for him and defensive, but I didn't take up for him.

Mary-Louise was wearing a royal blue skirt and a shimmery white blouse. She pressed in the cigarette lighter and looked over at me. "That dress is charming on you," she said.

"I didn't know what to wear," I said.

"Oh, the young can wear anything," she said. "You look like a dream."

As we drove out of Milledgeville and onto the Atlanta highway, she asked, "What do you know about ballet? Anything?"

"Not really," I said. "When I was growing up, ballet was what you took if you didn't take piano. Mama and Daddy thought piano would be more useful."

Mary-Louise laughed. "They were right about that," she said. "Now you can be my page turner. Wait until you see Nureyev. I wish you could have seen him with Margot Fontaine. They were partners for years."

Out the window I saw brown shacks with children running in and out. I turned my head as the car sped by, trying to see inside the doors. In one, I saw the white edge of a bed, the dark interior, and the children in the doorway looking out.

"Isn't that horrendous?" Mary-Louise said, glancing through the window. "Those poor people. How do you suppose they keep warm?" Then the scene changed to long broad fields of black-and-white cows, a few horses, and rows of pine trees on the horizon. "Look at that bucolic scene," she said. "Do you know that word *bucolic*?" I didn't, nor did I know the word *horrendous*. "It's similar to *pastoral*," she said. "Beautiful scenes, like some of Rembrandt's paintings or Wordsworth's poems about the lake country." I was quiet. Once again, I didn't know, and I was embarrassed by my ignorance.

Something about riding in a car and facing the road as the lines shoot under the car makes it easier to talk. The person is not looking at you. As we rode, I told Mary-Louise about my relationship with Ellen.

Her reaction was nonchalant. "Why didn't you leave Harvill?" she asked, "if you were in love with her."

"I don't know," I said. "I couldn't."

"Do you think you're a lesbian?" she asked.

"I don't think so," I said, flinching at the word.

"Well, don't ever try anything with me!" she said. "I like men." She then told me about her affair with the cartoonist Saul Steinberg, how she had sat on his knee in his studio. When she changed the subject, I was glad.

"I can't wait to see your reaction to the ballet," she said. Even that made me nervous, as if there were a correct or incorrect response, that my response may not be right, and she would think less of me. "Nureyev is sensational. That body, svelte and strong! Wait until you see him in tights!" She clicked her tongue, raised her eyebrow, and began searching in her purse for her cigarettes. When the car swerved over the line, she said, "Light me a cigarette, will you?" As I looked in her purse for her cigarettes, she told me about a man named Paul Wittgenstein who had only one arm but who played the piano magnificently. She said that composers wrote music especially for him to play.

We had dinner at the Abbey, an old Unitarian Church on Peachtree Street that had been changed into a restaurant. As we drove around the block, Mary-Louise told me what she had read about this place. "It was founded in 1968," she said. "The waiters wear monks' robes, and the bar is on the altar. A harpist near the altar plays everything from 'Ode to Joy' to 'Tara's Theme.' And we're going to have a three-course meal."

That night Mary-Louise taught me how to eat escargot, to spear it with my fork, to dip it in melted butter, to swallow fast. She ordered for both of us and chose Chicken Kiev and globe artichokes with Hollandaise sauce and butter. "When I called to ask about the menu and learned that they had escargot and artichokes, I knew that you had probably not had them and I could teach you! I hand-picked this place for us." She asked the waiter to bring the artichokes first. She taught me how to pull off the leaves and scrape the tender green pulp with my bottom teeth, how to then clean off the straw-like covering of the heart and eat the best part with my fork. She closed her eyes as she savored the soft center. "Oh, this is ecstasy!" she said.

After dinner, we hurried to get to the ballet on time. People wore fur coats and stood around holding plastic cups of wine. When we were seated, I settled comfortably next to Mary-Louise. The lights dimmed, a pale blue spotlight appeared on the stage, and the music and dance began. Nureyev flew across the stage, and Mary-Louise squeezed my arm and whispered, "Isn't he gorgeous!" When the swan died, I was mesmerized, as dying became an art and the creature folded in on itself as if it all had to be returned in the same box it came in.

It was the day of Mary-Louise's recital. The two of us practiced for weeks, and she had trained me well. She placed me into different areas of the sanctuary so that I could listen to the various pieces and give her feedback. I wasn't sure how to do this. I told her that her playing was beautiful, and it was, but I had to ask her what specifically she wanted me to listen for. She wanted me to tell her if the notes were clean, separate from one another; to listen to be sure the volume was right so that the stops were set correctly for the size of the sanctuary. I didn't feel I had the ear to know what she wanted, and if I did hear anything wrong, I wouldn't have had to courage to tell her. I was drawn to her and attracted to her. I wanted to please her, and I wanted her to admire me. At the same time, I was afraid of annoying her; her reaction could be volatile.

Several afternoons a week I sat in the dark sanctuary beside the stained-glass windows and watched Mary-Louise in the light of the choir loft, her whole body moving back and forth across the organ bench, her head nodding, and her voice shouting out when she did something she didn't like, sometimes slapping her hands together in a loud clap along with the word, "Damn!"

The first two pieces were by Bach. The first was called "Komm, heiliger Geist," and I loved it. The second was the "Fourth Trio Sonata in E Minor," and it had three sections to it, each one different from the other. My favorite was the third piece, which sounded like bells. It was called the "Carillon Sortie."

The remainder of the recital was something Mary-Louise called Avant-Garde music, and I didn't think the people in Milledgeville were going to like it. The music was dissonant, and Mary-Louise told me that it would be shocking. The composers were Vierne, Messiaen, and Ligeti. The final piece, called "Volumina" by Gyorgy Ligeti, was the strangest of all. It turned the organ into something different from anything I had heard before. It didn't sound like church music but, rather, like a horror movie. Mary-Louise asked me to help her with that one, and she listed my name in the program as "Sandra Holsenbeck, Assistant."

When the time came in the program for Mary-Louise to play that piece, I was to leave the audience, go into the choir loft, and sit beside her on the organ bench. Then I was to lean on the organ keys with my left elbow and with my right hand begin to turn off the stops until they were all off. Finally, I was to reach up and flip the switch, turning off the entire organ completely, while the two of us held down all the organ keys we could reach with our arms flat on the keys. The sound was a loud rumble that slowly died away until no sound was left at all. It felt as if we were conspirators, the killers of the sound. I couldn't imagine how the audience would react. Maybe some of the people from the music department at the college would understand, but they would be the only ones.

The last thing that Mary-Louise asked me to do for the recital seemed more difficult to me than being the assistant for the "Volumina," more than pulling the stops, more than listening from the sanctuary as Mary-Louise practiced. A few days before the recital, she asked that, at a certain time after the first Avant-Garde piece, the

Vierne, I stand and begin applauding loudly. This was an action that I could not imagine myself taking. It was not in my personality.

"I can't do that!" I told her. "I would be embarrassed! What if nobody starts clapping, and I'm standing there by myself!" Just thinking about it made me nervous.

But Mary-Louise would not be talked out of it. She waved her hand and said, "Don't be ridiculous."

On the day of the recital, I sat where she told me to, slightly left of center, about fifteen rows back. Slowly the sanctuary filled with people wearing coats and hats and gloves, for it was a cold day. Many of the people were probably there out of curiosity about this organist at the Methodist Church who wore purple stockings and gave big parties. People began to talk quietly among themselves. I was nervous about the final piece, but I was more nervous about standing and clapping, and, to make it worse, at the last minute, Mama came in and sat beside me.

Then Mary-Louise entered, wearing a shiny black dress. She bowed toward the audience and turned and sat down at the organ. As I listened, my neck muscles tensed as I dreaded the moment at the end of the Vierne when I was to stand and clap. Having Mama sitting beside me made it even worse. I hadn't been able to convince Mary-Louise that clapping in church was considered disrespectful. "It's a concert!" she said. At the end of each piece, the people sat quietly as Mary-Louise stood, nodded, and sat down again to play. At the end of the second Bach, she had begun to look angry, and as she bowed, she looked directly at me.

When she began the Vierne, I could feel my heart pounding. I felt hot and faint. I could see Mama's hands folded in her lap beside me.

And then it was time, as I heard the last notes of the piece. I stood straight up from my seat and began to clap loudly, my hands stinging as they came together. For what seemed a long time, I stood alone, clap, clap, clap. Then two or three others stood and began clapping. I began to clap louder, willing the others to rise. Slowly a few more rose to their feet. Mary-Louise stood at the front smiling and bowing as I continued to stand, clapping, feeling relieved. Finally, all but a few people were standing. Then I felt my mother pulling on my blouse, tugging lightly at first and then more insistently. I turned to look down at her, and she whispered loudly, "Sit down!" I clapped a few more times and then slowly sat down with the others.

Suddenly, anger flared up in me. "Don't do that!" I whispered to Mama, who looked as if I had slapped her across the face. Her mouth tightened, and she folded her arms across her chest. I was angry, and I sat and fumed and stared straight ahead, not even hearing the two Messiaen pieces. Then I caught the end of the second piece, and I recognized it as my cue to go into the choir loft to be ready to do my part with Mary-Louise on the Ligeti.

She was bowing to the audience as I entered the loft. When she saw me, she smiled and said, "Are you ready?" Then she told the audience about the piece she was about to play. She told them that it was, like the two previous ones, an Avant-Garde piece and that they might find it shocking. She introduced me as her assistant.

I sat beside her on the organ bench, and she began. The piece went exactly as planned. The music rose to a loud pitch. The sanctuary rumbled and vibrated with the sound. Then Mary-Louise and I landed together on all the keys with the length of our arms from elbow to wrist, pressing as many keys as possible, white and black, holding them down as the dissonant sounds spread throughout the sanctuary.

When she nodded, I began to turn off the stops, a few at a time. Finally, when I reached over and turned off the power switch, we held our arms down on the keys tightly as the sound died slowly. When the organ was completely quiet, Mary-Louise whispered, "Good!" and the two of us stood together and faced the audience. Everyone rose and began to applaud. Mary-Louise bowed and then moved to the side and gestured toward me as the people clapped for me alone. I saw Mama slip out the door. She would be mad and hurt for days. But Mary-Louise was smiling and proud, and she bowed her head toward the audience, the two of us having pulled it off together.

Afterwards at her apartment, we drank Manhattans and toasted our success. "I have a surprise for you," she said. "I'm taking you to the Big Apple, my treat."

A few weeks later we were at the Atlanta airport waiting for a Delta plane to fly us to New York. I had never been inside an airplane before.

At home in Milledgeville, Harvill was mad. When I told him that I was going, his face clouded to a dark red, he shrugged his shoulders, and said, "Do what you want. You're going to anyway."

Mama was also mad. She had never really quit pouting about the way I talked to her at the recital. "Some opportunities you can't pass up," I told her, to which I added, "Mary-Louise is paying for this trip, and this is my life!"

"You can't do just anything in your life that you want to if it hurts other people," Mama said, again.

"Who is this hurting?" I wanted to know, but Mama looked at me with that look on her face that said she hadn't been able to sleep for trying to solve problems in the middle of the night.

"I had a dream that I was lost downtown," she said the night before Mary-Louise and I were supposed to leave. "I felt like I was cut off from my family, and I kept wondering when anybody was ever going to notice that I was missing and come looking for me. You wouldn't be acting like this if it wasn't for that Miss Brown," she said. "You're being influenced, and not for the better. That music at that recital sounded like something that came from the devil. And you standing up and clapping in church like that."

In the airplane, I pressed the back of my head tightly against the seat, gripped the armrest with my hands, and closed my eyes as the plane began to move faster and faster. I felt myself let go inside as behind the black of my eyes, I pictured us, Mary-Louise and me, rising into the clouds as Mama's and Harvill's sad faces in Milledgeville receded into the background, becoming smaller and smaller until they were nothing but two dots.

When we arrived at the Plaza Hotel, I followed Mary-Louise through the lobby filled with gold, mirrors, and sparkle. She walked ahead of me, as if she were the manager. Our room overlooked Central Park. Mary-Louise stood at the window and said, "You see how innocent the park looks? But it's full of riffraff! No one would dare go in there at night."

Because we had only one afternoon, she rushed us back through the lobby, telling me about a book called Eloise at the Plaza, about a girl who lived there, how in the book the girl named Eloise played in the dumb-waiter, how she skipped through the lobby.

Outside on the sidewalk, we walked down Fifth Avenue, Mary-Louise taking my hand and leading me through the crowd, walking fast, pointing to the right and to the left. In Brentano's Bookstore, she allowed us to stop only once, briefly, at the travel books. "Have you ever seen a bookstore more wonderful?" she asked. "Or larger? You see how I told you we could spend hours here? But we don't have time. There is so much I want you to see, and I can only afford one night."

When we got back out on the street, a Women's Liberation march was in progress. The parade came around the corner and turned in front of us. Women filled the street, from one side to the other, passing out pamphlets. Jane Fonda was riding atop a car, smiling and waving. "Look!" I said to Mary-Louise. "Can you believe it! That's Jane Fonda!"

"Isn't this a riot?" she said.

One of the women came up on the sidewalk and said to us, "Come on. This is your march."

"Oh, what the hell," said Mary-Louise. "Let's do it," and she took my arm and pulled me off the curb into the swarm of women. We were swept along with the crowd as it moved slowly up the street. "Won't it be funny if we get on television?" she said, laughing. I imagined how we would look to Mama and to the people in the Methodist Church. We walked with the other women for one long block. Then she took my arm, pulled me back up on the sidewalk, and shouted into my ear. "That's enough of that. We've got a long way to go. I've made reservations for lunch at an Ethiopian restaurant, and I want you to see St. Patrick's and ride the subway."

As we walked up the street, we passed Saks Fifth Avenue and stopped to look at the mannequins in the windows. A bald man wearing a long robe passed us on the sidewalk, handing out flyers. A woman with a blue blanket spread out on the street was selling tee shirts folded in neat stacks. We passed a vendor selling hot dogs and another selling big soft pretzels. A man was sitting on a box banging on some upturned cans as if they were drums.

At St. Patrick's Cathedral, inside, scaffolding rose to the ceiling. We walked around tall columns and in and out of smaller chapels off to the sides. We gazed up at magnificent stained glass, the colors of red and blue covering Mary-Louise's upturned face. When either of us spoke, it seemed that our voices were absorbed into the open space. I had no idea then what a Roman Catholic cathedral would come to mean to me later in my life. I didn't even know then that I was supposed to genuflect toward the main altar.

For lunch we took a taxi to an Ethiopian restaurant that Mary-Louise said was the best. The restaurant was dark inside. Black-skinned waiters dressed all in white emerged from the back like ghosts. Nearby two men dressed as women hovered near a phone booth and then walked past our table, holding their heads high, looking as beautiful as the mannequins at Saks. Mary-Louise touched my arm, nodded toward the men, and said, "New York!" then laughed, rolled her eyes, and put her hand over mine.

We sat at what she called traditional Ethiopian seating, in low armless wicker chairs beside a short round table. She explained to me that we would receive Injera bread, a thin porous bread that we would use as utensils, tearing off small triangles and using them to pick up our food. She ordered for us and, while we waited, we sipped our wine.

Our food came on a large round platter that the dark, smiling waiter set between us. His white teeth flashed in the darkness of the room. A small plate to the side contained rolls of the bread, which Mary-Louise unrolled and showed me how to tear into small pieces. She pointed to identify each of the small different-colored portions of food. "This is Gomen," she said, "Ethiopian collard greens. This in the center is the salad that always accompanies the meal." It was an ordinary salad of iceberg lettuce with tomato and cucumber and an oil and vinegar dressing. "This is Doro Wat," she said, "Ethiopian chicken stew." She used her bread and picked up a bite. "This is delicious," she said. "Try it." Then she pointed to something yellow she called Kik Alicha, Ethiopian split pea stew. Last was a green portion that she said was Ethiopian lima beans. I took a piece of the bread and imitated Mary-Louise, putting the bread with the lima beans into my mouth. I was surprised at how good it was. Everything was good, and I continued to tear the bread and eat. We were both ravenous, not worrying about manners or how neatly we were eating the food between us. At the end of the meal our waiter brought us hot steaming towels to wipe our hands and mouths. He lifted the towels off a platter with tongs, clean white towels, almost too hot to touch, smelling slightly of Clorox.

When we were back on the street again, Mary-Louise led me down some steps, and we got onto a subway train. Along the sides above the seat in front of us were signs advertising shaving cream and cigarettes. Sitting under one of the ads was a dark-haired woman holding above her head a large sign from the Women's Liberation march. In tall black letters on the sign were the words, "Think Clitoris." The woman was about my age and was dressed in jeans, a white wrinkled shirt, and brown oxford shoes. I couldn't imagine having the courage to go out in public holding a sign like that. I thought that the girl must live somewhere close by, and I pictured her dragging her tired body home from the march, sinking down into an easy chair, and eating a sandwich. Somewhere on a table nearby would be the magic marker she had used to make the sign. Mary-Louise pressed my arm, and the two of us tried to hold in our laughter. How funny it was, the two of us riding on a subway together and sitting across from that sign. Mary-Louise whispered to me, "Only in New York! I couldn't have planned this day better!"

When I look back at the person I was then, I can see that I was trying so hard to become Mary-Louise that I didn't even realize that I was sitting directly across from myself. That girl was me, and I didn't even know it. In a different scenario, another time and place, a more aware myself, I could have gone home with the woman and her sign. We could have had a glass of wine and talked about the parade. But I didn't know myself, and I would have sat in her apartment like an uncomfortable stranger.

That night we had dinner at the Top of the Sixes and watched the lights of the city move by as we sat in the rotating restaurant. Mary-Louise pointed out the tops of buildings to me, the Chrysler Building, the Empire State Building. The twin towers were not yet built back then. I often wonder how Mary-Louise would have reacted to 9-11. She could have called it the Apocalypse and could have said it was in the stars. Perhaps the end of the world was near. She would ask her astrologer friends up north. After a few drinks, I began to talk about Mama, about how controlling she was.

"You're an adult," Mary-Louise said. "Why do you let her control you like that? Why do you keep going back for more?"

Suddenly it seemed as if Mama were hiding around the corner hearing herself being discussed. I didn't know how to answer, and I didn't know how to explain the feeling I got when I tried to stand up to Mama. Even now I am embarrassed when I look back at that time. I am sorry for that childlike adult woman—me—who was so unsure who to be in this world. We drank too much and walked along the sidewalk back to the hotel room arm-in-arm. On the street we passed people whose eyes were glazed and who looked as if they hadn't bathed or had anything to eat in a long time.

That night, between the sheets in the Plaza Hotel, where the bathroom had a heated towel rack, I scooted down and pulled the covers up under my chin. Mary-Louise was in the other bed. The draperies were open, and out the window we could see the lights of the city blinking on the ceiling. I could hear Mary-Louise breathing nearby.

"Thank you for doing this for me," I said aloud into the darkness.

"You're a dear girl," she said back to me.

"I love you," I said.

"Oh, for Pete's sake," she said, "Don't be maudlin."

As I drifted off to sleep, my head was spinning with the day—the swarm of women on the street, the open coolness of the cathedral, Mary-Louise taking my hand and rushing me along, leading me. I imagined myself with all my insides squeezed out, or moved aside, all the essence that was me, filled in with Mary-Louise, so that when I went back to Baldwin High School to teach, or when I went over to

Mama's, or when I went home to Harvill, I would look the same on the outside but on the inside, I would be someone else entirely. I had a strong homesick feeling that made me swallow hard and feel tight in my throat when I thought of my ordinary life of going to school to teach, going by Mama's, and going home to cook supper for Harvill.

The next morning I heard Mary-Louise stir, moan, and then say aloud, "Good morning! Are you ready for your first cheese blintzes? There's a deli down the street."

Mary-Louise was so tired when we arrived back in Atlanta that I drove us home from the airport. The roads were dark, and the headlights lit a short space in front of the car. Suddenly I saw a rabbit dash in front of us, and I felt the bump under the tires. I pulled to the side of the road, left the lights on, and got out and walked around to the front of the car. Mary-Louise got out too and stood beside me in the road in the yellow glow of the headlights. The rabbit was trying to pull itself out of the road, only its front legs working, its back legs dragging behind. I began sobbing. I heard myself moaning, my mouth saying, "No! No! Oh, no!" I scooped the rabbit into my hands and went to the side of the road. I put the rabbit into the grass, and it began to pull itself by its front legs into the dry brush. When I realized that the rabbit was getting away from me, I reached for it, to take it back, but it disappeared into the deep brown grass.

"It's a rabbit," Mary-Louise said. "You couldn't help it. It was that rabbit's time to go."

"No!" I cried. "I did it! It was my fault!"

"Your problem is that you think you have control over things," she said as we got back into the car. "You don't. It was in the stars.

Come on. Let's get home. These Georgia roads are too dark." She leaned over and put her hand on my back as I leaned forward and hugged the steering wheel, peering at the road ahead.

On Monday I was sitting at my desk at the high school. It was early, before homeroom, and in front of me were several stacks of papers I had to grade, assignments I had left for the substitute. One was a personal essay entitled, "Something I did that I regret." For students who didn't want to write on that topic, I left an alternate— "Something I did that I am proud of." The topics had grown out of a class discussion on Robert Frost's narrative poem, "The Death of the Hired Man," and the line, "Something to look backward to with pride, something to look forward to with hope." Another stack of papers was written on a creative definition of the word *home*, taken from the line, "Home is the place that when you have to go there, they have to take you in."

That afternoon I went to Mama's house for a visit. It was one of those days that I needed to tell Mama about school. I needed to reconnect with her, to feel the closeness of my mother, to feel that everything was all right.

"How was the trip?" she asked.

"It was okay," I said, sipping the lemonade she had brought to me on the front porch. I was moving forward and backward in the blue metal rocking chair. Mama was in the webbed lounge chair, her hands folded in her aproned lap. "But I'm glad to be home," I said. Mama said she was glad that I was glad.

"Miss Brown is different," I said, connecting.

"She's not like us," Mama said.

One day when I went by the church after work, Mary-Louise was not at the organ. I found her in her office, moving around frantically, putting things into boxes. Her green choir robe was thrown across a chair. She looked up when I entered. Her blonde hair was frazzled, and her eyes were dark with anger.

"What's wrong?" I asked, standing in the doorway.

"You mark my words!" Mary-Louise said, her voice dark and heavy. "This day I have put a curse on this church! You may not see it today or next week or next month. You may not see it for years. But this church will come to ruin!"

"What in the world happened?" I asked, my voice sounding small. I sat down in a wooden straight chair close to the door.

"I was fired, that's what happened!" she said. "That pious Mississippi bastard of a minister called me to his office this morning and fired me. He didn't go through the proper procedure. He didn't consult the board members. He just fired me!" The new pastor had only been there for a month. Mary-Louise had loved the previous pastor, but she and the new one did not like one another.

I looked through the doorway behind her. "Don't look," she said. "I don't care what they think!" She dropped a stack of music books onto the floor loudly and kicked the pile into the corner. The books cascaded and slid. She turned and pointed her finger at me. "If you and that choir don't do something after all I've done for you, there's a curse for you as well." She turned her back, bent over a box, and motioned with her hand for me to leave.

"Mary-Louise," I said.

"I need to be alone," she said. "I'll talk to you later,"

I left, but I couldn't go home. I didn't know where to go or what to do. I drove around town for a while, my hands tight on the steering wheel. Mary-Louise's voice, threatening, kept playing itself again and again in my head as a wad of cotton grew larger and larger in my chest. A curse. A curse. That afternoon she didn't even look like the person I had come to love. She looked hateful, even evil, and I was afraid of her.

When I got home, the telephone was ringing as I opened the back door. "What did I do wrong?" Mary-Louise asked, her voice no longer angry and demanding, but sad. "If I knew what I did wrong, I could understand."

"I don't know," I said. "You wouldn't play gospel hymns. You gave drinking parties. You know how they are." I was trying to make her laugh. Mary-Louise had often said to me, "That's what I love about you, Darling, you make me laugh." But this time she didn't laugh. She was silent except for a soft agitated sound that she was making in her throat. I heard her pause and swallow, and I knew that she was drinking.

"You are going to do something, aren't you?" she asked me. "If the choir gets together...he didn't go through the proper channels. Tell them that."

"What can I do?" I asked, feeling alarmed, fearing that this was going to be another of those tasks she gave me that I found difficult.

"Oh, God!" she said. She sounded too tired to explain. "You can go to the board meeting. You can get up a petition. You can ask around. If all else fails, you can take up a collection. I deserve that, at the least!"

I couldn't imagine myself doing what Mary-Louise wanted me to do. She had taught me many things, and because of that, she expected me to go to people, ask them to use their influence, even perhaps ask them for money. Singing beside people in the choir or being with them at her parties was one thing. Going to their businesses or their homes to ask for money was something else entirely. I read somewhere that if you pretend to be something you are not long enough, you will become that thing. I sat in the chair in the living room and tried to picture myself, confident, smiling, holding out my hand to people, first one and then another, like a politician. But when I imagined it, I saw myself standing before them, my head down, not remembering what I was there for.

Mr. Swanson was one of the deacons, but I had never been to his office at the bank. Albert Mason, one of the basses in the choir, was with the Georgia Power Company; Mama bought her hot water heater from him. Dr. Rutherford, a tenor, was a dentist who had a new brick office on the corner downtown. But he wasn't my dentist, and I had never been inside his office. In my mind I saw all of those people lined up to be visited, and I heard Mary-Louise's voice saying to me, "What have you done? How many people have you talked to? You are my only hope."

When I first walked into the bank, Mr. Swanson came toward me, shaking my hand, and saying, "Well, young lady, what can I do for you?" He knew my parents, and his words immediately reduced me to a child. I sat down across from him, and I said the words I had rehearsed, "I don't know whether you are aware of this, but Miss Brown has been fired from her job as our organist/choir director."

"That right?" he said, leaning forward. "I'm sorry to hear that."

"Yes," I said, "and I was wondering if maybe we as church members could get together and express our opinion to the board, if maybe that would help to get her reinstated."

Mr. Swanson didn't say anything but waited for me to continue.

"Or, if that doesn't work," I said, "we could take up a collection for her."

"Yes, yes," he said, rising from his chair and putting his hand into his back pocket, pulling out a checkbook. "That is a good idea. We've been fortunate to have such a fine musician here." He wrote me a check. Out on the sidewalk, I looked at the check. It was made out to Mary-Louise Brown and was for fifty dollars. He had written "donation" in the corner. It was a start.

At Georgia Power Albert Mason was selling a woman an electric oven. I sat down in a hard plastic chair to wait. Lucy Avant was sitting behind the counter, and she asked me, "How's your Mama?" She was one of the biggest gossips in Milledgeville.

When the woman looking at ovens left, Mr. Mason came toward me, his hand out. "Is there somewhere we can talk?" I asked him, looking at Lucy Avant.

"Certainly," he said. He led me to a cubicle with a desk and two chairs.

I sat across from him and said, "Are you aware that Miss Brown has been fired?"

"I'm sorry to hear that," he said. "But isn't that about how long our directors usually stay?"

"She doesn't want to leave," I said. "She wants to stay here in Milledgeville and continue being our director. The new minister didn't follow the proper procedure. He fired her without going through the board of directors. She feels that the choir members could do something to get her reinstated."

"I see," he said. "But I'm not sure, as a businessman, that I can get involved with that. I've known those board members for a long time. Then he stood and said, "You know, she has always been different. We've had some pretty music, and she's a hard worker, but I can't help but feel that she might be happier somewhere else. She doesn't really fit in here. We're simple people, and sometimes I think she thinks we're the Mormon Tabernacle Choir."

Suddenly I felt as if I were talking to the enemy. It seemed as if Mr. Mason may have been one of the people who were against Mary-Louise from the beginning.

"Well, could you make a donation?" I asked. "It's the least we can do."

"Sure!" he said, seeming relieved. He took out his wallet and handed me three ten dollar bills.

As I was walking out the door, he called after me, "Tell your Mama I said hello! Tell her we have some nice new ovens if she's ready to trade that old one in!"

Dr. Rutherford's dentist office looked like a private home. It had a white picket fence around it and shutters on the windows. Inside, the office resembled a living room you might see in "Better Homes and Gardens." The receptionist said that the doctor was with a patient and would be finished in about twenty minutes. I sat in the waiting room and looked at magazines.

Dr. Rutherford's response was, "I'll certainly be glad to do whatever everyone else is doing. Let me know what you all decide. I'll sign a petition or make a donation or something." Then he rushed back to his next patient.

Emotionally exhausted, I drove home. I had eighty dollars and a promise, and I didn't want to be in charge of this. I dreaded talking to Mary-Louise and listening to her demands, the blaming, and that sound she made in her throat. She wanted me to go to the board meeting, and I hated the idea.

As I went into the church the next evening, I could hear people talking inside, but when I entered the room, they got quiet. Seven men and one woman were sitting around a table in the center of the room. I sat in a folding chair against the wall. Soon after I sat down, the minister said to the group, "Is there any more discussion?" No one looked at me, and no one said anything. "Then I guess we'll call for a vote," he said.

"Excuse me," I said, standing. "Is this about Miss Brown? If it is, I would like to express my opinion about it before you vote."

"Go ahead," the minister said.

"Doesn't the choir have any input in this decision?" I asked.

Dr. Alberta Carrington, a retired psychologist from the college, said, "This young lady has been unduly influenced and is herself one of the reasons this action is necessary. Miss Brown is unstable, and she has a drinking problem."

"The only ways she has influenced me have been positive," I said. "She has helped me and many others."

But I could tell from Dr. Carrington's words that rumors had been circulating about our relationship. People thought that I was under her spell, and I was defiant. I tried to argue with them, but I heard in their voices that they didn't think I was thinking for myself.

Mr. Al Martin said, "She's influenced you. And not for the good either. I never knew your mother and father to drink at parties like that. Your daddy was a tee-totaler and a good man. The Baptist Church doors didn't open but what he was there."

I knew that I was defeated.

Over the next several days, Mary-Louise was like a dark shadow in my mind. Some days when I went to see her, I found her dressed and making a list of places she wanted to go to look for a job. Other days she was still in her bathrobe in the middle of the afternoon, saying that she had no energy. On those days, she sent me to the liquor store for Port, another thing that didn't feel comfortable to me, going to the liquor store, having grown up Baptist, my daddy a tee-totaler. She didn't want any visitors except me, and she didn't always want me. She reminded me to use the code when knocking on the door, the beginning of Beethoven's Fifth Symphony—dum-ta-da-dum, dum-ta-da-dum. Sometimes she came and let me in, and other times she ignored my knock. I thought that she was blaming me for not succeeding at getting her reinstated or getting a larger collection from the choir members.

One afternoon Mary-Louise was in bed, and she got up to let me in. She was wearing a white silk nightgown that flowed as she walked. Instead of sitting down at the Mother-of-Pearl table, she went back to bed and told me to come back there with her. She lay down and said to me, "Be a dear, and fix us a martini." As I went into the kitchen, she called out to me what to do. "The glasses are those long-stemmed ones in the cabinet above the sink," she said. "The olives are in the refrigerator. The gin and vermouth are under the counter. Fill the glass with gin, then put a drop of vermouth. Drop an olive into each glass." I followed the steps. "There's a round tray on top of the counter," she said. "Bring napkins from the second drawer." I carried the drinks on the tray into Mary-Louise's bedroom. I sat on the edge of the bed as we drank the martinis. I had never had a martini before, and the strong liquid burned all the way down to my stomach. It smelled like pine trees.

"I'm tired," she said. "I haven't found a job. My back hurts, and the doctor won't give me anything for pain."

I asked if I could fix her something to eat, but she said that she wasn't hungry. She said she wanted to die. "There's nowhere for me to go," she said. "Up North are all the Jews. Out West, the people are so bland. Down here in the South the people are such hypocrites. Darjeeling. I'll go to Darjeeling. Darjeeling is Shangri-la." I had never heard her sound prejudiced before, and her words scared me.

Over the next several days Mary-Louise made a plan. She decided to use all of her savings and take a trip around the world. She said it was something she had always wanted to do, and she decided that now was the time. She would board Thap Thim and stop the *Times* delivery. She said that she had checked with her astrologer friend up North and that her stars were favorable for travel. She wanted me to collect her mail regularly and to take anything that looked like a bill to her accountant. And she wanted me to drive her to the Atlanta airport.

On the way home from the airport, I imagined Mary-Louise on the plane going far away to exotic places. I thought of Harvill and Mama in Milledgeville, and in a way I felt relieved; life seemed easier and less complicated with Mary-Louise gone. During the time that she was gone, I picked up her mail every day, delivered the bills to her accountant, and told her in my letters which bills had come. I settled into a routine. I went by to see Mama after work, and she was glad to see me. She met me at the screen door, and we traded stories about our day. She told me she did a washing, baked some Amish friendship bread for her neighbor, how she lay down and took a nap with the door open, a breeze coming in.

Then Mary-Louise's letters began to come, sometimes four or five together in one day, sometimes none at all. Her letters were like reading a book. She suggested to me before she left that I read an Indian writer, Rabindranath Tagore, and she left me her copy of *A Tagore Reader*. I read a story called "The Cabuliwallah." It was a story about a fruitseller from Cabul who befriended a young girl despite her mother and father's suspicions that he may have devious motives. They had heard of peddlers who kidnapped young girls and carried them off in their bags. After being accused of stealing, the fruitseller went away to prison for a long time, but in the end I learned that he was just a father who was missing his own daughter who was miles away in another country. As I read, I imagined Mary-Louise in that exotic land. And as I lived my days in Milledgeville, in my mind I was aware that on the other side of the world was Mary-Louise and that she would return.

THE LETTERS: A SAMPLING
October, 1971, to February, 1972

From Frankfurt:
"I hope you got home safely. You were an angel to drive me to the airport. At last I am in Frankfurt, and I am exhausted. The flight to

London was delightful. I met a charming Englishman who wants to move his family to Georgia near Atlanta. I tried to tell him the score, but I don't think it made a dent."

From Kabul, Afghanistan:

"Friday I went alone with the hotel driver for a gorgeous trip to the Salong Pass. It is through the Hindu Kush, winding through gorges, mounting on an excellent road to eleven thousand feet up to the snows. The tunnel at the top, built by the Russians, is used by everything from taxis to petrol trucks to camel caravans.

"On the way home, we stopped off at the home of the driver's brother. The family were lovely, and we sat on the floor for tea. The brothers kept throwing a white tablecloth over my legs because a woman's legs are not supposed to be seen in a Moslem household. When I got back to the hotel, I found that the family had taken every bit of my money, even my traveler's checks. I dispatched the driver back to his relatives, and at about midnight the brother returned with my wallet, missing half my money. Then the thief expected a reward! Can you imagine!

"The next morning I went to the American Embassy. They were wonderful to me and said I had been lucky beyond belief and could not understand how I had gotten back alive from the Pass. You only travel by surface in this country with a large bus and armed guards. Four Americans have been murdered in the last two weeks in Kabul, and dozens and dozens are missing, probably buried somewhere in the mountains. The bulletin board at the Embassy is a horror, card after card requesting the whereabouts of someone's child, young travelers in their late teens and early twenties who disappear. There is absolutely no law and order in this country. The mountains are filled with wild tribes that attack any car unfortunate enough to be there at night. The American Embassy insisted that I move to the Intercontinental Hotel immediately, as my life was not safe at the Spinzer, where I was staying. The awful thing is, I know they were right. The Intercontinental is up on a hill, a bit removed from the city, and it is much more expensive. But at least it's safer.

"Have been able to buy almost nothing since it is impossible to mail anything from Afghanistan. It is a shame because there are lovely carpets and magnificent old musical instruments. I have never seen so many guns in my life. I would estimate, conservatively, 500,000 for sale in Kabul!

"Today I took the bus ride to Peshavar, East Pakistan, through the Kabul gorge and the Khyber Pass. This again was a dangerous affair. Your luggage rides on top of the bus, and you have to keep jumping out to make sure it's still there. The bus was filled with hippies smoking hashish. They looked ill, and there was a great deal of vomiting. A Pakistani boy asked me if people smoke hashish on buses everywhere in the world."

From Darjeeling:

"Here I am in Shangri-la. I met a nice American couple who live here in palatial luxury. The wife has been trying to get me to see Mother Teresa of Calcutta while I am on this trip. She says it would be a shame to come all this distance without seeing her.

"Goods here are reasonably priced. I would love to live in this city, but coping with the system would be horrendous.

"How are your stars? Mine are making me touchy and temperamental. Thank God I'm in heaven here in Darjeeling. One man at the hotel said to me, 'See Darjeeling and die!' Honestly, Sandra, I miss you, but I don't want to come back there!"

From Calcutta:

"The people in this city are much scrawnier and more emaciated than I imagined. I think Calcutta is like New York, an impossible situation without a dictator.

"I visited Mother Teresa today, and I can't describe to you how I feel. There is a staff of seven and about 150 sick and dirty children. All I could do was stand there and say, 'What can I do? Why won't someone tell me what I can do?'

"Then one of those gentle Indian sisters told me that they needed blankets for the winter. Today I am going to buy as many blankets as I can afford and get someone to help me carry them up there. The look of those people, the way they live their lives. I don't know how to tell you, but I have a lot to think about.

"I bought blankets and ten yards of 54-inch width heavy flannel, all for $14, and I paid a young man to help me carry it all back up the hill. Mother Teresa herself came over to thank me. Her face is a pattern of wrinkles. When she took my hands into hers, her hands were rough, like the bottom of a rusty bucket. When I became aware of my soft hands, how protected they are for my music, I wondered what I've been doing with my hands all this time. Sometimes I feel like the most useless human being on the face of the earth."

From Saigon:

"There are no words to describe Saigon. The tragedy of this country, the look of pain and suffering in every single person's eyes, is something you never forget once you have seen it. The city looks as though, after years of war, it is ready to crumble away. Nothing, of course, has been cared for. I am staying at the Majestic, an old French hotel on the harbor. It is the second best hotel in town and is old, dusty, and dirty, like everything else.

"The bombing went on all night long. The well-taped windows rattled like mad. They bombed Sunday and Monday during the day, and at night it sounded as though they were a block away.

"The harbor is fascinating. It is narrow; when the destroyers turn around, it looks as though they will touch both banks.

"The marketplace is indescribable, certainly the most fascinating black market in the world where the choicest goods anywhere are for sale. Unfortunately, it is also dangerous. One cannot wander far in Saigon.

"The people are beautiful. Saigon is an entirely Eurasian city, and it is easy to see how the French spent their time while they were here! The fragile, delicate features mixed with the Southeast Asian polyglot is unique in this part of the world. It is touching to see the butterfly girls pedaling up and down on their motorbikes. There is a general sweetness and hopelessness in everyone. This may be because there is talk that the Americans may be leaving, I do not know. Certainly they have no hope for their future. As you know, the war did not stop. I don't think anyone really expected anything different, certainly not the Vietnamese. On Sunday, the 'peace-keeping' forces moved into the hotel, obviously enjoying themselves but slightly confused as to what they were supposed to do. On Monday Agnew's entourage and CBS moved in.

"I expect to be home near the end of this month, utterly exhausted and thoroughly broke, but with many thoughts in my head and incredible memories. I do not mind coming home, but how I am going to withstand the pettiness and small-mindedness of Milledgeville after all I have seen, I do not know."

My life in Milledgeville continued as usual. We went to eat with Harvill's parents. I took Mama to Wal-mart to look at some cloth. Mary-Louise wrote me about Indian batiks, and as I fingered the material at Wal-mart, I imagined women in long sarongs with red dots painted in the center of their foreheads, a place for the soul to move in and out. Time went by with rainy Mondays and crinkly grocery sacks, cartons of strawberries and fresh haircuts, pages of books and Harvill's warm soft undershorts fresh from the dryer, leaves falling and crunching, brown grass and sweaters, Santa Claus and evergreen, gold garland and blinking lights, nativity. My days at school were students and teachers, wrinkled faces, freckled faces, bitten fingernails, a ring in a nose, unlocking doors, walking up and down steps, seeing my reflection in a window. In my mind was an image of movement, Harvill, Mama, and me shifting here and there in a small space, the cubbyhole that was Milledgeville.

I imagined Mary-Louise at the end of a long bridge, her blond hair and white skin moving in and out among the dark eyes, dark hair, dark skin, dusty dirty poverty, open mouths, hungry bellies, screams of children. All day I carried with me the darkness of the east, the exotic smell of far-away places, dusty feet walking in sand. No matter how many grocery aisles I walked down, no matter how many meals I cooked, no matter how many miles I walked, a cord connected me to the traveler far away who I knew would return. I shielded myself from the complications that I knew her return would bring.

While Mary-Louise was in Japan in February, it snowed in Milledgeville, more snow than since the time of George Washington, the newspaper said. The schools and businesses were closed, and Pennsylvania loaned Georgia its snowplows. It snowed and snowed, and I stood at the window of our double-wide and watched as peace settled in and all rough edges smoothed out, all colors turned to white. I put on my denim bell-bottoms, gloves, and knit cap and went out. I lay in the snow, its softness around me. I waded through it, breathing the frigid air deeply into my lungs. With a big spoon I scooped the top layer off and went inside to make snow ice cream with sugar, vanilla, and milk. I threw my jeans into the dryer and stood, looking out the window. As soon as my jeans were dry, I put them on and went out again.

Once Mary-Louise called, collect. The connection was bad, and I couldn't catch the name of the country she was calling from, but still she stayed on the line, not talking, wanting to hear news of Milledgeville. Hadn't anything changed? Anything at all? Hadn't anything happened worth telling her? I had not intended to tell her anything bad, but in the silence, in an attempt to fill it, I blurted out the thing I had meant not to tell, that one of Mary-Louise's neighbors down at the end of her street, an elderly woman who lived alone, had been raped and killed, presumably by her yard man. Mary-Louise's silence was so long that I called out, "Are you there? Are you still there?"

"Horrendous, horrendous," she said, making that sound in her throat loud enough to hear over the static. Then she said, "I'm really annoyed that you told me that. Why did you tell me such terrible news when I'm far away?"

"It snowed here," I said, getting away from the subject that had annoyed her.

"Yes," Mary-Louise said, distracted. "Mrs. Johnson dead. I can't believe it. What a horrible thing. And on my own street." Then another long silence.

"Listen, Dear," she said. "I'll pay you for this call. I'll be home soon." Thinking of her coming home gave me a heaviness, a feeling of dark draperies to push aside, tall grass to wade through, and a low ceiling, too short to stand up under without bumping my head.

Coming in at the airport gate, Mary-Louise looked like a stranger to me. Her hair had grown long and stood out around her face. When she saw me, she waved and smiled. "Hello, Darling!" she said and came toward me, holding her arms open. I hugged her, and then she pushed me out at arm's length. "You look marvelous," she said. She was in a good mood, and I could smell whiskey on her breath.

"Let's go have a drink," she said. "It will take a while for them to get all my luggage in anyway."

In the airport bar, Mary-Louise leaned toward me, patting my arm, and said, "I've missed you!" Then, suddenly serious, she looked down, stirred her drink, and said, "I can't describe to you the things I've seen. I feel as if my whole life has been wasted."

"What do you mean?" I asked, but she changed the subject and said she would tell me bit by bit, not all at once. She had to think first; it was all so new.

When the packages began to come in containing her purchases from the trip, she wanted me to come over. I helped as she opened them one at a time and spread the treasures around her apartment. Across her bed she laid long starched batiks in animal prints with matching borders. In piles on the tops of tables, bookshelves, and chests were bracelets, necklaces, beaded bags, and satin pin cushions. Pushed into corners and lying in rows were brown woodcarvings of Madonnas, Buddhas, and sacred cows.

In the center of her hallway was a long oriental rug that she had had made in Afghanistan, especially for Harvill and me. It was in bright shades of red and blue on a background of gray. Facing one way was a phoenix and in the opposite direction, a dragon. She said the rug was a symbol of eternal life.

She bought a carved wooden mask for Harvill and, for me, some batik cloth and beggar's beads, composed of semi-precious stones strung by people on the streets and sold for almost nothing. The beads were smooth and in colors of teal, green, gold, and amber. I put them on, and they were heavy and cold against the back of my neck.

She rolled up the Oriental rug and laid it beside the door so that I wouldn't forget to take it with me. She cleaned off the mother-of-pearl table and got us a glass of Port. We sat there the way we had so many times before. The items she brought from foreign places surrounded us, the exotic smell of them in the room. I thought of my first days in Mary-Louise's apartment when she began to teach me about the world outside of Milledgeville. Now she had brought the world to her apartment.

We lit cigarettes, and I realized suddenly that I was tired and sad. It seemed that I had been sitting in this room for years and going back and forth from Harvill to Mama to Mary-Louise. The conversations we had were deep, making me think, the laughter, long and loud and secretly ours, the humor ours. My cheeks became tired from smiling.

The red and blue packages lying around the room like a flea market were alien and unfamiliar. I felt lonely, misplaced, and homesick.

"I can't ever play the organ again," Mary-Louise said, "not after all I've seen," shaking her head, blowing out smoke.

"Why?" I asked, my mouth dry and thick, tired of smoke.

"Music doesn't mean anything," she said, "not to people whose stomachs are empty. I could play the organ in India until I was blue in the face, and no one would hear. I'm going to find something else to do, something that will be useful."

"Like what?" I asked.

"I don't know," she said. "I have credentials, a good college degree from Barnard. Surely I can do something. Social work. Or nursing. I could go back to school and study to become a nurse."

"You could," I said. "But what about your talent?"

"I'm going to rest a few days and then begin studying my options," she said. "I've been talking to my astrologer friends up North. They see me in a helping profession. They are going to help me." She looked over at me. "You should know. You're in a helping profession." She leaned forward and set her drink on the table. "You should go," she said. "I want to sleep."

The next day at school I assigned my class a paper to write. They were to create a conversation between Hamlet and Huckleberry Finn, a discussion about right and wrong. Should Hamlet kill the king in prayer or wait until later and kill him in adultery? What do you think, Huck? And what about Huck? Should he turn Jim in? It is a crime to protect a slave, but is it a sin? What a discussion the two would have! These were the kinds of writing ideas I created for my students. I put two unlike things together to see what would happen. Two unlike things, like Mary-Louise and me.

When the telephone bill came, it contained the collect call Mary-Louise made from her trip. The call cost two hundred dollars. When I came home from work, Harvill was already there, going through the bills at the dining room table. He was mad, and he stood up and faced me. His neck was red and splotched, and his eyes looked tired. "You've got to make her pay for this call," he said, shaking the bill at me. "We can't afford it, and it's her responsibility." When I thought about it, I agreed that Mary-Louise should pay for the call. Two hundred dollars was a lot of money for Harvill and me.

The next day after school, I gave the bill to her. I pretended that I assumed she would want to see it, to pay it. "I thought you'd probably want this," I said, sitting on the love seat across from her.

Mary-Louise took the bill in her hand and looked up at me, angry. "How can you ask me to pay this bill? I've lost my job. I've taken this expensive trip, and I have no money. I can't believe you would ask this."

"We can't afford it," I said. "Harvill said that I should ask you. I'm sorry. I'll try to work it out." I didn't tell Harvill about her reaction, and I decided that I would try to pay it myself out of my check.

I didn't go by Mary-Louise's the next afternoon. Her depression was heavy on my shoulders. But when I got home that afternoon, she called and told me that she had gotten a job teaching music in the school system.

But teaching is mine, I thought.

She had met with the school superintendent. She was to begin immediately, taking over for a music teacher who was pregnant. I couldn't imagine it. "I told you I wanted to be in a helping profession," she reminded me. "This way I can be involved with music but help the children as well." I had misgivings, but I didn't say anything. I was looking forward to the freedom Mary-Louise's job would give me.

But after the first few days, she was exhausted and complaining. "Can you come over?" she asked.

"Those buildings are old and dirty!" she said that afternoon, nibbling on cheese crackers and sipping wine. "How do you stand it? And these children are far behind those in the New York schools."

I felt protective, distancing myself. "I like it," I said. "They do the best they can with the money they have."

"And the bugs!" she said. "I can tell you if I see one cockroach, I'm quitting!" Mary-Louise was terrified of the large roaches in the South. Once when she found one in her bathroom, she called her electrician to come kill it.

"I can guarantee you that you will see cockroaches in the public schools!" I said, laughing.

One afternoon, I found her in her bedroom crawling around on the floor, looking for something. She sat back on her ankles and showed me what she had in her hand. It was a wooden statue of the Virgin Mary holding the baby Jesus in her arms. The Virgin had a carved wooden crown on her head. Mary-Louise pointed to the statue's hand where a tiny hole was empty. "The scepter is gone," she said, "and there is a chip out of the crown. My grandmother brought me this carving from Italy years ago," she said. "It's old and valuable. I've knocked it off the mantle. The pieces are on the floor somewhere."

I got down on my hands and knees beside her and began to feel around on the floor. I found the small round scepter under the desk, but I couldn't find the chip from the crown. Mary-Louise took the scepter and fitted it back into the Virgin Mary's hand. Then she looked up at me and said, "Here, help me up."

I stood and gave her a hand up and told her that I had to leave. As we walked to the door, Mary-Louise said, "I'm going to look for another job. Maybe social work." She held the wooden statue in the crook of her arm, as if holding a baby, and stroked the sharp edges of the Virgin's carved dress. As we stepped out on to the front porch, she said, "If that works out, fine. In the meantime, if I get too tired, I'll commit suicide. My stars have me under strong suicidal aspects right now."

I had been looking out toward the street, but when she said that, I was suddenly angry, and I turned to face her. "How can you say that?" I asked. It seemed to me that if you knew what your stars were, you should be able to do something to change them. If you were standing on the tracks when the train was coming, you could get off. You didn't have to just allow things to happen.

"You haven't lived long enough to know the score," Mary-Louise said. "I'll talk to you tomorrow." And she waved me away and closed the door.

Several days later when I went by, she was listing her possessions on a yellow legal pad. "Would you like this cloisonné vase?" she asked me. She pronounced it vahz. "It's valuable. Or my fur? You'd look ravishing in it." I had seen her full-length mink coat hanging in her closet. At any other time it would have been laughable to imagine me wearing the fur in Milledgeville, Georgia, or anywhere for that matter.

I may as well be wearing an Indian sari or a gorilla suit. But that day it wasn't funny.

"Mary-Louise..." I began.

"The Mother-of-Pearl table is going to Claire Coci, an organist friend of mine up North. I'm writing her address and phone number down for you."

"Mary-Louise, you don't need to do this," I said. "You don't have to. You're going to get a job you like. You'll see." For the first time, our age difference mattered to me. I was too young to have to carry the weight of the knowledge of what Mary-Louise might do. I resented her putting this burden on me.

One night we were talking on the phone when I heard the receiver drop. I called loudly, "Mary-Louise! Are you there?" I couldn't hear any response; yet, the phone was still off the hook and the line open. I got in my car and drove over. Harvill was mad, but that was nothing new. We barely spoke any more but just passed each other in the hallway. The windows to Mary-Louise's apartment were dark. I pounded on the door...dum-ta-da-dum, dum-ta-da-dum. I didn't hear any response inside; I called her name loudly twice. "Mary-Louise!" Knock, knock. "Mary-Louise!"

Then I heard her voice on the other side of the door. "Please!" she growled. "Everybody in this house is going to hear you!"

"It's Sandra," I said, pronouncing my name the way that she did.

"What do you want?" she said, unlocking the door. Then she pulled the door open and leaned around, her nightgown on, her face white and puffy. "Do you know what time it is?" she said.

"I heard the phone drop, and then you wouldn't answer," I said. "It scared me, the way you've been talking."

"Oh, God," she said, exasperated. Then, her voice softening, "Come in for a minute." She went back to her bed, and I followed. The phone was still off the hook, and I placed the receiver back in its cradle. She sat down on the edge of the bed and motioned for me to sit beside her. When she began talking, her speech was slurred. "You know, Dear, when I heard you knocking then, it occurred to me that I never told you about the beginning of Beethoven's Fifth."

"My code for knocking on your door."

"Yes," she said, "but I wanted to tell you this. There's a myth that Beethoven meant for it to sound like the approach of death. Or fate knocking on the door."

"Really," I said. "Did you mean that when you chose it for my code?"

"Oh, I don't know," she said. "It was a theory. A student of Beethoven's said it, but Beethoven poo-pooed the idea. Then Beethoven's first biographer liked it so well, he stuck it in there, and everybody attributed it to Beethoven."

"That's interesting," I said, and then, "You're not still thinking of killing yourself, are you?"

Mary-Louise shrugged. "It's an option," she said. "It's always been an option. My drawers are full of suicide notes I've written over the years. Somehow life seems easier if I have a way out."

"I really hope you won't," I said. "What would I do without you?"

"You'll be fine," she said.

Mary-Louise complained about her job in the schools every time we talked. "The principal of the school is illiterate," she said. "You should hear the way he talks." I tried to encourage her, but it seemed as if her mind was made up. After a while, I didn't know what to say.

"At the faculty meetings," she said, "the principal drops all his consonants and makes crude jokes. He is condescending to the teachers." I tried to say things that would make her laugh, but she said, "Yes, well," and then was quiet, making that agitated sound in her throat. "And the cockroaches are everywhere."

I began to hope that she wouldn't call, and I dreaded going by her apartment after work. She was down, and I didn't know how to lift her back up.

"The children won't be quiet long enough to sing," Mary-Louise said to me the next time she called. "And when they sing, they scream."

"I know that must be hard on you," I said.

"I simply must get something else," she said.

"Have you heard from any of your job applications?" I asked.

"Not yet," she said.

"You'll probably hear something soon," I said.

Mary-Louise didn't say anything but stayed on the phone, silent. I was sitting on the edge of the bed. Harvill was in the living room watching TV. He had already had his shower and was lying down on the sofa in his pajamas watching an old re-run of "Columbo." I could hear the television. My arm was getting tired from holding the phone.

"The books I have to carry from one classroom to the other are too heavy," Mary-Louise said. "I don't have the strength to lift them, and that principal won't find me a cart."

"Why don't you let the children help you carry those books from one room to the other?" I asked. "They are the age where they like to help the teacher. They would love to help you carry those books." It was a simple, spontaneous suggestion, a helpful idea. I didn't realize what a moment that would be.

Mary-Louise shouted into the phone, sudden and loud. "Oh, Saundra, don't be an idiot!"

Before I knew what I was doing, I slammed the telephone receiver into its cradle. It made a loud satisfying noise. When I sat down on the edge of the bed, I could feel my heart pounding in my ears. The sounds coming from the living room seemed wrapped in cotton. Idiot! Idiot! Idiot! The word thrummed in my head.

When I took my hand from the receiver, it stayed in the curved position, and I held it in my lap and looked down at it the way a mother might look at her own hand after slapping her child in the face. Idiot! Idiot! Saundra, don't be an idiot! I imagined myself re-dialing Mary-Louise's number, hearing myself say, "I didn't mean to do that. It was an impulse. I didn't like you calling me an idiot." For a moment, I could have done that. Instead, I let the moment pass. Soon it would be too late to take it back. I got up and walked away from the phone.

Suddenly, the house looked different to me, the way the street looks different outside after leaving the picture show. I closed my eyes and held my hands above my head. A door closed. I let Mary-Louise stay behind the door.

As I left the bedroom and stepped into the hall, the phone rang. I jumped and took a deep breath. I let it ring several times.

"Hello?" I said.

"What are you doing?" Mama asked, her voice pleasant.

"Oh, nothing much," I said. "Watching TV." With the phone to my ear, I lay back on the bed, free.

That night I dreamed that I was floating on a raft in the middle of a huge ocean of black water. The raft was almost too small for me to be able to hold on. All I had with me were my keys. The keys kept slipping out of my hand and falling into the deep water, and I kept grasping for them, catching them each time before they drifted out of reach in the black water.

A few days later I received a note in the mail. It was written on yellow lined paper in Mary-Louise's scrawling handwriting. All it said was, "Put my books in a brown paper bag, and leave them at my door." I knew that it was over, and the sad, heavy thud of ending was tinged with a sense of relief. I put the *Quest for the Historical Jesus* in a brown paper grocery sack on the bottom and then on top of it layered the boxed set of Proust's *Remembrance of Things Past*, Dostoevsky's *The Idiot*, Rabindrinath Tagore's Complete Works, and the *Bhagavad Gita*. I put the bag in my car and waited until Mary-Louise's car was gone, then parked on the street in front of her apartment. I quietly set the bag in front of her door. It occurred to me to put a note inside, but I didn't know what I would say, so I left the books there with no message.

A month went by, and I didn't hear from her. The Methodist Church got a new organist, but I didn't go to church. I began taking some after-school courses at Georgia College as part of my Master's Degree. I had time now.

One day I was walking along the sidewalk on Montgomery Street headed to class. I was passing Mary-Louise's house, looking straight ahead, when I heard her coughing. Out of the corner of my eye I saw her beside her open car door. She was kneeling down trying to put some books into the back of the car. I heard my feet hitting the sidewalk, determined, moving forward; I did not want to be drawn into her web again. My arms were swinging at my side. She was bent down, maybe wanting help, maybe needing me to run over to offer. I didn't know if she saw me. The scenario played itself out in my mind, one of two. Oh, thank you, darling, how good it is to see you again, I've missed you. The other, I'm fine, leave me alone, I don't need you. I kept walking, the coughing, the blonde hair, the desperation beside me, then behind me. I kept going, leaving her behind, standing up for myself, not being manipulated, feeling independent and defiant, the figure beside the car receding into the past.

Another month passed before I received the call at school. Later I couldn't remember the exact words. Did the person say, "Mary-Louise Brown committed suicide last night," or "Mary-Louise Brown killed herself," or "That former organist took her own life"? Whoever it was said that she had taken twenty seconals. She had accepted a job as a Social Worker in Griffin, Georgia, and someone was to pick her up that morning and drive her. She left a note on the door for him to come in, that the door was unlocked. She locked Thap Thim in the closet because she knew that cats eat the faces of the dead. By the time the man found her, rigor mortis had set in. The nurse in the pathology lab when they brought her in at the hospital had been one of the members of the Methodist Church and a friend, and she screamed and fell to the floor when they took the sheet off Mary-Louise's face.

She did it kept going through my head. *She did it.* I ran down the hall, gasping for breath. I pushed open the door of the counselor's office. I sat on the sofa and said aloud again and again, "She did it."

Throughout the following days, when Mary-Louise was cremated, when she was buried in a single grave at the back of the cemetery next to the Cuban refugees, near other people who had no family, I moved forward with no feeling. Mary-Louise's favorite hymn, "Ah, Holy Jesus," which she called *Herzleibster Jesu* was sung at her memorial service at the funeral home. "Who was the guilty? Who brought this upon thee? I crucified thee!" I thought that I should feel blame or responsibility, but I didn't feel anything at all.

Was Mary-Louise in Nirvana, or in the concentric circles somewhere on her way? Would she come back one day, like a prisoner released from jail, and would I be glad to see her, or else wonder where in my life I would put her, with all her demands of time, energy, attention, and obedience? Would she be forever there, looking over my shoulder? What about the curses she promised to leave behind? After I hung up on her that day, did she put a curse on me as well? Or the day I passed by and didn't help her? Would I recognize the manifestation of a curse if I saw it?

Mary-Louise left a note for Rose Baugh, the only friend in Milledgeville that she had kept. In the note, she blamed no one. Rose asked me to help her clean out Mary-Louise's apartment, and I did. We were afraid to throw anything away without looking at it first. What if Mary-Louise had composed a piece of music that should be offered to the world? Day after day we emptied drawers and shelves into tall brown garbage bags. I lined the bags up across the back seat of my car like friends and took them to the extra bedroom in our double-wide. Each day I passed by the room and looked in. It seemed to me that the bags were filled with bones.

Finally, I went into the room and began. I knocked one of the bags over to its side, and the contents spilled out. She had thrown nothing away. Sitting in the middle of the floor, my legs stretched out in front of me, I began to go through the contents of her bedside table. There were five medicine bottles, a Milledgeville telephone directory, a small green disposable flashlight, a dozen paper notes—grocery lists, people to call, things to do, and lists of possessions, all in Mary-Louise's handwriting. In the midst of the pile were a jar of Mentholatum, pens and pencils, a box of hairpins, an open package of lifesavers, a tube of red lipstick, two unopened packages of Vantage cigarettes, a roll of astrology charts, and two calendars with notes written on them, one old and one new. The first calendar contained notes about Mary-Louise's life before Milledgeville, notes about her father, when his medicine was due, when his doctors' appointments were scheduled. I found lists of students' scheduled piano lessons, names that were Northern and strange to me—Kolodzeski and Weiss. The other calendar was one Mary-Louise had used in Milledgeville. It contained notes about doctors' appointments with names I recognized and notes to herself, go buy more purple stockings.

I slid across the floor, moving into each stack that tumbled from the bags. From Mary-Louise's dresser drawer were rolled up stockings in pink, mauve, and silver, pajamas and a long blue nightgown. I picked up the gown and stood up. I was already stiff from sitting too long. I took the gown into the bedroom and stood before the mirror. I held the gown in front of me and looked at myself. I put my face into the gown and breathed deeply for her scent. Then I folded the gown and put it into my drawer on top of my cotton nightshirts.

Back on the floor again, I found a brown envelope containing glossy prints of Mary-Louise in concert, a younger version of herself in a black evening gown, bowing beside the grand piano on stage, long-stemmed roses cradled in her arm, her smile, her blonde hair curled loosely. In another envelope were flyers from Town Hall and Carnegie Hall, "Mary-Louise Brown in Concert." In glossy black-and-white photographs, she moved through cocktail parties, wearing her mink coat, her flirtatious smile, a Manhattan glass in one hand, a cigarette in the other.

So many possessions we accumulate in our lives! I thought of my own—my books and records—my lists of things to do. I would be judged by what I left behind. From a shoebox tied with a ribbon were two pairs of cloisonné earrings the size of silver dollars, one white glove still shaped like Mary-Louise's hand, her mother's death certificate, and her own childhood report cards. A small paper book of Saul Steinberg's drawings contained inside the front cover an original Steinberg drawing of Mary-Louise herself, sitting on a piano bench with antennae coming out of her head. Inscribed around the drawing was Steinberg's handwritten message, "Happy Birthday, Mary-Louise."

I picked up a small oblong box. Inside was a pair of old eyeglasses with round gold frames. The earpiece was off on one side, and only one lens was in place. I lifted the glasses gingerly out of the box and curved the one earpiece around my right ear. Holding the other side with my left hand, I closed one eye and looked around the room. The lens was scratched and cloudy, and everything in the room was askew. Through those glasses all Mary-Louise's belongings in their colorful piles became a puzzle with many pieces missing.

The last item, lying on the floor in front of me, was a small black book. In gold embossed letters on the front were the words *My Prayer-Book*. Inside the front cover was an inscription, "To Baby Mary-Louise on her First Birthday from Grandmother Elizabeth." As I turned the pages I saw short daily readings: "Seeds of Contemplation," "Finding Perfect Peace," " The Power of Silence," and "Total Abandonment to God's Will." Further on, I read prayers to Saint Joseph, to Saint

Patrick, to the Blessed Virgin Mary, to the Sacred Heart, and to Saint Alphonsus Liguori. Near the end were sections entitled, "Praying the Rosary" and "The Stations of the Cross." I held the open book in my palms, put my face into it, and breathed in the dark musty smell, something foreign and old. I did not know at the time how those readings would later become such a deep part of my life.

As I laid the prayer book on top of a pile, a handwritten note fell out. It was a quote to Mary-Louise's father written and signed by Swami Vivekananda himself: "May I be born again and again and suffer thousands of miseries so that I may worship the only God that exists, the only God I believe in, the sum total of all souls—and, above all, my God the wicked, my God the miserable, my God the poor of all races, of all species, is the special object of my worship."

That was the conundrum that was Mary-Louise Brown. The Catholic and Ramakrishna ancestors, the astrology, the music and the "helping" profession, and the many suicide notes containing lists of all her worldly possessions, mixed in among the prayers. She was the person whom I tried hard to become, to fill in the blank of myself, but it hadn't worked, and I was as misplaced in my world as she had been in ours.

CHAPTER FOUR: THE DIVORCE

"The only thing more unthinkable than leaving was staying; the only thing more impossible than staying was leaving."
— Elizabeth Gilbert *Eat, Pray, Love*

The year after Mary-Louise's death, Harvill and I moved through the house like strangers. We worked, we came home, we ate separately, we went to bed; each of us clung to our own side, trying not to touch. The television playing was the only noise. We were polite. I began to imagine a single life, myself having chosen to be independent, to make my own choices, to read and write, to choose to be a woman alone, as Mary-Louise would have said. But the road from where I was--to there, was as wide as the ocean and filled with the big obstacle of words having to be spoken aloud. I imagined saying to him, "I want a divorce," but the knowledge that everything in the world that I knew would change with those words made them impossible to say, the wall between the words not having been spoken and having been spoken impossible to see around, the moment postponed day after day, month after month, each day the same as the day before.

One Saturday afternoon a married couple came to the house selling burial plots and pre-arranged funerals. We sat at the dining room table and listened as they explained how much money we would save by planning in advance, how secure we would feel with the knowledge that everything was decided. But neither of us could imagine a future in which we would be buried side by side. Even sleeping side-by-side held little life any more.

It had been a long time since we had made love, and Harvill had quit trying. We never even kissed. We weren't mad; we just weren't close and didn't have anything to talk about. One day I found under Harvill's sink in his bathroom a pasteboard box filled with sleazy black-and-white pornography. Naked women stood with their legs apart, showing everything. I lay across the bed for a couple of hours turning through the pages of the magazines, feeling disgusted and yet sexually aroused enough to keep looking. Instead of throwing them away and letting Harvill wonder where they were, I slid them back under his sink and never told him that I had seen them.

One day I came home from the grocery store after teaching all day. The back of the car was filled with a dozen brown paper sacks of groceries. When I pulled under the carport, I saw that Harvill and his red-headed female cousin Clydie were standing near the back door talking. I spoke to them when I got out of the car, and they spoke back. Then I began taking the groceries in, walking past them each time with a grocery bag in each arm, having to put a bag down to open the screen door for myself. Each time I passed by, they moved slightly to the side to make room for me, but neither offered to help with the groceries or even to open the door for me. With each trip I got madder. Clydie was standing there with her white freckled arms folded across her stomach, and Harvill was smoking and shaking his left hand. I was furious with both of them. After taking in the last bags, I slammed the back door of the double-wide.

Harvill came in as I began to put away the groceries. When he began to help me unpack the bags, he commented on the items. "We don't need these beans; we've already got three cans." And "These are too expensive; they are a lot cheaper at that Food Lion out on the highway." I looked at him but didn't say a word.

When the last grocery bag had been folded and stuck into the cabinet, when the countertops were empty, I turned to Harvill and said, "I have just bought groceries for the last time." It was not the words I had been harboring, "I want a divorce." It was not the other words I had been trying out, "Harvill, I'm not happy being married." It was nothing but one simple sentence, "I have bought groceries for the last time." But it was a beginning, and saying those words made the later words easier to say.

Several times I chose a day, but on that day, I awoke hot, anxious, and sick, and I looked at Harvill in his white tee shirt lying beside me, his cherry mouth open, and it seemed that I couldn't hurt him that day. I wasn't mad at him any longer. I didn't want to be married, but for some reason I felt responsible for him. Saying those words would be the end of what had once been a dream for me, a future of being a wife and a mother. I didn't know how to make my feelings sound rational to Mama, to his family, to other people. Who of them would understand the words, "I don't want to be married"?

One day in the front yard I saw a brown and black beagle-mix dog standing there whining with a Cheezits box stuck over its head. I guess the poor thing had tried to reach one cracker at the bottom of the box and got its head wedged. I walked slowly up to the dog and pulled the box off its head. As the dog ran off, I said out loud, "I know how you feel, buddy. Wedged tight."

Finally, on a Saturday afternoon, without having planned that day, I jumped in and blurted out the words. It was almost Spring, and the first shoots of grass and weeds had been shooting up in the yard. Harvill had been outside running the lawn mower over the grass, and he came in to get another beer out of the refrigerator. He had had to buy the beer for himself, for I had stuck to my plan not to buy groceries again. Except for his beer, the refrigerator was almost empty. He was standing in the light of the open door enjoying the coolness against his hot skin when I said, "Harvill, don't you think we ought to have a talk?"

That was it. Those were the words that came out of my mouth. Harvill came and sat down at the table beside me as if he had been expecting this time to come. I don't remember the words that came after that. I probably followed with, "Don't you think we need to get a divorce?" or "I'm not happy, and I don't want to be married anymore." But Harvill went along with it. He was agreeable. My relief was incredible. I was on the other side of the big impenetrable word wall.

For the next few days, I was in a good mood. The decision had been made. We would get a lawyer and start the ball rolling. I would be the one to move out. We would divide up our things. I was finally going to get to move on with my life.

One day when Harvill came home, he said, "These last few days have been good. If it was like this all the time, maybe we could make it."

I was washing dishes and looking out the window at the back yard. What he said startled and frightened me, and I didn't say anything for a minute. But then I turned and said, "I still wouldn't want to have sex." That statement seems strange to me now, given what I know--not strange that it was true but strange that I said it, how I didn't consciously realize the implications of what I said. And for the days after that, I pretended not to be happy.

We systematically worked together dividing things up. From a set of eight green Francoma pottery dishes that I had chosen for my "everyday china," we each took four. We both liked them, with their green centers, the faded-to-brown edges, the rustic look they had. The "good china" was Belcanto by Syracuse, milky-white with a thin silver rim and raised flowers around the edge. This, too, we divided down the middle, as well as the crystal glasses with their flaired tops, the water glasses, the tea glasses, the short squatty dessert glasses with stems. He agreed for me to have all the silver, Prelude by International. It seems strange to me now that brides back then chose "patterns," as if I would ever be the kind of woman who would entertain with the silver and the good china. It was as if setting up housekeeping required a wedding and choosing a pattern and having a china cabinet with all the good stuff lined up and propped, proof that your marriage was a solid one.

We divided other things up by family. Anything that came from Holsenbeck aunts, uncles, or cousins, he took. Anything that came from Worshams or Fordhams, my mother's maiden name, I took. The cherub flower arrangement with the trailing green grapes on the top of the Magnavox television set, I took, because one of my mother's friends, Miladean, gave it to us. Harvill kept the television set because his father had given us that. The most difficult part was dividing up the Christmas ornaments. We both cried with sentiment as we separated them into two piles. Each year for five years we had dated the ornaments we chose for that year—the Micky and Minnie Mouse pair for our first Christmas together in 1969, the yellow duck for 1970, the Mrs. Santa Claus for 1971, the silver rabbit, the blue angel with feathers, the gold star. We sat side by side on the floor beside the Christmas box, and I still remember Harvill's stubby fingers holding the small silver pitcher ornament labeled 1974. "Could I have this one?" he asked. Dividing the ornaments meant giving up the years, making the separation real.

The morning I had chosen to leave, I awoke with a sense of dread. The sun was coming through the crank-out windows of the doublewide trailer. As I lay in bed and looked around, everything in the room took on a purple tinge of sentiment. It would be sad. In the closets were Harvill's clothes, in the drawer, his undershirts and the tee shirts that I loved to smell, fresh and white from the dryer.

Divorce is grief. Change is grief. The loss of anything you are used to in your life is grief. I did love Harvill. But I didn't love him like a husband; I loved him like a brother. And, while I had not decided on any label to call myself at that time in my life, I knew that I would never be happy trying to make that marriage work. I was leaving someone I cared about, and I was hurting him deeply. I was breaking up the family unit that included his parents and all his cousins and aunts and uncles who lived clustered together on Holsenbeck Hill.

I packed my belongings in boxes from the grocery store and the liquor store and drove to Mama's house where I would stay until I could find an apartment. Mama asked me to bring in the liquor store boxes first because she didn't want the neighbors to see them. My books and phonograph records were most important to me, and I brought them in quickly to prevent the records from warping in the heat of the car. It took me many trips back and forth, and I piled the boxes in the middle of the back room at Mama's, a room we called The New Room because it had been added on. It had been Daddy's getaway place. A single bed was pushed against the glossy, orange-varnished, pine-paneled walls. Mama had had her sewing machine against the window at the end of the house, and when the new room was built, she lost the window she liked to look out as she sewed. I don't remember if it caused an argument; I just remember that Mama lost her window when Daddy gained his private room.

As I sat on the twin bed, the boxes in front of me, an ashtray on the end of Daddy's desk that was pushed up against the bed like a bedside table, the memories of my father surrounded me. The small bathroom was the place where Daddy gave me the only spanking he ever gave me, egged on by Mama at the supper table when he told her that I had refused to mind him in the barbershop. Daddy never spanked us. Only Mama did it, so when she said to him at the table that night, "Why don't you spank her then?" I wasn't worried. Sitting in my Daddy's room after the divorce, I remembered back to that night when I pulled my child-sized rocking chair up beside the tall wooden round-top radio, as tall as I was. "Story Hour" came on after supper every night. It began with a song that I later learned was "March of the Toys" from Babes in Toyland. "Da-da-dum-dum-dum, da-da-dum-dum-dum." I was rocking and listening when Daddy came into the room. He stood tall over me, his thin frame and bald head leaning over looking down at me. He motioned for me to go into the bathroom. I got up, put my hands on my hips, and big-stepped into the bathroom, showing him in my smart-alecky way that I wasn't afraid of the spanking that was to come. In the bathroom he fingered the razor strop that he used, to sharpen the straight razor to shave his whiskers. He told me to bend over. I turned my back to him and bent over. It's strange to me now that I don't even remember the only spanking my father ever gave me. All I remember is Daddy standing in the bathroom door watching me as I walked away and then turned back to look at him. The spanking itself is a blank. There was me, high-stepping into the bathroom, then a blank, and then me walking away, having been spanked.

Mama didn't like my smoking in that room in front of her, or even smoking at all. It makes me sad to think of it now; after all, she had let me back into her house and had given me a place to stay. She felt sorry for me, and she was glad that I was out of the unhappy marriage. She set her mouth firm and didn't say anything as I stubbed out my cigarette in front of her. Spraying Raid on the floor in a circle around the outside of my belongings, she said, "These grocery boxes have cockroach eggs in them." I remembered the nights when as a child I had gone into the kitchen and turned on the light for "kitchen water," the roaches scurrying across the green-and-white tiles and under the counters. Coming back into the same house automatically turned me back into the child I was then, back into the house where my name would once again be Worsham and not Holsenbeck.

When the divorce papers came, the papers that spelled out in no uncertain terms that the marriage between Harvill and me would be as if it had never existed, I was sad about the ending, but happy about the beginning. I didn't know how starting over was going to look. I didn't know that years later I would have to go to my safe deposit box and retrieve that official paper to prove that I was, in fact, divorced and free to be married again—to the woman I loved.

When I finally got my own place on the first floor of the Carrington Woods Apartments, I filled my car with the boxes and drove back and forth across town again and again, piling the boxes into the corners of my new efficiency apartment on Briarcliff Road. It was the first home I ever had entirely to myself.

The more boxes I carried in and set on the floor, the more excited I became. It was a furnished apartment with a small kitchen, a living room and dining room combination, and a bedroom with a big walk-in closet. It was all I needed, and it was mine. I set up the record player in the living room and put the six books I was reading and my journal on the coffee table in front of the sofa. I put my writing desk that Daddy had made me in the bedroom against the wall. Into the closet I lined my clothes, hip-hugger bell-bottoms, sweaters, and vests in all the bright colors I liked. That first afternoon I put Helen Reddy on the record player and sang "I Am Woman," as I stood in the middle of the room, put my hands over my head, and turned in a circle.

One night I was sitting alone in my apartment, reading a story from the *New Yorker*. Something about the description of a character, the way her hand swept her hair out of her eyes or the way she moved her mouth, made me think of Ellen. I began staring into space, remembering her, remembering us. I closed my eyes and imagined her soft face against my cheek. I felt a deep longing to see her. I wondered where she was and if I would be able to find her. The last number I had for her was listed in my pink address book. I had listed her under a blank, no name. I suppose I was hiding her completely, so that if I was suddenly killed in a car wreck, Harvill or Mama wouldn't know that I still had her number.

But that night I dialed Ellen, and she answered. When I heard her voice, it was as if we had never separated. She lived in Columbus, Georgia, and we made a plan to meet on Saturday at the Ramada Inn in Macon, almost halfway between us.

I got there first, and I parked in front of a window. As I got out, I saw my reflection, and I wondered if Ellen was inside, seeing me. I didn't see her green Camaro in the parking lot, but I realized that she may have bought a different car by then. I wondered if she would like how I looked. After Mary-Louise died, I let my hair grow to my shoulders in a blunt cut, and I had dyed it dark brown, covering up the salt-and-pepper hair I had inherited from Mama and the Fordham side of the family. I put on a white pantsuit that had been Mary-Louise's, and I had my photograph taken at a studio. I wore gold octagon-shaped glasses, and, with my longer hair and straight bangs, I looked like Cleopatra. I don't know who I was trying to be with that look. I guess it was one of many identities I tried out over the years. But the week before the night I called Ellen, I had my hair cut short, allowing the gray to begin to show. I wasn't used to the way I looked yet, and in my pocketbook I had one of the "Cleopatra" photos. I wanted to see what Ellen thought about that look.

I went inside and took a booth beside the window, in front of where my car was parked. As I waited, I wondered where this would lead. Was I finally ready to commit? I had packed the long blue nightgown that was Mary-Louise's. It had a deep V-neck that I thought looked sexy. During the time that Ellen and I were involved, I had yearned for us to have unlimited time together, when we weren't looking at the clock, when we weren't sneaking around, time to explore our bodies uninterrupted and unafraid. But now I was afraid. I knew that when I saw her, I would be taken in. I would want her, as always. I asked for a menu and looked at it, but the soon approaching Ellen hovered over my head. Just as I was deciding on a club sandwich, I saw the familiar green Camaro pull into the lot beside my turquoise-blue Toyota Tercel with the orange stripe. She knew my car.

She looked the same, as she strode toward me. I stood and, after she hugged me, she held me at arm's length and looked at me. Her wispy hair fell across her forehead, and her eyes looked at me in that shy way she saved for me, a loving look that melted me and made me hers. We sat across the table from one another, and I felt safe, like falling into cotton, being with her again, all the longing rising to the surface. She told me that she was with someone, a student who had seduced her after graduation. "Isn't that wild?" she said. I was jealous. I had imagined that she would wait for me, that I was the only one in the world for her the way that she was for me.

We ordered from the menu. I ordered the club sandwich, and she ordered a hamburger and French fries. But when our food came, we picked at it and didn't eat. It seemed that we had to pass through a wall to be back where we were, when we separated in the restaurant bathroom that day.

I was still nervous about running into someone I knew from Milledgeville. Macon was only thirty miles away, and people from Milledgeville often came to Macon to shop. But I didn't think they would come to a hotel unless they, too, had something to hide. When we finished eating and were ready to check into our room, we went separately, rather than standing at the check-in counter together. I went first, and by the time Ellen got to our room, I had hurriedly jumped into the shower. I heard her come into the room, and I wondered if she would come into the shower with me, but she didn't.

When I came out of the bathroom, Ellen smiled and met me in the center of the room. I fell into her arms, and when we kissed she said, "I'm going to have to teach you how to kiss again. You've forgotten." I realized then that I was damaged, that I had become wounded and fragile.

I opened a bottle of wine I had in my suitcase and poured us each a glass. I clicked my glass to hers and said, "To us."

When Ellen went into the bathroom to take her shower, I closed the black-out drapes in the room, shutting out the slowly dying light of the afternoon. I put my glass of wine on the bedside table, let my gown slide to the floor, and got into bed and snuggled down under the covers. The room was cold, and the covers were warm. I lay there and thought of Ellen's body the way I remembered it, her heavy breasts in my hand, my fingers touching the warm wet place between her legs. I was anxious to let go, to give in.

When the running water of the shower went off and the bathroom door opened, I saw Ellen's dark shadow enter the room and felt her raise the covers and get into the bed with me. Her body slid next to mine, and her hand ran down my side. "You are completely naked," she whispered. We began to kiss and touch the way I imagined. At last, after the years had passed, I once again held her breasts in my hands.

But there was much I didn't know, that I had suppressed in trying to live another life.

"Go down on me," I whispered to her, the way I had imagined. She raised the covers, and I squeezed her hair in my fists as I felt her tongue touch me. My mouth opened, my back arched, and my head pushed back into the pillow. At last. At last.

But when it was my turn to make love to her, I found that I couldn't. Something in my script had gone awry. "I'm sorry," I told her. "I can't." I was a scattered person, half of me here, half of me somewhere else.

Ellen hugged me, told me it was okay, told me that everything was going to be all right and that we were going to be together. She said that she was going to explain to her partner that she had reunited with her first love, that it was fate that we had found each other again. She had always been honest with her about me, she said, that we might meet again one day. We slept curled together; I was an actor in a movie that could not be shown in public, not shown to children.

The next morning at breakfast we made plans. She would talk to her partner at home in Columbus, and I would talk to my mother. I would be open about my feelings. I would convince my mother that I had my own life to live. I would be determined and focused about what I wanted for my future. I would not hang my head and beg forgiveness the way I had that night in the double-wide trailer when Harvill called Mama and she came over and fixed oatmeal. I would explain my feelings to Mama, and she would try to understand and give me her blessing. After all, she was my mother; she wanted me to be happy, right? Ellen would help me heal and find myself.

As we parted in the parking lot, we exchanged something we found in the backseat of our cars as a promise. She gave me a pewter beer stein. I can't remember what I gave her. As I look back on that day in the sunny parking lot, I see her hand putting the beer stein into my hand. But when I try to remember me handing her something, it seems as if I'm handing her a blank, something clear and see-through and intangible. It was the last time I would see her.

III.

CHAPTER FIVE: THE COLOR OF THE WHEAT FIELDS

"It's a puzzling thing. The truth knocks on the door and you say, 'Go away, I'm looking for the truth.' And so it goes away. Puzzling." --Robert M. Pirsig

1975...

The call to Ellen was short and sad. "I can't do it," I said.

"Can we keep in touch?" she said.

"I don't see the point," I said.

I had promised God never to kiss another woman. I don't even remember the call to Mama. It was just a silence into which I had said, "Never mind. It won't happen."

The day after the Telling, after my night of arguing with God, after calling Ellen and Mama to take back everything that I had said and done, I went to school to teach, even though I had had no sleep. My eyes were red, my face was puffy, and I felt ravaged. I knew for certain that in only a period of a few days, my life had changed forever.

In 1972, when I went back to Baldwin High to teach at the school I had graduated from, my former teachers had become my colleagues. I tried to learn to call my former English teachers, Mrs. Hodges (who gave me three demerits for inattention in class) and Mrs. King by their first names, Margaret and Elaine. It did not come naturally to me to do so, and I often forgot, turning myself into their student again.

One of my former teachers was Miss Elizabeth Horne, whom the other teachers called by her nickname, "Teeny." She had been my chemistry teacher in high school. I was a terrible chemistry student, but I admired Miss Horne. Every day in her class I daydreamed, not listening to her lecture or lab demonstrations; yet, she didn't criticize or penalize me. Instead, she stayed after school to explain to me privately what she had already taught in class. I still had trouble understanding the electron configurations, but she was persistent. She had a way of making the difficult seem easy. I had seen her talking to other students about their problems, and she was never judgmental. She listened, and many students, especially those who were different or didn't fit in, were devoted to her. When I was in high school, the other students had said that she was a Catholic who walked to the seven o'clock Mass every morning from her home a block away from the church. Daddy had told me that when he was walking downtown from our house on Doles Boulevard to his barbershop in the mornings, he sometimes passed Miss Horne going into the Catholic Church, the round doily on her head and a prayer book in her hand. What impressed me then as her student was what she did when she gave us a test. She didn't monitor us. She passed out the test, and then she went back into her chemistry stockroom and worked. It was remarkable that the students never cheated in her class, even though we weren't being watched. It was as though when she left the room, she left God in charge. Because we knew she trusted us not to cheat, we never cheated.

Seven years later, as a teacher at Baldwin High, I ate my sack lunch every day in one of the classrooms along with Margaret, Elaine, and Miss Horne—Teeny. I learned over those lunches that Teeny's father had died a year earlier, that she had a beagle named Pup Dog, that she grew gardenias and hydrangeas that she brought to school in a mason jar, and that she lived with her mother in Carrington Woods, a few blocks around the corner from the Carrington Woods Apartments where I lived. I had also noticed that students still chose her to talk to about their problems, and she was still listening and not judging.

The day that I went back to school after the Telling, Teeny stopped me in the hall. "Are you okay?" she asked.

I shook my head. "Not really," I said.

"Stop by my room this afternoon if you want to talk," she said. No one else that day had noticed or questioned why I looked upset, but Teeny Horne had.

After school that afternoon I went into her chemistry classroom. I sat in a student desk and watched as, wearing her white lab coat, she moved around her room, wiping off the black lab tables and putting away Bunson Burners and microscopes. As I watched her while she worked, I remembered the many afternoons only ten years earlier that I had stood beside her at that lab table trying to understand as she explained about electrons. Now here I was, waiting to talk to her about an entirely different subject, and I didn't know how she would react. I was raw, with no defenses, and I was one of her misfits who needed help. At that moment I had no mother, no husband, no friend or lover, no identity, no church.

When she had finished with her work, she came and pulled a student desk in front of mine. She folded her hands in front of her and leaned forward, quietly listening before I even began to speak. Her face was as kind as I remembered it from high school. Her hair had gotten grayer, and her eyes were deep and dark behind her glasses. There was no barrier around her; she was completely open to whatever I was about to say.

I twisted my hands in my lap. I looked down at the desk, then out the window. When I began to speak, my words came pouring out. The more I talked, the more difficult it was to speak through my tears and my closed throat. I told her about Ellen, about our affair during the time I was married to Harvill. I told her about my divorce and about my reunion with Ellen. And I told her about the Telling and about the night before that I had spent wrestling with God. I was amazed at her openness, for I thought that as a Catholic, she would frown upon divorce, even more toward adultery, and a relationship between two women. I thought that she would try to tell me right from wrong or guide me in the Godly direction. She was twenty-five years older than I. I could have still been her student. She could have been my mother. Instead, she was listening, and that afternoon I emptied myself of my sadness and guilt. When I stood to leave, she stood with me, and I hugged her and thanked her for being so kind to me.

Many days after that, I picked up my things after my last class and stopped by Teeny's classroom to wait for her and to talk. She didn't seem to mind having me there. One day as I was standing to leave, she stood too and we hugged. It was like every other day, but on that particular day, the hug lasted longer than usual. Her hug was warm and nurturing, and when we pulled apart, she said, "We're going to have to be careful about this."

A loud gong went off in my head. I had no idea that she was feeling that way about me. And as soon as I knew, I was drawn to her more than ever.

A couple of days later when I got home from school, I picked some of my violets and made them into a bouquet, the stems wrapped in aluminum foil so that the rose, pink, and purple colors reflected in the silver. I walked the three blocks to the house where Teeny lived with her mother. When she answered the door, Teeny smiled, and I could tell that she was pleased that I had come. She asked me in, and I handed her the nosegay I had made.

I was surprised at the way Teeny's mother looked. She was pushed back in a recliner with her knees bent, her legs spread apart like a frog, an afghan covering her legs. Her hair was steel gray and wild, flat in the back as if she hadn't brushed it all day. She was holding a cigarette in her right hand, and the smoke circled her head. She looked up at me with a frown, and I knew immediately that she didn't like me.

It wasn't until years later that I learned that Teeny's mother had warned Teeny about me, had assumed something, had told Teeny that it takes a lifetime to build a good reputation that can be lost in a moment. Then she told Teeny about a girl who lived in Milledgeville years ago who was run out of town.

But that day I didn't know any of those things. All I knew was that Teeny and her mother didn't appear to fit together. The mother was earthy and worldly with a raucous laugh and raspy cigarette voice. Teeny seemed good and focused on Heaven. She introduced her mother to me as "my mother, Willette." I learned later that Teeny had never called her mother anything other than her first name, that even as a toddler, she called her mother "Willette." I decided years later that the only mother Teeny ever had was the Blessed Virgin Mary.

Teeny led a student interdenominational faith group that met before homeroom in her chemistry lab. The students came to her to request the club, and she agreed to be the advisor. The students named the club "Pi Epsilon Alpha" for "Faith, Hope, and Love." All were welcome, and the president of the club was a Jewish student. Every Thursday morning, Teeny went early to the Goodie Gallery to bring doughnut holes to the students for the meeting. On November 6, 1974, when she arrived at school with her doughnuts, one of the most devout students was not there, and all of the other students were crying. The student, whose name was Mandy, along with her father, Carswell Carr, had been killed the night before by a serial killer named Paul John Knowles, also known as "the Casanova Killer" because of his good looks. Mandy's mother, a night nurse who was a friend of my mother's, having been in nurse's training with her, came home early that morning to find the scene. Teeny and the students spent the meeting that morning in prayer. The reports of the killing were all over the television and the newspaper. The scene was grizzly and bloody. The newspaper said that Knowles had killed at least eighteen people throughout the United States and that he had not been captured. Knowles had stabbed the father, who then had a heart attack before Knowles strangled Mandy. The home where the Milledgeville crime occurred was in Carrington Woods, a white split-level a few blocks from my apartment, a house I passed when I walked to Teeny's.

That night, and many nights to follow, I lay awake in my bed, stiff and terrified, my eyes open. I was afraid to move, fearful that if I turned on the light, my sheets would be covered with blood. I began to dread being alone in my apartment at night. One day, after four days of no sleep, I went down to Teeny's classroom at the end of lunch. She was in her stockroom wearing the white lab coat, a curl loosely hanging over her forehead. She was labeling small brown bottles and placing them on the shelves. When I stood in the door, she looked up, smiled and said, "What can I do for you?"

"What do you do when you get afraid?" I asked her. "I haven't been able to sleep since the thing with Mandy."

She answered quickly, lifting her shoulders in a shrug. "I just turn it over to the Holy Family," she said. Her answer was that matter-of-fact.

"Really?" I asked. "Is it that simple?"

"Yes," she said. "It works every time."

I went home that day with that simple answer on my mind--the way she shrugged, as if the answer was obvious. The Holy Family was not something often mentioned in the Baptist Church where I grew up, nor the Methodist where I had known Mary-Louise. And since Mary-Louise's death, I had not gone to any church. The Holy Family to me meant the scene at Bethlehem in the manger. But before I left that day, Teeny had said the prayer, "Jesus, Mary, and Joseph, I give you my heart and my soul. Jesus, Mary, and Joseph, assist me in my last agony. Jesus, Mary, and Joseph, may I breathe forth my soul in peace with you"--her soft voice saying the words, her head bowed, her hand on my shoulder as we stood together in the stock room. I lay in bed that night flat on my back, my fists clenched down by my sides, and closed my eyes. I said the words, "Jesus, Mary, and Joseph, help me not to be afraid." And I slept through the night with no fear.

Over the next several weeks, I continued to walk around to Teeny's and her mother's house several times a week. Sometimes I passed her house after dark in my car when she was outside walking Pup Dog in the front yard where, she said, "Pup Dog likes the smells better." On those nights I pulled over to the side of the road and walked up and down the edge of the yard with her. We talked about school and our families. She told me that her mother was controlling and jealous of church and her friends, that when the Catholic School was still in Milledgeville, her mother complained when Teeny drove the nuns back and forth to Atlanta. I agreed that my mother, too, had always seemed jealous of my friends.

When I visited Teeny and her mother in their home, Teeny was always friendly and tried to think of things that would bring Willette and me together. "Sandra teaches at the high school and was once in my chemistry class," she said.

"Uh huh," Willette said, blowing smoke out of the side of her mouth. "Teeny's had a lot of students over the years."

"She's a great teacher," I said.

"Yes," said Willette. "She ought to be. She spends all her time on her teaching or the church one. She doesn't know how to say no," she said, looking at me and frowning.

One day in Teeny's room after school, I sat and watched her as usual. With a dishtowel in her hand, she moved her arm in circles on the countertops, wiping up water or spilled chemicals from the experiment she had conducted with her high school students that day. As we were leaving, I said, "I've got a Southern Living Willette might enjoy. It has a lot of recipes and flowers. I'll bring it by this afternoon."

Teeny stopped wiping the counter and looked at me. "I need to talk to you about that," she said. "Willette doesn't want you to come by the house any more, at least for a while." I stood and looked at her, surprised at what she was saying to me. "I hate like everything to have to tell you this," she said, "but she's old and set in her ways, and there is no point in trying to change her now."

I was immediately hurt and panicky, rejected by both Teeny and her mother. It was as though Teeny didn't want me either and was using Willette as an excuse. Or that she didn't consider me important enough to fight for. I didn't know what to say, and I'm sure she saw the hurt on my face. "Why don't I come by your apartment?" she said. I was relieved and happy. She was not shutting me out of her life.

Over the next few weeks, Teeny came by my apartment after school. Willette thought she was still at the high school when she was with me. If I knew she was coming by, I didn't go by Mama's. There we were, ages twenty-seven and fifty-two, wanting to spend time together, yet feeling that we had to hide it from our mothers. We were friends, and yet something about our friendship was shameful and needed to be hidden.

On those days we grew closer. At the time I would not have known to call my feelings for her an attraction, although now I realize that it was. We sat side by side on the sofa. We held hands, and I put my arm around her shoulders. She had a short forehead with a widow's peak, and I traced my finger along her hairline and smoothed her wirey eyebrows with my thumb. We looked into one another's eyes in a way that was more than friendship. A few times we kissed, quickly on the lips, never lingering, a peck, the way you might kiss a friend hello or goodbye. I was more drawn to her than I was to Ellen or to Mary-Louise, for with Teeny I admired her goodness. She had been my teacher, and her love surprised and honored me. The quiet, vulnerable way she looked at me turned me to mush.

One day she said, "This is a galloping horse. But I sure do like its gallop." When she said that, I knew that she was feeling the same intoxicating attraction that I was. I looked forward to every visit, and each day when she arrived, I began to dread her leaving.

"Have you ever thought that you might be gay?" I asked her one day.

"I've noticed that tendency," she said. She told me about Tom, a Catholic boy she had dated, a fine young man that everybody thought was perfect for her. She and Tom put the missals out into the pews before Mass began and straightened up after Mass had ended. They often joined the priest and a small group of parishioners in the rectory to listen to opera on the record player. The priest then had loved opera too and had many recordings. One of Teeny's favorites was "La Traviata." She explained opera to me, the way that the production was composed of music, dance, and theater, the way that the soprano's aria was intended to show off her voice, that in one long piece, the soprano might be singing only "Please pass the bread" in a foreign language. As in the way that I had been absorbed in watching Mrs. Matthews conduct an oral recitation and Mary-Louise conduct the choir, I loved watching Teeny as she listened to music, the way she closed her eyes and moved her head slowly from side to side, going to a place in her head where I wanted to be.

Everyone expected Tom and Teeny to get married. "But I knew that I wasn't the marrying kind," she said. "Tom would go to Willette and try to get her to make me marry him, but she would tell him that she couldn't make me do anything I didn't want to do." She laughed at the irony. Teeny learned years later that Tom and his wife had had ten children. "That could never have been me," she said, shaking her head.

"Did you ever think about becoming a nun?" I asked her.

"I thought about it," she said. "But I knew that I couldn't stand living in community with a lot of other women. I need my privacy and time alone. Plus, my father was an alcoholic, and every time I started to move somewhere else, Willette said, 'Go on off and leave me here with this alcoholic,' and I felt guilty and couldn't leave. I guess I could stand giving in to Willette easier than I could stand feeling guilty." Of course, I understood that comment completely. Sadly, our fear of standing up to our mothers was one of the things we had in common.

One Saturday afternoon she came by my apartment after she had been to Jewel's Beauty Shop to get her hair done. On her way to the beauty parlor, her car had drifted into another lane, and she had a mild fender-bender. She told me that the accident had been God speaking to her, warning her that she was on a dangerous path. Although she never said this aloud to me, I knew that her mind had wandered to a daydream involving me. That afternoon she told me that we were on a slippery slope and that we needed to be careful. "I need a friend," she said. "I don't need a lover. Besides, it's wrong."

I knew that Teeny Horne was the one I wanted in my life and that the only way I could be with her was to allow our relationship to be on her terms. She drew the line at the quick kiss on the lips and a hug, never lingering. That was the fixed line that was drawn that day. I intended to change myself into a person who was not gay; she intended to accept herself as who God made her, but to follow the church's rules. We would be a good fit, and neither of us would have to feel guilty about our relationship.

One afternoon we had been reading together Antoine de Saint-Exupery's *The Little Prince.* She had read aloud the passage, "Love does not consist of gazing at each other but in looking outward together in the same direction." Then she said, "This is all wonderful, but you have a lot longer to kick around this old world than I do." I knew that she was committing to me and that we would be together for a long time. But, because of our age difference, she was worried about my being left on Earth without her.

My answer to her was paraphrased from *The Little Prince.* "Because I have known you, the color of the wheat fields will always be more yellow." She accepted my answer.

She knew that I had grown to need her, and she said to me, "You can't need anyone but God. You love and enjoy people on earth, but you can't need them." One day she said to me, "I wish you wouldn't wear your hair so short." She immediately reprimanded herself. "I never should have said that. I'm sorry." She shook her head, exasperated with herself. Years later, she said, "I wish you would let your fingernails grow longer." It was remarks like these, I realize now, that let me know that Teeny was more aware than I was of how the two of us would be perceived by others. The Catholic Church called it "scandal," something that, whether true or not, could create thoughts of scandal in others. It didn't seem to matter much what you were doing; what mattered was what it looked like you were doing.

But I did let my hair grow longer and later, my fingernails. I wanted to please her. And I wanted to become a good person, the kind of person that she was. I had promised God that I would. I had promised God that I would change myself, that I would not be gay. And over the next two months, I began my transformation. My reaction to Mary-Louise's death, and disposing of all her possessions, as well as the feeling I had that I was beginning my life as a new and changed person, caused me to begin to clean out my own possessions. It seemed to me that many things had become a heavy burden, as if I were carrying my past around on my back. One day I collected all of my high school and college yearbooks, took them to the large dumpster in the apartment complex, and hurled them over the edge. I heard them land with a thud in the bottom. I was purging my past, wiping it clean.

Next, I took all my clothes except for a couple of pantsuits to the Salvation Army. I had orange bell-bottoms and a short wool vest with ruffles; yellow and pink plaid pants with a matching yellow sweater; a long black dress with a V-neck that had belonged to Mary-Louise. I set up the sewing machine on my dining room table and began to make myself new clothes. Teeny wore solid-colored double-knit pantsuits with white shells. I bought sewing patterns and double-knit cloth in solid colors for elastic-waist pants and long-sleeved jackets with buttons and a collar. I laid out the material and the thin paper pattern on my bed and trimmed the pieces. Then I began to sew. I made one pantsuit after the other, all alike, all solid colors like Teeny's. As I sewed, I listened to Lily Pons sing opera, *Lucia de Lammamoor.* When Teeny came over, I put on the Lily Pons record, and as she listened, she closed her eyes and moved her head from side to side, lost in the music. I could not take my eyes off her when she was listening to music. Her favorite piece was "the mad scene." It is ironic to me now that I sewed clothes making myself become the spitting image of Teeny, twenty-five years older than me, dressing myself like her, trying to become her, while listening to the mad scene.

I knew other women who talked to their mothers and who went on with their own lives, letting their mothers come to terms with their daughters coming out as gay. But I wasn't able to do that. Perhaps I was weak and childlike. I can't explain. I wanted to demolish the side of myself that my mother couldn't love; I wanted the guilt to go away. Teeny was the perfect model, a truly good person.

One day I took the black Catholic *Prayer-Book* I had found in Mary-Louise's belongings and drove to the Catholic Church. I felt drawn to see inside this church that meant so much to Teeny. I parked in front of the post office and walked around the corner to the front of the church. I walked up the steps and put my hand on the metal handle and slowly opened the large wooden door. The Catholic Church door was always open. The door creaked as I pushed it and walked inside. I closed the door behind me and breathed deeply the foreign smell of incense. The church was empty. Under my feet was a carpet runner in colors of red and blue. I walked down the center aisle to the front altar where I knelt on a carpeted step and rested my elbows on a white marble railing. In front of me was a wooden altar covered with a white cloth and behind the table a gold container with a pointed top, like a small house. I had heard Teeny call this the tabernacle. I sat down in a pew about halfway back on the left. I don't know how long I sat there, but I read from the *Prayer-Book* and prayed. I asked God to show me where he wanted me to go in my life. I asked him to help me be as good as I could possibly be. This was my mantra during that time, that I could become as good as I could be. To be good meant not feeling guilty, to wipe myself clean, not to give my mother or God any reason to be displeased with me or ashamed of me. I wanted to learn what "good" meant; I wanted an Absolute Truth, a definite right and wrong. I didn't want to be unsure about what pleased and displeased God. Mama's lists of wrongs could be something as simple as: Don't drink wine. Don't do anything that will embarrass or hurt your mother. In order to be free of guilt, I needed to have God's list, which might be a different list from Mama's. To go by a different list meant weaning myself. If I could follow God's list, then I would not follow Mama's list, but I would still be right, still be clean and not guilty. Later I would joke that I became a Catholic so that I could drink, dance, and gamble.

In the back of the church I found a pamphlet advertising something called a "Serendipity" workshop to be held in Atlanta the following weekend. I went home and sent in my registration fee and made plans to attend. I don't remember much about the workshop. It was one of those touchy-feely days where you discuss things in groups. What I remember most is a Catholic Priest who was in my group. I had never been up close to a Catholic Priest before. His name was Father Thomas Kenny. He wore all black and the white clerical collar at his neck. He was a big man with dark graying hair and gold-rimmed glasses. His voice was deep, and he spoke softly and warmly. The workshop was not held by Catholics but was interdenominational, and Father Kenny did not "talk Catholic." But something about this man stayed with me after the retreat had ended when I was back home in Milledgeville in my apartment.

On Tuesday after the workshop, I received a phone call. "This is Father Drohan," the voice said, "from Sacred Heart Catholic Church. You left your *Prayer-Book* in the church. I saved it for you if you want to come to the rectory to pick it up." I was glad that I had written my name and phone number inside.

I didn't know what to expect as I drove into town to the priest's house. When I got there, a red-faced silver-haired man met me at the door. He was wearing black pants and a black shirt with the white collar. "Come in," he said, motioning for me to enter the living room. Over the fireplace was a large color picture of a Pope. I think now that it must have been Pope John XXIII since Teeny told me that Vatican II had happened by then. That day I was wearing a necklace with a mustard seed pendant on a gold chain. The priest looked at my necklace and said, "Don't worry, it will grow." When I looked puzzled, he said, "Your faith. It will grow." He gave me back the *Prayer-Book*, and I left. That was the first time I had ever been inside the Catholic Church rectory.

After the Serendipity Workshop, I wrote a letter to Father Kenny and told him that I wanted to know more about the Catholic Church. He mailed me two books, Thomas Merton's *The Seven Storey Mountain* and another book entitled *Christ Among Us: A Modern Presentation of the Catholic Faith*. On Easter Monday, the day after Easter, I sat down at the dining room table in my apartment and began to read both books. As I read, it seemed that everything I read sounded like the Truth.

I began to ask Teeny questions. She was cautious; she didn't want me to be what is called a "Personality Catholic," someone who becomes Catholic because they admire or love a particular Catholic person. I told her that I was interested in taking instructions to learn more than I could read in books. She began to take me to Mass with her whenever Willette didn't go, which was often. I stayed in the pew while Teeny went with the other Catholics to the altar rail to receive the Eucharist, and I received in my heart what Teeny called the Eucharist of Desire. In *Christ Among Us* I read, "By frequently taking part in the Eucharist we are gradually transformed into Christ. We begin to shed our weaknesses and assume something of his own strength." I wanted more than anything to be able to receive the Eucharist, to have the Risen Christ inside me, to become strong like that, strong like Teeny.

After Mass one Saturday evening I said to Father Drohan, "I want you to make me a Catholic."

"We can make you a Catholic," he replied.

I began to receive instruction every Saturday morning in the rectory. I took a notebook with me, and, as the silver-haired priest talked, I sat on the sofa across from him and took notes. When Teeny came by after school, I told her everything I had learned that week. She said she was re-learning many things that she had grown up with but had forgotten. Mama's reaction was, "You've been a Baptist, and you've been a Methodist. All this skipping around. I hope you'll find something and stick with it."

At the time I was disappointed that I was entering the Catholic Church after Vatican II. I wanted to experience the old ways, the Latin, the way that Teeny grew up. I wanted the rules. I read The Lives of the Saints, and I felt drawn to the flagellations of the monks of old, to the rocks in the shoes of Flannery O'Connor's character Hazel Motes, to those who wrapped their bodies in barbed wire, to the stigmata, to the levitations in ecstasy of St. Teresa of Avila. The more solidly I could follow the rules, the better person I would be. My spirit yearned for that moment when I could go to the altar and the priest would place on my tongue the Holy Bread that would strengthen and fortify my soul and cause me to glow from the inside out.

At one point it seemed that my head was spinning with the many Jesuses in the Catholic Church: The Holy Infant in the arms of his mother, the Sacred Heart of Jesus, the Infant of Prague. Teeny told me about a time in the past when there had been two infants in the church, on one altar, St. Joseph holding the babe, and on the other altar, the infant in the arms of his mother: twins. In the Baptist Church was only the one Jesus. As I learned more about the Catholic Church, it seemed as if there was a Baptist Jesus and a Catholic Jesus, and I struggled to bring them together in my mind as one.

I didn't know the Virgin Mary. I prayed, sitting on the bed in my apartment, "Mary, this is Sandra. Are you there? You don't know me, but I would like to get to know you." With the Absolute Truth inside me, I memorized the prayers: The Hail Mary, the Angelus, the Morning and Evening Prayers, the *Prayer of the Miraculous Medal*—"O Mary, Conceived without Sin, Pray for us who have recourse to you." There were even more Marys than there were Jesuses—the Mother of Sorrows, Our Lady of Lourdes, Mother of God, Queen of Heaven, Queen of the Holy Rosary. I memorized the Rosary, and Teeny and I began to say it together.

In my apartment, I set up an altar near the front door in the corner beside the sofa. I used a small table from my childhood birthday parties, and I covered it with a white tablecloth. On the table I put a two-inch framed picture of the Sacred Heart of Jesus, a holy card that I had found inside the black *Prayer-Book* that had been Mary-Louise's. I loved staring at the picture because it seemed that I could see straight into the kindness in Jesus' eyes; he brought me comfort, forgiveness, and acceptance. His eyes looked like Teeny's eyes, understanding and caring like hers. Beside the framed picture I put a small vigil candle and a crystal bowl of matchbooks. In the dark of my apartment I knelt there twice daily, my knees digging into the pattern of the carpet, the only light in the apartment the flickering of the candle. In those moments I saw my life stretched out in front of me, a life dedicated to Jesus, and I felt loved by him and by my friend Teeny, the good Catholic.

During that time I also quit smoking. I had smoked throughout college and during the time I was married to Harvill. I had half a carton left of Vantage cigarettes and a small brown-and-green suede cigarette case. I went into the bathroom of my apartment and threw the case into the trashcan under the sink. I ripped open the cigarette packs inside the carton and flushed all the cigarettes down the toilet, a handful at a time. I said to my friends, "I have quit smoking." I didn't say that I was trying to quit; I said that I had quit, even though my last cigarette was the day before. At school the friends that I used to smoke with in the faculty lounge ragged me, but I held firm, and I stopped going where I knew they would be smoking. I took deep gasps of fresh air, and I found that the fresh air satisfied me in a way that smoking never had. I was cleaning out my lungs the way that I was cleaning out my soul.

By the end of the summer I had finished my instructions, and I was ready for my First Confession and First Communion, which was to be on August 31, 1975. Kneeling in the dark confessional, the shadow of the priest through the grill, I said what I had been taught, making the sign of the cross: "Bless me, Father, for I have sinned. This is my First Confession." My list of transgressions was long: I confessed my relationship with Ellen during the time I was married to Harvill and our reunion later. I confessed stealing a bathmat from the Plaza Hotel in New York City when I was there with Mary-Louise, cheating in my tenth grade history class, stealing a book of ee cummings' poetry from the college library, having sex with Harvill before we got married, pouring salt on a slug when I was a child, not stopping a friend from committing suicide, and talking back to my mother more times than I could count. I confessed not going to church and feeling far away from God. It took me a long time to finish my First Confession. I ended it the way I was taught, "For these and all the sins of my past life, I am heartily sorry." Father assigned me five Hail Marys as my penance. In addition, I wrapped the white Plaza bathmat in a box and mailed it anonymously back to the hotel in New York City. Teeny had told me that after my first confession, I would feel as though I had wings on my feet, and she was right. I had wiped my past clean.

My first Communion was during Mass. As Father consecrated the Host and the altar boy rang the bells, I bowed my head deeply and said in my mind the words that Teeny had taught me, "A Thousand and One Welcomes!" As he consecrated the chalice, I thought the words, "You said it, and I believe it!" Teeny was my godmother, and she stood with her hand on my shoulder, promising to keep me on the narrow path, as I renewed my Baptismal promises. As Father Drohan placed the Host on my tongue, I thought I would faint, I hoped I would levitate, and when I returned to the pew and knelt there beside Teeny, saying in my mind the "Prayers after the Eucharist," I felt completely happy. For my First Communion present, Teeny gave me a rosary, a crucifix, and a card in which she had written, "Congratulations to a strong and brave soldier of Jesus Christ!" the same words that she had been told as a child, when she received her own First Holy Communion.

In the Catholic Church, to be "one of those women," as my mother had said the day of the Telling, meant taking a vow of celibacy. It was unspoken, but Teeny and I took that vow. The two of us were one, in every way but that. We went to Mass together. We stood side by side facing the altar, our voices blending in the responses, our hands making the sign of the cross together—up, down, left, right.

I loved the Liturgical Seasons. When Advent began on November 30, 1975, Teeny taught me the St. Andrew prayer and the Novena of nine prayers that we would say each day of Advent: "Hail and blessed be the hour and the moment in which Jesus Christ was born at midnight in Bethlehem in piercing cold. In that hour, hear my prayer and grant my petition through the merits of Jesus Christ and His most blessed mother." We read the Advent readings together every day. On Christmas we gave one another something she called "Spiritual Bouquets." Each of the years that followed, we made Spiritual Bouquets for each other, and each year, they took different forms. She gave me a construction paper Christmas tree she had made that contained paper windows through which I could read the prayers she promised to say for me: 10 Hail Marys, 15 Ejaculations, 25 Sacred Heart Prayers, 10 Masses and Holy Communions, 25 "offer ups." The term *ejaculations* made me laugh. It meant a short, expressed prayer, sudden and heartfelt: "Jesus, Mercy!!" or "Help my unbelief!" or "I give you my heart and my soul!" The offer ups meant that she would offer up to God for me the times when she had to put up with Willette's demands or a student's frustrating behavior. In addition, we got a men's small wooden Brut cologne box, turned it on its side, and collected straws from the side of the road. We put the straws into a small vase and set it beside the wooden box, the "manger." We kept the manger and the straws in her chemistry stockroom. Throughout Advent, as we offered up the aggravations connected with teaching and everyday life, we put a straw in the manger. At Christmas we had a small plastic Baby Jesus to place in the manger. We wanted to use up all the straws before Christmas so that the holy infant would have a soft bed to lie on. On Christmas day we exchanged our presents and lit the candles on a birthday cake for the Baby Jesus and then sang Happy Birthday to him.

Christmas was hard for me because I always came second to Willette. Teeny and I planned a time that we were going to exchange our presents, but at the last minute someone dropped in to visit with Willette, and Teeny didn't call to tell me she would be late. I stood at the window and watched for her car and was disappointed that our private Christmas was not happening at the time we had decided. She never had the nerve to tell Willette outright that she was going to have her Christmas with Sandra.

Throughout the Advent and Christmas season that first year, Teeny kept saying, "Wait until Lent!" And she was right. In the Protestant church, I had never experienced Lent. During my first Lent in the Catholic Church, Teeny and I went to the church on Friday afternoons after school to say the Stations of the Cross. Using the

---

words of St. Ignatius of Loyola, I heard in more detail than ever before the agony our Lord went through at Golgotha. No prayers in the Protestant Church had ever included that kind of detail. We walked around the church together and stopped in front of each station. At the tenth station we read aloud from our book, "When our Savior had arrived at Calvary, He was cruelly stripped of His garments. How painful this must have been because they adhered to his flesh and with them parts of his bloody skin were removed. All the wounds of Jesus are renewed. Jesus is despoiled of his garments that he may die possessing nothing. How happy shall I die after casting off my evil self with all its sinful inclinations? I will not count the cost but will struggle bravely to cast off my evil propensities."

Holy Thursday during Holy Week ended up being my favorite night of the year, more than Midnight Mass at Christmas and more than the Easter Vigil. Holy Thursday was the night in which the Lord was moved from the central place on the altar to a side altar, representing the night in which Jesus instigated the Eucharist and was crying out to the Lord in the Garden. On Holy Thursday the choir sang, "Humbly let us voice our homage for so great a Sacrament!" And, "What our senses fail to fathom, we believe by faith's consent!" The belief in the Real Presence—that the bread and wine became the real and true body and blood of Christ—was my favorite belief. It was miracle and mystery.

On my first Holy Thursday Father Drohan was going to have feet washing. His altar boy was Eddie Tamayo, who was a clutzy little boy. His cassock was hiked up on one side by the cincture (the rope around his waist.) Father had filled the church crystal punch bowl to the brim with water, and from the side door of the altar, Eddie entered with the heavy bowl. As he walked, he wobbled from side to side, sloshing water on the altar floor. He set the bowl in the center where various people from the different organizations of the church—the choir, the Knights of Columbus, the St. Vincent de Paul Society—would sit in chairs to get their feet washed by the priest. Sitting behind Teeny and me was Ann Smith, a pillar of the church. During the feet washing, Ann leaned up between Teeny and me and said, "That's the wedding punch bowl! The weddings will never be the same."

Not long after I became a Catholic, a problem presented itself to me. I found that my own body tempted me: I wanted to touch myself. Sunday afternoons were the worst. In the quiet of the afternoon in my apartment, I gave in. I thanked God for such a wonderful feeling, for making our bodies capable of such ecstasy. But after it was over, I knew that I had committed a mortal sin. I got into my car and drove into town to the rectory and told Father Drohan that I needed to go to confession. I was afraid that a train would hit me as I crossed the tracks toward town, and I would go straight to Hell. Feeling humiliated, I forced myself to say the M word to the old silver-haired priest face-to-face in the rectory. Holding a box of Kleenex out to me, he said that it was good that I was crying, that God loved the tears of a penitent sinner. He assigned me five Hail Marys and a Firm Purpose of Amendment and said that I should try to avoid this sin. Each time, I promised myself that I would not do it again. When I told Teeny about it, she said, "You're not sorry. You're just sorry it's wrong." As usual, she was right.

How could twenty years go by so fast? We were teaching, and we gave ourselves to that. We loved the church, and we gave ourselves to that. I lived alone, and she lived with her mother. I divided my time between my mother and Teeny. A quote on a greeting card says, "Don't live the same year seventy-five times and call it a life." But I did live the twenty years much the same; it was my life, and I was as happy as I knew how to be. The years were divided into seasons: the Liturgical Seasons of Advent and Christmas, Lent and Easter, and the long Ordinary Times. Life went by like a merry-go-round, the same horses passing by again and again.

In 1976, I bought a house of my own on River Ridge Road, about two miles from Robin Circle where Teeny lived with her mother. The yellow-and-white house was on a street in a small neighborhood. On my left lived a young couple, Hazel and Sandy Dennis, who had three children, two boys and a girl. On the right lived Dena and Danny Burgess and their two children, Brad and Ashley. I changed the house to suit me. I hired a man to install new double-paned Andersen windows, gray vinyl siding and black shutters, and I had the carport enclosed to turn it into a garage, so that I would feel safer when I came in at night, the automatic door coming down behind me, closing me in.

Teeny and her mother worked regularly in their yard, but Teeny called me a "hot house flower." After I bought my own home, I became determined to turn myself into a gardener. Sitting inside and looking out the new bay window, I planned my yard as if I were an artist painting a picture. The bay window was the frame. In the center I placed a birdbath and surrounded it with Shasta Daisies. Behind the birdbath, I planted a purple plum tree that had pink blooms in the spring and then purple leaves all summer. Near the birdbath I put up a bird feeder. On three tall pine trees, I nailed bluebird houses. Starting at the left side of the fence and moving around to the right, I used the pointed end of the hoe like a paintbrush and drew borders for flowerbeds. I sat down on the ground and scooted along, pulling grass and weeds all day until my hands were rough and bleeding. At night I slept better than I ever had, my body aching from working in the yard. My hands developed the rich smell of earth, my fingertips a crisscross of scratches. I planted shrubs along the edges of the yard, and when they grew tall and I cut them back, the neighborhood children came and stood beside me asking for the branches to use for their clubhouse. When they wanted me to come see it, they told me that I couldn't come inside. You're too big, they said. They piled the branches up against their side of the fence and, on their hands and knees, they burrowed in, opening up a small room with branch walls that they could peep through. I told them what a fine clubhouse they had built.

A black miniature poodle, an orphan, arrived at the high school one day and adopted me. I named her Maggie, and she sat in front of the bay window for hours each day looking out. From her post, she watched the yellow, black, and white Evening Grosbeaks when they came in the winter. In the spring bluebirds built nests in the houses, year after year. Each season meant two sets of families. I watched as the mother sat on the eggs, her face in the round doorway. With binoculars I watched as the babies began to try their wings from inside the birdhouse and as they flew for the first time to the edge of the roof where their mother sat coaxing them to join her. In late summer, the whole family returned and splashed together in the birdbath.

One day I saw a snake's head in the birdhouse where the bluebird mother had been sitting. I called my neighbor, Danny, and he came over with a Styrofoam cup filled with gasoline. He tossed the gas into the birdhouse door, and the snake came straight out into the air, its stomach filled with the bird eggs. With a hoe Danny knocked the snake to the ground where he chopped it into many pieces.

I developed in myself the peace of living alone, the quietness in the house, the time to be inside my own head. Some nights I sat in the rocking chair in the living room, the lights out, feeling the comfort of my own solitude. Two miles away Teeny and Willette watched television in their own house. On Saturday mornings I got up early to plan my lessons for the week. I sat on the sofa and read many books. I wrote in my journal about the books I was reading. I turned the back bedroom into my office, and I put there a desk Daddy had made for my room when I was a teenager and was first beginning to write. On the desk I put an old Royal Standard Typewriter where I began to write stories and send them off. Several years later I replaced the typewriter with an Apple IIe so that I no longer had to re-type whole pages when I made a mistake.

On many days after school, Teeny came over. We sat side by side on the sofa and looked at the yard through the bay window. I made pineapple daiquiris in the blender, and we drank them and held hands and talked, watching the cardinals at the bird feeder. Teeny taught me the names of the birds: the black-capped chickadee; the purple finch--a female sparrow dipped in cranberry juice---, the gray tufted titmouse, the red-winged blackbird. I always dreaded her time to leave, when we would hug and kiss quickly on the lips.

I enjoyed teaching. One day when my back was turned as I was writing on the blackboard, a student threw a Warriner's grammar book at me. Warriner's was the Bible of teaching grammar back then.

The book slammed against the blackboard close to my hand, and immediately the bell rang and the students ran out. Trying not to cry in the hall, I hurried to the counselor's office. That was the beginning of my learning how to be a better teacher. Soon I had planned a writing class in which students wrote plays and acted them out in front of one another. Then I taught students to make puppets out of socks and cotton batting, had the shop class to make us a stage, and the students who were usually afraid to stand up in front of a group could be good actors as, on their knees behind the stage, they let their puppets act out their parts. I invited the elementary students from the school next door to come over to see our puppet plays, and when the plays were over, my students gave their puppets to the children. Years later, when one of my students appeared in the Police Beat section of the newspaper, I told Teeny, "I remember what his puppet looked like." Down the hall Teeny taught Chemistry in her lab and continued to be a good listener for her students.

In 1981, I began the *Rain Dance Review*, a literary magazine at Baldwin High, a project that lasted for twenty years until I retired. The magazine published all ability levels of students, from Special Education to Advanced Placement. The students in my *Rain Dance Review* class went around to the elementary and middle school classrooms throughout the county and led writing activities with the children. In the spring each year we held an autograph party for the authors in the magazine. The *Rain Dance Review* was my heart, and I always said that if I never did anything else worthwhile in my life, I had at least done that.

Anytime I got a big idea or wanted to start something new that was at all risky, Mama discouraged me. Sitting on her sofa after school one day, I told her my idea about starting a literary magazine at Baldwin High. I told her we could send out letters asking for support from community patrons and see who would respond. "That sounds like a lot of trouble," she said. "You already don't have time to do the things you want to do now. It sounds time-consuming." But I was Mr. Toad from *Wind in the Willows*. When I had a new project, I put my whole self into it. As I told Mama about my current project, my voice rose, and she patted the air with her palm, saying, "Lower your voice" and thus, "Lower your enthusiasm." But I didn't usually listen. And, like Mr. Toad, I had to have all the accoutrements to go along with my project. When Mr. Toad became a motorcar driver, he had to have the gloves and hat. When he became a chef, he needed the tall white chef's hat. When I decided to do yoga, I bought all the DVDs, as well as the yoga chair, the yoga blanket, and the yoga clothes. When I was lifting weights at the gym, I had to have the leotards and the Jane Fonda outfit, along with the gloves with the fingers cut out.

One day I learned that my next-door neighbor's brother had died. At her kitchen table Hazel told me that she was one of triplets, that she had two brothers. One of her brothers was a football player, and the other had died from AIDS. He was sensitive, she said, and he was her best friend. He was manager of a flower shop in Atlanta. Then she looked up at me. "Why does God make someone gay?" she asked. "Why would he do that to someone?" I told her that I didn't know. I didn't say anything about myself, for by then I had convinced myself that the word did not apply to me.

Dena, the neighbor on the right, had been a mermaid at Weeki Wachee Springs in Florida. I remembered as a child going to see the mermaids. I was mesmerized as I sat and watched the beautiful women behind the glass, wearing their mermaid tails, and swimming gracefully in circles. I thought it would be wonderful to be a mermaid when I grew up. My favorite comic book had been "The Little Mermaid." I was fascinated with the mermaid who was trapped in the water longingly looking toward the shore, always on the outside looking in, unable to be with the one she loved. Dena and Danny built a swimming pool in their small back yard. I watched as the big bulldozer shoveled again and again, the hole becoming bigger and bigger as the mounds of red dirt piled up in the edge of the woods. The pool took up the whole yard with only a small row of grass between the fence and the pool. In the summer Dena taught swimming lessons, mothers bringing their babies for the "Moms and Tots" class. I sat on my back porch and watched as, at the end of the class, the mothers took their babies out to the end of the diving board and dropped them into the deep end of the pool, then hurried to lean forward with their arms as the babies swam to the side to be lifted out.

One day when I got home from school, Maggie was standing at the end of the sofa almost pointing, if a poodle can point. Every muscle in her body was taut, and I couldn't persuade her to move or interest her in a treat. When I looked behind the sofa, I saw a brown rabbit, missing half its white tail. I put Maggie into the yard and moved the sofa, then picked up the rabbit and put it into a box. When I called my veterinarian, she said that I should take the rabbit into the woods and leave it in a protected, shaded area, that the rabbit would either live or die but there was nothing she could do. I remembered the night I hit the rabbit when Mary-Louise and I were driving home from the Atlanta airport in the dark, the way that Mary-Louise told me that I had no control, that it was the rabbit's time to go. I guess she felt the same way about herself, that she had no control over taking her own life, that it was her time; astrology said so. I took the rabbit into the woods and left it, and I never went back to check. I remembered reading Cervantes in college, when Don Quixote built himself a mask out of cardboard. When he had finished making his mask, he struck it hard with his sword, and the mask broke into many pieces. When he re-did it, Sancho Panza asked him if he wasn't going to test it again. "I'm sure it's fine," said Don Quixote. I was sure the rabbit was fine.

In 1982, two big things happened. I had a hysterectomy, and I was chosen Teacher of the Year for the State of Georgia. The day before my hysterectomy, Father Drohan told me that he didn't think I should have it, that I might want to have children one day. He told me a story about a Catholic woman with a grapefruit-sized tumor who had a child before she had the tumor removed. I told him that I didn't think I was going to have any children, but he wouldn't relent in his disapproval. As I lay in the hospital waiting for the next morning when I would be put to sleep for my surgery, I told Teeny how worried I was that the priest didn't approve. I was afraid that I would die during surgery with what the priest considered to be a sin on my soul. Teeny called Father Drohan and insisted that he call me and put my mind at ease before I received anesthesia. Father Drohan called me in my hospital room past switchboard time. He had gotten through by telling them it was an emergency. He told me that night that he hadn't meant to worry me and that I had his blessing for my surgery. When I look back on that time now, I see a childlike me who saw the church as her parent, who needed permission for everything.

When I was chosen Georgia's Teacher of the Year, Mama and I rode to Atlanta with the School Superintendent for the festivities, and I was given a painting containing blue hydrangeas, my name and "State Teacher of the Year." But I never felt worthy of the honor. I kept looking over my shoulder wondering when the real me was going to emerge and everybody would know that I was faking being a good teacher. There were many other good teachers at Baldwin, especially Teeny. Teeny was happy for me, but I kept thinking that it should have been she who won, not me.

In 1985, we got a new priest at the Catholic Church. He had a thick Irish accent and a mop of dark hair streaked with gray. He had a wonderful sense of humor and an infectious laugh. He did not want any "quiet" masses, and he asked that I play the organ for the Saturday night vigil Mass. I had taken piano lessons as a child, and I had turned the pages for Mary-Louise; but I had never played the organ. The main organist taught me how to play the pedals with my left foot, and I became the Saturday night one-legged organist and cantor. Every week I practiced the Psalm and the hymns for the week, and singing felt like praying to me. The organ was at the back of the church in the balcony, and Teeny always sat upstairs and sang with me. Willette stayed home.

One evening when I drove into my driveway, a snake was stretched across the pavement. Without thinking, I drove over it, then put the car into reverse and backed over it again, then forward, and then reverse. Finally, I pulled into the garage and put the door down behind me. The next morning, when I went out to get the newspaper, the snake was in the neighbor's flowerbed beside the road. Its body was bruised and broken, but its head was up. The snake looked directly at me as if to say, "Why did you?" I panicked and called Danny to come over and kill the un-dead snake that was probably suffering because of me. It never occurred to me back then that I had also tried to kill a part of myself, a part that was still un-dead.

I was always aware that I came second to Willette. Any plans that Teeny and I had could be changed without warning if company dropped in at her house or if Willette had something she wanted her to do. I knew that Teeny would never stand up to her mother; I used to pray, not that her mother would die, but that Teeny would have some time left to live her own life. Of course, I wanted that life to be with me.

In 1989, Willette died of congestive heart failure. I knew that Teeny loved her mother, but I don't remember ever seeing her cry, not at Willette's funeral and not at any other time. She was stoic like that. After her mother's death, Teeny began to clean up and re-do her house. She had the walls painted to get rid of the yellow stains from Willette's cigarette smoke. She replaced the draperies and bought new furniture. She began to be herself, to do what she wanted when she wanted. On Friday nights she began cooking for a group of us: two widowed sisters who lived together across the street from her, and for my mother and me. Before we left her house each Friday, Teeny gave us what she called "service pans," leftovers in divided melamine plates with lids. On those nights Mama brought a suitcase and spent the night with me. She slept on the sofa in the living room because it was more comfortable for her than in the guest bedroom. Maggie jumped up on the sofa with her and slept stretched out against her leg with her neck over Mama's ankle. As she had many years ago on that night when Harvill found out about Ellen and me, Mama always brought her blood pressure instrument with her in a plastic grocery sack. On Saturday morning early, when I was trying to sleep in, she got up and began rattling that grocery sack, getting her stuff together to leave. I could hear that sack rattling all the way to my bedroom. It was as if the noise pierced through to my eardrum. Finally, she let herself out and drove home, and the noise stopped.

The Liturgical seasons in the church came and went. It was comforting to know what would always be, and Teeny and I developed our traditions. In the photo albums that I kept year after year were photos we made before we went to Midnight Mass to sing with the choir, of the Easter Triduum beginning with Holy Thursday and ending with the Easter Vigil. Year after year the choir of eight people practiced the same songs as last year. For the season of Advent we awaited the coming of the Baby Jesus as we read the readings every day and said the Saint Andrew Prayer, put straws in the Brut box manger, and made Spiritual Bouquets for one another. For the purple season of Lent we "offered up" school aggravations. Teeny gave up the milk in her coffee every day but Sunday. She said that "you could get used to hanging if you do it long enough" and that milk one day a week kept her wanting it. I gave up Breyer's vanilla bean ice cream and wine throughout Lent, so that every time we sang the hymn "These Forty Days of Lent" and got to the last verse that said, "An Easter of unending joy we may attain at last," I thought of ice cream and wine instead of the Resurrection. I was happy with Teeny as my friend and the Church as my focus, and I enjoyed the peace that came with being good.

One day at school in 1992, I received a phone call from the front office. When I answered, it was Werner Rogers, the State School Superintendent. He said, "Congratulations, Sandra, I would like to inform you that you have received a Milken National Educator Award." I had never heard of the Milken family nor of a National Educator Award. I had not applied for anything. I remember sitting there at the desk in the main office as teachers passed by and hearing those words in my ear. He immediately followed with, "You can't tell anybody; it's to be a surprise." He told me that the award meant that I would receive $25,000 and that in March I would be flown to Los Angeles to receive my award and attend the Milken Conference. I could take someone with me. When I hung up the phone and walked down the hall, I was squealing inside with what I couldn't tell anyone. Twenty-five thousand dollars was more money than I could even imagine, and he said that it didn't have to be used for school, that I could use it for whatever I wanted. "How did I get it?" I asked. He told me that it is a secret and that I would never know how I got it. My sister Linda flew with me to Los Angeles that year, and Michael Jackson was the main entertainment, singing "We Are the Children" on stage with about fifty children surrounding him. I remember walking across the stage and receiving my check from Lowell Milken, Linda in the audience taking pictures.

With the money, I made a down payment on a house around the corner from Teeny on Robin Circle. I fixed the house the way I wanted with old black-and-white photographs of my ancestors along the hallway, my study in the big room with the tall windows, and irises and bluebird houses in the backyard, although unfortunately the bluebirds didn't follow me to Robin Circle. Teeny and I ate our evening meals together and worked in one another's yards. In the evening we watched TV at first one house and then the other.

On Saturday nights she came to pick me up for the Vigil Mass and brought her Chihuahua, Itsy Bitsy, to stay with Maggie until we got back from Mass. Each Saturday night after Mass I made us an omelet with tomatoes and green olives, and we ate off lap trays and watched the antics of "Mrs. Bucket" in "Keeping Up Appearances" on PBS.

One day I heard from my hairdresser that someone had said in the shop, "Miss Worsham and Miss Horne have been lovers for years." I was shocked, dismayed, and frightened. How could I be good and be accused of what I wasn't doing?

But we did have our tender moments. When I washed her hair in the kitchen sink, her gray hair turned dark and straight and was slicked flat to her head as the warm water ran into it. I poured on the shampoo and scrubbed and rinsed and then wrapped the thirsty white towel around her head. Then I played the childhood game, "Where's Teeny?" Sliding the towel to the side of her head, I uncovered her lips. I kissed those soft pink lips, touching quickly before she drew back, that line having been drawn many years before and never crossed, never violated.

CHAPTER SIX: IS EVERYTHING ALL RIGHT?

"Mother is the name for God in the lips and hearts of little children." ---William Makepiece Thackaray, *Vanity Fair*

1995

I was susceptible to my mother's moods. If she was sad, I thought it was my fault; many times it was. If, when I was a child, we went downtown and, once again, unable to resist seeing how things felt, I reached across the counter and touched items in the stores, I was in trouble. Mama was silent for hours, while I worried and asked her again and again, "Is everything all right?"

"There are some things that saying 'I'm sorry' won't make all right," she said. It seemed that I waited hours to be forgiven. I stood behind her as she washed dishes at the kitchen sink, looking up at the side of her sad face, waiting for her to turn and smile, signifying that the wait was over. Finally, I asked again, "Is everything all right yet?" I wondered what things saying "I'm sorry" couldn't make all right. It wouldn't bring a dead person back to life. Did my mother think I would commit a murder? Years later, I realized that I had committed a murder, for I had buried a part of myself. Saying I'm sorry couldn't make that all right.

In January of 1995, one night at our Friday night suppers at Teeny's, Mama said to me, "Look at my stomach. It's never been this big before." Mama had always taken pride in her flat stomach. I looked up at her, standing beside me at the table, and put my hand on her abdomen, that place from where I came. It was huge and hard. I couldn't believe I hadn't noticed it sooner. That night when we got over to my house for her to spend Friday night as usual, she also showed me that her legs had begun to leak fluid through the pores. Both her legs were hard and wet from the knee down, her slick skin stretched so tight that it looked as if it would split open.

The next week I took her to her doctor, and he was puzzled about what could be causing the bloated stomach and the leaking legs. He sent her for an ultra-sound of her abdomen. As Mama lay flat on her back on the table, I sat in a chair nearby. She was small and silver-haired, eighty-four years old, with an abdomen that looked as if she were nine months pregnant. "What am I looking for?" the young technician asked as he moved the wand around on her stomach. He looked over his shoulder at me.

"Can't you see how big her stomach is?" I snapped at him. When I said that, Mama gave me the look.

Years later, I would learn that my sister Linda had never gotten any spankings. I couldn't count the number of spankings I got.

"Why didn't you get any spankings?" I asked her.

"All Mama had to do was look at me," she answered.

When she said that, I remembered myself, the child Sandra, her hands on her hips, saying to Mama, "There you go with that look again!" The day of the ultra-sound, I got the look.

Because the ultra-sound didn't show anything, we went to Dr. Keith Garnto, a brilliant doctor in town known for being the best diagnostician around. He wrote Mama a prescription for fluid to be drawn from her abdomen at the hospital. I stood in the corner of the bright white lab that day while Mama lay on a table, her bare stomach rising into the air. Again and again the nurse inserted a needle into

Mama's abdomen in different places and filled vials with liquid. She lined capped vials into a wooden holder near where I stood, leaning against the wall. I watched as the vials became a row of different shades of pink and red, the fluids from my mother's body. I was breathless with fear. The sheet under her became wet with the fluid leaking from her legs.

Three days later I received a call on the English Department telephone at school. It was late afternoon, and I had been grading papers in my room. One of the teachers came to tell me that I had a call. I stood in the empty room with the phone to my ear and heard Dr. Garnto say, "The fluid was filled with tumor cells. It is reasonable to assume that it originated in the ovaries."

"What can be done?" I asked.

"She's too fragile for surgery or chemotherapy treatments," he said, "and the tumor is too far advanced." He carefully did not use the C word; I guess the word *tumor* is a euphemism for the word *cancer*.

"What would you do if she were your mother?" I asked.

"I think I would make her as comfortable as possible and let her have quality time. Hospice would be a viable option."

"How long do you think she has?" I asked him.

"Well, of course, doctors don't really know that. But I would estimate weeks to months."

I hung up the phone. The words *weeks to months* screamed in my ears. I stepped into the hallway. The janitors had already dimmed the lights, suggesting to the teachers that it was time to go home. The teacher who had called me to the phone was not there any longer. I needed someone to tell. I ran down the hall looking into each empty room; no one was there. I went into my classroom, put my head down on the desk, and sobbed. Dr. Garnto had asked me to tell Mama.

I got my things together and went to my car. All the way across town I beat the steering wheel with my fist and cried out, "It's too soon! It's too soon! We need more time!" When I got to Mama's house, I parked the car in the driveway, as I had many other times in my life. I sat in the car and remembered the day of The Telling, that day that had been the moment of change in my life. As I had that day, I dreaded what I had to tell Mama. It was one of those "Mama, I have something to tell you" occasions, those words that Mama dreaded hearing from me. I got out of the car and went to the door and rang the bell. The screen door was hooked, and the French door was closed, for it was a cold day in January. Beside the door hung a brown shriveled begonia with an empty bird nest in the center. Every Mother's Day I gave Mama a hanging basket that she hung there, and every summer the birds returned to build. Every year she watched the mother and the new babies, gave me reports about their progress, and let me know when the tiny birds had left the nest. It was time to take this dead basket down, but I didn't.

I peered through the door and rang the bell. Mama's silhouette came from the kitchen and down the hall toward me. The evening sun was coming through the windows in my sister Linda's room and flooded yellow rays around Mama's dark approaching figure, making her look like the icon of the Virgin of Guadalupe in the Catholic Church. When she moved into the light of the living room, I saw that she was wearing her apron and held a spatula in her hand. I could smell chicken frying.

"The doctor called?" she asked, looking at my face as she let me inside. She sat down in her pink velour chair, and I sat on the sofa in front of her.

I nodded. "It's cancer," I said. "He thinks it's ovarian."

She put her hand to her mouth. "Well, I knew it was something," she said. Then after a few moments of silence, she continued, "In a way I'm relieved. At least it's not Alzheimer's or a stroke." Mama's biggest fear had always been "not being herself." She took her blood pressure instrument almost everywhere she went and took her pressure several times a day. Dr. Garnto had told me that if you had to have cancer, ovarian was a good kind to have. It usually stayed contained within the abdomen and didn't break loose and go to the brain. It didn't cause a lot of pain and people kept their mental faculties up until the end. I told her that.

"Well, supper's ready," she said, getting up, walking with the spatula down the hall toward the kitchen. Ever since a fall had activated arthritis in her left hip years ago, her left leg was shorter than her right. In order to walk straight around the house, she wore two different slippers. I followed her, passing my childhood bedroom on the right and the telephone table at the end of the hall beside Linda's old room.

"He suggested we go with hospice," I told her over supper, a drumstick in my hand. On my plate were butter peas, white creamed corn, and a refrigerator biscuit cut open and covered with brown gravy. Mama was an expert with corn, sitting on the back porch scraping each ear until her face and arms were covered with thin sliced kernels and splotched with white corn milk, the ripe smell of freshness filling the air over the galvanized tub that she straddled.

"Did he say how long I have?" she asked.

"He said only God knows that," I told her. "Do you want to spend the night with me tonight?"

"Yes," she said. "We'll need to call everybody."

At home, while Mama lay on the sofa with my dog Maggie at her side, I called Linda first. She cried, of course, and I cried, the two of us together on the phone from Georgia to Kentucky. Next I called my first cousins, the ones in Macon and Atlanta. Because Mama was the last living sibling in the Fordham family, all the cousins had gravitated to Mama, their last aunt and the last connection to their own mothers. There were eight siblings; I had many cousins to call. They would then call their children, our extended family.

That night when I lay down in my bed, I began to sob. I lay there on my back and longed to go to Mama where she lay on the brown couch and cry and let her comfort me. I tried to be an adult, to hold it back. But then I thought that one day she wouldn't be here and I wouldn't be able to go to her. I went to the family room and knelt on the floor beside the couch. I put my ear against her chest and said, "I don't want my mama to have cancer."

She rubbed my back in big circles and said, "Honey, I don't want to have cancer either."

The next morning on my way to school, I left her in her house on Doles Boulevard. As I drove down the street, I remembered the many times I had ridden my bicycle down that hill, my hands out, riding free, my mother standing on the front steps in her apron watching me and afraid I would fall.

The following Thursday the hospice nurse came to see Mama for the first time. She was a stout white woman wearing teddy bear scrubs with a stethoscope around her neck. Five earring studs lined her left ear. She carried a clipboard on her arm; her elbows looked like my aunt Alma's, round and dimpled. When I let her in, she shook my hand, said her name was Louise, and then went straight to Mama, who was lying down on the sofa. Sitting beside Mama, she leaned toward her and said, "I'm sorry you're so sick."

"Well, it's just one of those things," said Mama. Louise looked closely at Mama's wet legs and dabbed them with gauze that she took out of her bag. I didn't realize until that moment how relieved I would feel, to have the nurse there, taking over and treating Mama so tenderly. After she finished her examination, Louise sat down in the chair next to the sofa and began to explain to us about hospice--that Mama would receive no treatments or anything intended for a cure, that her treatment would be palliative. She explained that they would keep her pain-free, that they would send someone to bathe her, and that they would provide a chaplain and a patient advocate.

"Who will be her primary caregiver?" she asked, looking at me. Mama looked at me, questioning.

"I will," I said.

"Which will be your funeral home?" she asked, a shocking question to me.

I paused and looked at Mama. "Moore's," I said. It was the funeral home that buried Daddy, that would one day bury me.

"How much does this cost?" Mama asked. A Depression baby, she was frugal. It embarrassed me when we went out to eat and the waiter asked, "Would you like any sides?" and Mama asked, "Does it come with it?" I had a spending problem, still do. Any time I went to see Mama, she looked me up and down and asked, "Is that new?" What she meant was, "Have you been spending money again?" When she read a menu, she chose her order by the price rather than the item. She ordered water with lemon on the side, and she prided herself on making her own lemonade at the table with artificial sweetener from a bowl.

"It's covered by your Medicare," Louise said. Mama smiled and gave me a thumbs-up.

Then she looked at me and said, "I hate for you to have to do this. Why don't you put me out at Green Acres?"

I waved my hand in the air, signaling, Don't even suggest that.

Louise put a dedicated phone number sticker on the telephone and told us to call any time, day or night. She handed me a small booklet entitled *Gone from my Sight*. I quickly tucked it into my purse, not ready to read a book with that title.

Over the next few days, I began to read books about near-death experiences. I wanted to read about where Mama was going. Each book I read described the near-death experience in the same way, traveling through a dark tunnel, at the end of which was a bright white light that felt like pure love, a sense that all those you loved who had died were there, surrounding you with love. None of the people who had had this experience wanted to return to our dimension, and when they came back, all they said was that love was all that mattered. Next, I read Gilda Radner's book, *It's Always Something*, about her own experience with ovarian cancer. I wanted to know what Mama would go through. Last, I read Rosalind Carter's book on caregiving in order to know what to expect and how to prepare myself. I told Linda on the phone, "This is an important journey, and we need to do it right." Carter's book told about the series of losses that Mama would go through and that, in turn, Linda and I would go through with her. She would lose her ability to walk, to go to the bathroom by herself, to bathe herself, to sleep, possibly to think. It could happen in any order. Carter wrote that as caregiver, I should take care of myself, or I wouldn't be any good to Mama.

As soon as the church bulletin listed "Edna Worsham" with "ovarian cancer" beside her name, people from the church began to come to see her. Every day when I went by to pick her up after school, the house was full. I was tired, and I wanted everyone to leave so that I could take Mama to my house and get some rest. But she was entertaining company. Everybody that came brought something edible, and the refrigerator began to fill with congealed salads, pies, and puddings. It frustrated me to open the refrigerator door and see so much that would go bad if not eaten. One day when I went by, only a couple of Mama's friends were still there. On the buffet table in the dining room was a bowl of sweet potatoes that looked as if it had been there several days. Candied sweet potatoes were Mama's specialty, the dish that everybody wanted her to bring to the church suppers. The bowl was covered with swarming fruit flies, and for some reason seeing it there made me angry. I took it to the living room where Mama was visiting with her friends, and I said, "What are you saving this for? There are fruit flies all over it." Mama was embarrassed, but I was tired, and that bowl of sweet potatoes infuriated me.

"Set it back in there," Mama said, waving her hand, dismissing me.

But I didn't. I took it into the kitchen and with a spoon, I raked it into the garbage can. Such a small thing, but it was an act of defiance that felt good to me. It was something I could control. When I went back into the room and told Mama that I had thrown away the sweet potatoes, her mouth turned into a thin slit, and I saw that she was angry with me. Nevertheless, I had done it, and I couldn't take it back. When I look back on that day now, it seems ironic that I couldn't stand up to my mother with the big things, but I had the courage to throw away some three-day old sweet potatoes with fruit flies. That day, one thing felt as big as the other.

One of the first actions I took after Mama's diagnosis was to look in the *Union-Recorder* to see if Milledgeville had a cancer support group. I found one that met at a local doctor's office the following Tuesday. When I got there, the room was empty, containing only a long table with chairs and a box of Kleenex in the center of the table. I sat down at the end of the table and waited. Soon a young woman entered and sat down across from me. She had blonde hair pulled back into a low ponytail and square glasses. She did not say anything about my being the only person there, nothing like, Oh, well, since no one came, we can't have the meeting. On the contrary, she smiled and acted as if I *were* the meeting. She said that her name was Jeannie.

"Tell me about your life right now," she said, leaning toward me.

Immediately, my throat tightened, and I couldn't talk. When I finally said, "My mother has cancer," she asked me to tell her about it. I told her about the day they drew the fluid, about the weeping from her legs, and about hospice coming. She listened intently as I talked, as if the whole meeting were intended for me. I learned that Jeannie was the coordinator for the hospice volunteers.

Then she said, "This may sound strange to you now, but this time will be the most beautiful, quality time you will ever have with your mother." When I looked surprised, she continued, "Most people never know when they are going to die. When you know, as with hospice, you have time--time to ask all the questions you want to ask, time to be together with the knowledge that every minute is precious, time to say 'I love you,' time to say 'Thank you.' Make good use of this time," she said. "You will always treasure it. Keep a journal, and take pictures every day. Use this time to make memories." When the hour was up, I thanked her, and she gathered her things and walked with me to the parking lot. "Call me anytime," she said, "day or night." I couldn't believe that this complete stranger was telling me that I could call her in the middle of the night.

I created a system for Mama's weeping legs. I bought Pampers, set up the sewing machine, and cut the diapers into long strips, cutting off the elastic edges. I trimmed the Pampers over the trashcan because the material inside that collects the liquid fell out like sand. Then I strung the diapers together end-to-end and sewed them, making long strips that we would wrap around Mama's legs. I began at her ankles and wrapped the strips around and around until I reached her knee where I pinned a large safety pin. On top of the Pampers, I wrapped brown ACE bandages and secured them at the top. It worked. When Mama stood up to walk, the wrappings stayed in place. And at the end of the day when I removed them, they were heavy with the fluid that had drained all day from her legs. Dr. Garnto said I should get a patent for my idea. Soon I taught Louise and the nurse's assistant, Lynn, how to wrap Mama's legs. When I got home from school each day, I sat down at the sewing machine and made more. She used them up as fast as I could make them.

I asked Dr. Garnto if there was a way that he could regularly drain the fluid from Mama's abdomen. He said that it would have to be done every day and that it would make Mama so weak that she would deteriorate much faster. I read on the Internet that a tube could be inserted into her abdomen and then re-routed through her system, an experimental method. But that method would cause excess stress on her bloodstream, also causing an earlier demise.

Each afternoon when I picked Mama up to come sleep at my house, it was more difficult for her to move. Her legs were so heavy that she could hardly lift them to walk. She stood up and then looked down at her feet and said, "Move, feet." When she lowered herself into the passenger's seat of my car, she couldn't lift her feet inside, so I lifted them for her, first one and then the other. It was the same thing when we got to my house. I lifted each foot out of the car and then up the two steps to the door. I remembered the Rosalyn Carter book describing the losses we would face.

One night Mama wanted to take a bath, and I walked her into the bathroom and helped her get into the tub. Her swollen legs were like logs, and we could only move a few inches at a time. When I was a child, she used to ask me to wash her back for her. I remembered standing beside her that night in our bathroom on Doles Boulevard, wetting the washcloth in the tub water and rubbing the bar of soap over it, then squeezing the cloth over Mama's shoulders as the suds ran down her back. "Oh, that feels good," she said that night as the warm soapy water ran over her shoulders. But when I tried to get her out of the bathtub, her feet kept slipping, and I had to put washcloths under her feet to get traction. When we got her out on the bathmat, I dried her all over, her shoulders, her back, and under her atrophied breasts. I squatted down as I dried each of her legs and her feet with the big bunions causing the toes to point toward the left and the right. I always thought that her feet were misshapen because her daddy went to town to buy shoes with only their length measurements, not their width. But now that my own feet are beginning to take the shape of my mother's, I know that it must be hereditary. As we were walking slowly back to her chair, she said, "Well, I'm not going to do that again!" From then on, the nursing assistant bathed her in her chair.

One night Mama took a laxative, and the next morning as I was walking her into her house for the day, the laxative began to work. It was the biggest mess I had ever seen, and I didn't handle it well. "Where are the newspapers?" I shouted. "What should I do?" Later I was ashamed of myself, and I re-wrote the scene in my head. In my revision, I said, "Don't worry, Mama, we'll get it up. It won't be a problem at all."

That day at school, one of the English teachers stuck her head into my classroom and said, "How are you?"

"I'd give a million dollars for a cup of coffee," I said. The teacher went away and returned with a cup of coffee, a doughnut, and a handful of daffodils. I cried with gratitude.

After another week of going back and forth, Mama said that she thought it was time for her to start staying with me. We locked up her house, and she moved to my house for the duration. As she walked out the door, she turned around and said matter-of-factly, "Bye, house." And then, "I hope my friends will know where I am." I promised her that I would let them know, and I called the church office, her Sunday School teacher, and a few members of the Widow's Club, a group of women who got together once a month for a potluck, to let them know that Mama had moved to my house.

Soon people began coming to my house all day and evening. The front door was always flagging. I found a sitter to stay with Mama during the day while I was at school, and when I came home, the refrigerator was filled with food that would go bad if it wasn't eaten.

Before Mama came, when I lived alone, my refrigerator never had anything in it but a carton of milk, bread, cheese, flour, cereal, and sugar. When people started coming, they interrupted my schedule, and they got in my space. "Why do you have the flour in the refrigerator?" one of Mama's friends asked, laughing at me.

"So it won't get weevils," I said, aggravated that people were asking about how I ran my personal home.

"Then why the sugar and the cereal?" she asked. What I wanted to say was, "That's none of your business!" Instead, I answered, "Keeps the ants out of it."

"Well, I've never heard of keeping the flour and sugar in the refrigerator," she said, shaking her head.

We ordered Meals on Wheels to be delivered every day, but Mama often didn't eat it; when I got home from school, I ate Mama's leftovers for my supper. It also irritated me that I had to run the dishwasher more than once a week, sometimes every day. Living alone, I ran it on schedule every Saturday. It was the same with the washing machine. But almost every day there were enough towels for a wash. I felt like an old turtle, set in my ways, with everybody trying to get under my shell.

After a while Mama had accumulated a pile of ACE bandages that needed washing. When I washed and dried them, they came out of the dryer wadded up in wrinkles. I set up the ironing board to try to iron them straight so that we could wrap them around Mama's legs on top of the Pampers. But every time I put the iron on the bandage, the elastic stuck to the iron, and I had to rip it off.

When Linda and I were small, Mama hired a small black woman, about five feet tall, to come to iron for us. Her name was Annie Clark, and she ironed the ruffles on the dresses we wore to Sunday School.

I remember lying on the floor coloring in a coloring book and hearing the steam and the thud the iron made as Annie put the point into the tiny pleats. Annie liked hot Coca-Colas in the green bottles and peach snuff that Mama bought for her at the grocery store. As I tried to iron the bandages, I thought to myself, Annie would know how to do this.

Finally, I set the iron on the ironing board and sat down in a chair and cried. It was impossible. It was all impossible, all the dishes in the sink and the clothes in the dryer and the food in the refrigerator and the people coming in and out, always having to smile and be welcoming because Mama was pleased to see them. I cried for ten minutes, and on my shoulders were the wadded bandages and food going bad and the doorbell ringing again and again. Then I went back into the laundry room, wet all the ACE bandages, and clothes-pinned them around and around on the drying rack. The next morning they were dry and straight. Another problem solved.

As I look back now on those days when Annie worked for us, I remember the day I learned that Annie couldn't read. I was lying on the floor reading a book when I came to a word I didn't know. I think the word was *tenacious*, and I said, "Annie, what does t-e-n-a-c-i-o-u-s spell? Annie laughed but wouldn't answer me; I yelled out to Mama in the kitchen, "Mama, make Annie tell me what this word spells!" How could I as a child use that term *make*? Mama *make* Annie?

Mama said, "You leave Annie alone." It was also that day that Mama told me after Annie left that I didn't have to say "Yes, Ma'am" to Annie, a statement that I puzzled over. Annie was my elder, like Mama's friends Mrs. Vincent and Mrs. Stembridge. And why didn't I call Annie "Mrs. Clark"? Mama and Annie were about the same age and yet, Annie called Mama "Miz Wooshum," but Mama called Annie by her first name. These were the subtle things about growing up in a segregated South. I was never aware of prejudice in my home, no "N" word, no deliberate racism. But yet, Don't say "Yes ma'am" to Annie. Don't call her "Mrs. Clark."

Mama often needed me in the middle of the night, but I couldn't hear her when she called. I gave her a bell that Teeny had used with Willette. "Ring this when you need me, okay?"

Mama looked up at me and said, "Why don't you give me a grocery sack to rattle? That seems to wake you up pretty well!"

For breakfast each morning, all she wanted was Campbell's chicken gumbo soup. When I opened the can and poured it into a bowl, the smell of that soup in the morning made me nauseated. She also repeated the same questions off and on all day: "What time is it?" "Where's my pocketbook?" "Where's my walking stick?" and "Where's my blood pressure instrument?" As the weeks went by and she began to be cold all the time, her question became, "Is the heat up high enough?" It was March and becoming hot in Georgia. When I came home from school, the hospice sitter was there, and the heat was set on eighty. Because I couldn't sleep if my room was too hot at night, Teeny and I got the painted window unstuck in my bedroom, and we raised the windows and closed the heat vent in my room. I slept with the window in my bedroom open all night; yet, the first thing Mama wanted to know the next morning was if the heat was up high enough.

In my prayers at Mass, I offered it all up to God. During the Our Father, I held my palms upward and imagined resting in them everything that was bothering me, picturing Mama in her duster and hairnet, all in a package rolled in a big black ball of yarn, safety pins and unpaid bills and undeposited checks and rotting grapefruit, and wadded towels and long strips of Pampers heavy with Mama's fluid. I stuck all these things into my imaginary ball of yarn and pictured it turning to white as I put it into the lap of Jesus and asked for the ability to be the best caregiver that I could be for my mother. I asked for superhuman strength. I will only need it temporarily, I said, but please make me Superwoman this one time in my life.

On Holy Thursday, I sang with the choir, a song called "Remember Me." The words were meant for Jesus: "Soon I will be gone from you; I must die as it was prophesied." As I sang, I could think only of Mama, and it was hard to keep my voice from cracking. Then we began the Easter Triduum, the three days leading up to Easter. On Good Friday Mama took a laxative; I spent the day sewing together Pampers, emptying the basin, and spraying the room. Hospice suggested pouring Scope mouthwash into the potty to cut down on the smell, and it worked. Mama was exhausted.

With the Easter Vigil came the lighting of the Christ candle, the Old and New Testament readings, the singing of the Psalms, and the blessing of the fire and water. The choir sang, "O Death, Where is Thy Sting?" I prayed, Dear Jesus, please help me to remember the peace, love, and joy which is not of this earth but which is of you and Heaven. And I continued to pray for superhuman strength. On Easter Sunday Mama woke up from a deep sleep and called out to me, "Is everything all right? I don't want to be worried about anything."

Mama began waking me up almost every night. I was so tired at school that during my planning period, I locked the classroom door, put my head down on the desk, and took a nap. When I got home, it was hot, and Mama was still freezing. The sitter had her wrapped up in blankets, but immediately my hairline became wet with sweat.

Mama had spent all day calling people—old friends, her doctor, her dentist, thanking them and telling them all good-bye. I was barely putting one foot in the front of the other, and the only way for it all to end was to lose my mother.

One day hospice sent a music therapy student from the college. Her name was Araminta, and she was a beautiful blond from one of the Scandanavian countries. Working with Mama was to be part of her internship. She was to help Mama make a recording to leave behind for Linda and me. She came once a week, and Mama looked forward to her visits. On the tape Mama recited every poem she had ever learned in the one-room schoolhouse she attended in Dublin, Georgia, where she grew up. When I came home from school, Mama was sitting in her chair with Araminta by her side. Between them on a table was the tape recorder. Mama had recited "Hiawatha" and "Abu Ben Adhem" all the way through, all the words.

In early May, Linda and her husband Tom came, bringing a blue lift chair recliner that Tom's mother had used before she died. They put the chair in the middle of the family room, and Mama settled in. The chair became her most comfortable place.

While they were here, Mama wanted us all to go to the Baptist Church because it would probably be the last time we could all go together. "I want to go, but what can I wear?" she said. She couldn't wear a skirt because of the wrappings on her legs.

"Why don't we all wrap our legs with ACE bandages?" Linda said, laughing. Instead, we all decided to wear pants.

That day I saw many people that I remembered from my childhood in that church.

"Where have you been?" asked Pete Cheeves, a jolly man who always had a cigar in the corner of his mouth.

"Pete, I've been Catholic for years," I said.

"Awe, you too pretty to be a Catholic," he said, patting my back.

I guess he thought that I'd become a nun, and in a way, I guess I had.

We sat down on a pew about six rows from the back. Both Linda and I were remembering our time in that church, the times that we had been in Girls Auxiliary and were progressing through our Forward Steps. I only made it to Queen and received my cardboard crown. But Linda made it all the way to Queen Regent in Service, which meant that she had a scepter that looked like a fairy's wand and a green satin cape that tied in the front. As we sat there, each of us in our own reverie, I remembered a woman who used to go to that church named Ella Humbert, who always wore hats with feathers. She had large hips, and she walked down the aisle with her butt cheeks bouncing. I leaned across Linda and asked Mama, "Is Ella Humbert still living?"

"I guess she is," Mama said. "There she goes right there." I looked up and saw Miss Humbert walking down the aisle with her feather bouncing on top of her hat. Linda and I got tickled, and we tried to hold it in, but Linda snorted in spite of herself. Mama whispered loudly, "You girls behave, or I'm going to have to take you home."

The next week Mama wanted us to take her to the bank so that she could go into her safe deposit box. Linda, Tom, and I walked into Century Bank with her, and she went up to the desk and said that she needed to get into her lock box. In the back room, we stood beside her as she lifted the lid to the box and began taking items out. She took out Daddy's death certificate, her car title, war bonds, and many certificates of deposit that had been maturing over the years. Underneath it all was a soft rolled-up cloth that rattled as she set it down, her silver—spoons, forks, knives, and large serving pieces. She began to cry and shake her head. "You two are going to be all right," she said to Linda and me. "All these CDs will add up when you cash them, and this silver's worth a pretty penny. Your daddy and I came from poor families, and we had to work hard." After the trip to the bank, Tom drove back home to Kentucky, and Linda stayed.

Teeny's Chihuahua, Itsy Bitsy, was getting old and got sick one day, having to be taken to the vet. I was teaching my last class of the day, a prep class for students who had failed the Georgia writing exam three times each. During class, the telephone in my classroom rang. When I answered it, Teeny told me that Itsy Bitsy had died during the night in her crate at the vet. Teeny was distraught at the thought of her baby dying alone.

When I hung up, I put my face into my hands and sat at my desk. My students knew that my mother was sick, and they sat quietly, watching me. When I looked up, I said, "My friend's dog died."

Before the students could stop themselves, they began to look at one another and giggle. They tried not to laugh, but the tears rolled down their cheeks as they covered their mouths. When the bell rang, they filed out, their heads down.

I sat at my desk for a minute, and shortly I heard a knock at the door. "Come in," I called.

The door slowly opened, and the students sheepishly came back in. "We're sorry, Miss Worsham," they said. I couldn't believe they had waited and returned; it was the last class of the day, and they had buses to catch.

One day I came home with fever of 102 degrees. I had read in Rosalind Carter's book that caregivers often get sick. I put the telephone beside Mama's chair, and I slept in my bedroom for ten hours. It was a luxurious, restful sleep, but I had crazy dreams. In one I was trying to drive a car, but I couldn't control it. The seat was pushed back too far, and the mat kept slipping up. I couldn't press the accelerator or the brake. In another dream, my house was being blown by a strong wind. I stood and watched as all my possessions flew out the windows and doors. "Too much loss! Too much loss!" I kept crying, and then in my dream, I saw Mama flying by. I grabbed hold of her duster hem and held on as tightly as I could. When I woke up, my fist was squeezing the sheet into a wad. When my fever broke, I lay and dozed, remembering how it was to stand on Mama's front porch and press my face to the dark screen door, how I could see Mama round the corner from the kitchen, her silhouette coming down the hall toward me as if emerging from a tunnel.

After I recovered, Mama went down fast. She began to be awake all night and didn't want to be left alone. Hospice brought an oxygen machine that whirred constantly. I soon learned that the machine was filled with those roaches called water bugs. I sprayed around it with bug spray the way Mama had sprayed my boxes in her house after my divorce; then I called the pest control man. Something that appeared perfectly innocuous on the outside was hiding something sinister underneath, like cancer. When my Aunt Alma had bone cancer, Mama and I were in the waiting room at the hospital in Atlanta when I heard someone call across the room, "Don't any of us know what we're carrying around with us." I looked over at Mama sitting in her wheelchair with the oxygen tube hooked over her ears and thought shit, shit, shit.

One of the teachers at school asked me one day, "What are you doing for Lent?"

"Surviving," I answered, thinking of the water pouring from Mama's legs, the water pouring from Jesus' side. The water was rising higher and higher in Mama's body. I could feel it in her back, squishy, like a sponge. Eventually, she would drown from her own body fluids.

Louise, the hospice nurse, taught me how to put Mama on the potty chair. "You get her to link her hands behind your neck," she said, "and then you use momentum to swing her gently in one quick motion from one seat to the next." But Mama wouldn't let go. She kept her hands firmly gripped on the arms of the wheelchair, her elbows locked, bracing. She was either scared that she would hurt me, or she was afraid to relinquish control. Finally, hospice brought the Hoyer lift, the last piece of their equipment that we hadn't used. It was a contraption made of shiny metal pipes and a canvas sling. The sling went under Mama's butt, and big chains with hooks were attached to the sling in four places and then to the frame. A hydraulic pump raised Mama into the air where she swung as I rolled her to the potty chair and lowered her to the seat. Mama's world was composed of the reclining lift chair, the wheelchair, and the potty chair, and she needed help getting from one to the other. The Hoyer lift was the connection between the three parts of her world.

One day when Araminta came, Mama sat in her wheelchair and sang hymns to the tape recorder. "I always wanted to be able to sing," she said, but her voice was thin and reedy. I tried to memorize the sound as she sang "Amazing Grace," "Fairest Lord Jesus," "What a

Friend We Have in Jesus," and "How Great Thou Art." Then she told Araminta that she wanted her to record Linda and me singing "Whispering Hope" so that it could be played at her funeral. Araminta played the piano while Linda and I stood behind her and sang. Mama sat beside us in the wheelchair, and in the background was the whooshing sound of the oxygen machine. Araminta would have to filter out that sound before the funeral.

One day I came home to find Mama sitting in the front doorway in the wheelchair. The bottom of the chair was extended, and her outstretched legs were covered in a pink and blue striped blanket from our childhood. The yellow sun was illuminating her silver hair and her face and gave her an otherworldly look. Hospice was there, and they took her picture to put on the front cover of their new brochure.

Because Mama was awake all night and needed help, Linda slept on the sofa at Mama's feet, and we moved a single bed into the room for me to sleep on at Mama's side. That way we could always be available when she needed us. One night Mama woke up needing to go to the potty. We attached the Hoyer lift and lowered her to the potty. On the way back to her chair as she hung in the canvas sling, she said, "I don't think it's going to be long now. I don't know why we can't just talk."

"Should I call hospice?" I asked, panicky.

"I don't think it will be tonight. I may be around a long time, but I may not have the strength to talk," she said as we lowered her back into the lift chair. "Get something to write with," she said, and then, "Write this down." I sat at the end of the single bed with a pad and pen, and Linda sat on the sofa, listening.

Mama sat with her eyes closed, talking softly, her hands resting on her protruding stomach. "I want a light-colored casket that looks outstanding. I want to wear my pink suit." At this point Linda jumped up and went to the back and brought Mama the blouse she had bought for her to wear. It was in a box with tissue paper, a white blouse with tiny pearls sewn to the bodice. She put it into Mama's lap, and Mama nodded and looked up at Linda. "That's real pretty," she said. Then she continued, and Linda sat back down on the sofa, the blouse by her side. "If my friend Jerry wants to put a corsage on my shoulder, let her. I want the casket blanket to have a few pink rosebuds and the rest pink and white carnations with some of those pink lilies I like that smell good. I think they are called Stargazers." I took notes, writing as fast as I could.

"I want that scripture from Revelation to be read, the one that says there shall be no night there and God shall wipe all the tears from their eyes." I thought of the expression in the Catholic Church from the "Hail Holy Queen"—"weeping and mourning in this valley of tears." Mama had had a lot of things to make her cry: losing her younger brother Herman to epilepsy when he was alone at the State Hospital--they put epileptics in the mental hospital back then, and Mama couldn't think about Herman's death without crying. She never got over Daddy's death at only age fifty-seven, and she cried for him often, from 1966 to 1995. When she and Araminta made the recording, Mama sang, "Good Night, Sweetheart," to Daddy and "Bye Baby Bunting" and "You are my sunshine," to Linda and me. She never believed that people in Heaven knew what was happening to us on earth because if they did, she reasoned, then Heaven would be sad.

"But they know the whole story," I told her, "so they aren't sad." But she was never convinced. She had lost all her siblings and many of her closest friends. And then, of course, there was me. I had been a reason for her to weep and mourn.

"I want the last song to be 'Blest Be the Tie,' and I want all the verses sung. Then in her weak voice, she began to sing, "When we asunder part, it gives us inward pain, but we shall still be joined in heart and hope to meet a-gain." She pronounced *a-gain* to rhyme exactly with the word *pain.*

"Girls," she continued, "I don't want this to be painful for you, but it's just as important to prepare for death as it is to prepare for life. Please don't hold any resentment for anything people did or didn't do during this time. Do you have any questions you want to ask?" I couldn't think of any then because I had been trying hard throughout her illness to ask the questions I wanted to ask.

Linda asked, "Did we breastfeed?"

Mama answered, "Sandra did, but you wouldn't have anything to do with it. I think you were waiting for some rice and stewed tomatoes," Mama said, and laughed, opening her eyes to look at Linda.

She began naming the possessions that meant something to her and telling us who to give them to. The hand-embroidered picture in the drawer in her back bedroom was to go to Aunt Alma's children. The amethyst ring would go to our cousin Juliette. The cut-work tablecloth went to Linda. The amber bowl with the rose in the bottom, Aunt Alma brought from the World's Fair; she said that I could keep that. She named the glass pitcher with the cut-glass squatting, the crocheted tablecloth, the Dutch doll quilt, Daddy's pocket watch, the chenille bedspread. "You two can divide those up," she said. In one drawer was a child's dress that had belonged to a cousin named Ola, who had died young. Aunt Alma had tatted a neckline you could run a ribbon through. "You might want to put that in a shadowbox," she said. She told us to divide all the photographs from the desk drawer and put them into stacks by family. "I have some real pretty clothes," she said. "Give them away to any of my friends who can wear them. Then sell or donate the rest."

She put her hand up to her cheek and said, "Life is just a book, and this is the grand finale." Then she looked from Linda to me and said, "You have both been a joy to my life and a joy to your daddy's life. You have both looked after me. I don't know what I would have done without Linda when I had my neck surgery, and I don't know what I would have done without Sandra during this time. Don't either one of you think you have outdone the other. You haven't ever let me down."

After that night I didn't go back to school. Mama lost interest in the television and didn't care about reading the *Union-Recorder*, even though she used to read every word. Over the next few days, she slept most of the time. Her breathing was shallow, and she hurt in the center of her chest.

One day when Linda had gone to the grocery store and hospice was not there, Mama asked me, "Is everything all right? Between us?" It was ironic to me that she asked me the same words that I had always asked her, needing her reassurance that she was not mad at me, that I didn't have anything to feel guilty for. Her patting my hand and saying, "Yes, Honey, everything is all right," could give me such relief and take away my anxiety. It would never be spoken, but I knew that Mama was referring to the day of the Telling and to that unspoken thing between us, the source of my shame.

"Absolutely," I said to her. "Everything is fine between us."

On May 16, 1995, Mama was different. She whispered that she was too tired to talk. The hospice nurse told us that the fluid had moved to both lungs. For the next week and a half, Linda and I took turns helping her onto the potty chair, wiping her, or, if she had taken a laxative, cleaning her up. "I'm sorry you are having to do this," she said to us, and we answered, "How many times did you have to clean us up?"

On Monday, May 29, Mama slept all day in the lift chair, her breathing shallow and her voice weak. We had to lean in to hear her. On the morning of Tuesday, May 30, she wanted to sit up in her wheelchair, and as the day progressed, people began to come. All day cars parked along the street, and people streamed in and out. Some people thought that so many cars meant that Mama had already died. They drove by slowly and then telephoned the neighbors to ask if anything had happened to Edna Worsham. "Something happening" was a euphemism for death. So many visitors came that Linda and I kept some of them waiting in the living room and let them in to see her one or two at the time. They sat beside her, and she whispered to them as they leaned close. When they left, they were weeping or looking down shaking their heads. She was the Queen on her throne giving blessings all day. It was as if people were having an audience with the Pope.

Mama slept through the night, but the next morning her arms were so weak that she could hardly lift them. When I sat down beside her, she shook her head and said, "Poor Annie."

"Mama, do you want me to call Annie?" I asked. She nodded.

I dialed the number, and when Annie answered, she was almost deaf and couldn't hear me at all; she put her granddaughter on the phone. "Mrs. Worsham is sick," I said. "She may not be with us much longer."

In about thirty minutes, the doorbell rang, and there stood Annie on the stoop with her son Danny beside her. She had on her bedroom shoes, and her hair was tied up in a bandana. She looked even smaller than when she had worked for us.

As soon as Mama saw Annie standing in the entrance to the room, she lifted both arms high in the air for the first time all day. Annie sat down on the end of the single bed where I slept and took Mama's hands into hers. They sat there quietly, Mama's white hands entangled in Annie's black ones.

"Annie, I'm so glad you came," I said.

"Dis Miz Wooshum," she said, looking at me. Everybody in the room was crying. As Annie started to leave, Mama raised her left arm up slowly and pointed to her cheek. Annie leaned down and kissed her.

That night Mama threw up what hospice called black coffee grounds, a sign that she was bleeding internally. The next night she vomited oceans of green bile. Why, I wondered, does death have to be ugly? Why can't people be lifted up on a soft white cloud and float straight to Heaven? *O Death, there is thy sting!* But it was true that both the coming and the going into and out of this world are violent, bloody, painful, and ugly—birth, as well as death.

The last day, Mama didn't eat anything all day. Hospice said it was the body's way of shutting down, of preparing itself. She had company that night and much noise and commotion. She seemed agitated; I got her the methadone that hospice had provided in case she got in too much pain. She had not used it at all. When I came to her with the dropper, she asked, "What is it for?"

"It will calm you down," I said. She nodded, closed her eyes, and opened her mouth to receive the drops on her tongue. Later, after everyone had gone except for Linda and me, we sat and watched Mama sleep. Then I went to sleep on the single bed, and Linda lay down on the sofa.

Suddenly, I woke up and knew that something had changed. Mama's mouth was open, and we could see her bottom row of teeth. She was too still and was not breathing. When I called Linda, she came to Mama and grabbed her arms and pulled them again and again. "No! No!" she kept saying, too loud in the quiet room.

I called Teeny and she came over, made the sign of the cross, and said quietly, almost to herself, "Eternal rest grant unto her, O Lord, and let perpetual light shine upon her, with all your angels and saints forever, for thou art merciful. May the angels lead her into paradise: may the martyrs come to welcome her and take her to the Holy City, the New and Eternal Jerusalem."

I called hospice, and they came and then called the funeral home. They pronounced the time of death at twelve a.m. on June 1, 1995. "It's probably better to wait in the other room while we take her," the funeral director said. "People usually prefer to do that." Linda and I went into my bedroom and sat on the bed side by side, cold and shaking, hugging our knees like little girls.

After the funeral home left with Mama's body and hospice left with the wheelchair and the potty chair and the Hoyer lift and the pads and the leftover pills, Linda and I sat on the sofa staring at the empty blue lift chair in the room. The hospice nurse had offered to leave some of mama's sleeping pills for us, but we refused them. I sat in the room, trying not to move at all, not to twitch my finger, not to blink, to disappear. The clock continued to tick, and time passed, fifteen minutes since Mama died, thirty minutes since our mother died, an hour.

In the refrigerator were still the dishes brought before it happened. Now people would begin to bring food, in the Southern custom, because that is what people do. I dragged the kitchen garbage can to the open refrigerator door and raked everything into it. Containers that had to be returned, I emptied and stacked in the sink. In the clothes dryer I found the remains of a wash that the hospice volunteer had done before she left. It contained Mama's blue housecoat, three bath towels, six dishcloths, and in the bottom the pillow that had been under Mama's left arm. The pillow print was covered with red-and-black cats, and the stuffing had become lumpy in the dryer. I squeezed the pillow in my hands and put it up to my nose. I pressed it to me and breathed deeply. It smelled of soap and Downy, and not of my mother.

With the pillow in my hand, I went to the back of the house. I pulled back the sliding doors to Mama's closet and walked into the clothes hanging there, putting my face into them and taking deep breaths. I slid to the floor and put my hands into the shoes, the terry cloth slippers. I opened my mouth wide and wailed. When it was finally light outside, I was sitting on the toilet staring down. As I focused on one spot of the green carpet and then another, faces began to emerge. A feeling in my stomach felt like a thud, something hollow, a wooden sound. The silence after a death.

The next day Linda and I went to the funeral home to make arrangements. We stood in the room of caskets as the director showed us first one and then another, telling us the benefits of each. I saw one that was the same as the one Mama's friend Commie Berry had had. I remembered sitting at Commie's funeral with Mama at the Hardwick Baptist Church. The casket was a vanilla white color with pink flowers on the corners. Mama had leaned over to me as they rolled Commie's casket in and whispered, "That's a real pretty casket, but it probably costs too much." Another time she said something similar when I was helping her to pick out a car. We were in the Toyota showroom when she noticed a pearl white Avalon. She went over to it, leaned her head in, and said to me, "This is the color casket I want." That morning at the funeral home, Linda and I chose the white one with the pink flowers. It was one of the most expensive in the room, and, knowing how frugal Mama was, Linda and I laughed, pleased with ourselves. Mama wasn't there to stop us, and we had spent a lot of money on her casket without her permission. Gotcha!

The Saturday morning of Mama's funeral, the neighbor had a yard sale next door. Looking out the front window at the cars lined up and down the street in front of my house, the people traipsing back and forth across the lawn, I thought how inconsiderate it was for the neighbor to be having a yard sale on the day of my mother's funeral. I slipped a pair of jeans over my nightshirt and went out the front door. On the property line I met a tall blonde woman with a take-charge look on her face.

"Today's my mother's funeral," I said, accusingly. Red splotches appeared on the woman's cheeks. She put her hand on my arm.

"I'm sorry," she said. "I didn't know." She brushed a strand of hair back from her forehead and then pointed back toward the house. "We're having to put my mother in a nursing home." There we were, the mother of the living and the mother of the dead standing on the property line. And I would have given anything to change places with her.

The funeral was on June 3, the day of Mama's and Daddy's wedding anniversary. Mama looked pretty lying there in her pink suit with the white blouse Linda had bought for her. "She looks just like she's sleeping," people always say, but of course no one ever really looks that way, lying there with their glasses on. And the undertakers can never get anybody's mouth right.

All our cousins came from Atlanta and Macon. We walked in to "Fairest Lord Jesus," as Mama had requested and out to "Blessed be the Tie," the last verse. And they played our recording of "Whispering Hope." Araminta had managed to soften the sound of the oxygen machine. The minister talked about reunions, how all the family came together for a death. I remembered Aunt Alma's funeral when one of her grandchildren looked at her lying in her casket and said, "Granny sure knows how to throw a party, doesn't she?" And the minister talked about the anniversary that was being celebrated in heaven that day when Mama and Daddy were reunited after twenty-nine years. I imagined my eighty-four-year-old silver-haired mother, dancing with my fifty-seven-year-old father to their song, "The Waltz You Saved for Me" by Ferlin Husky.

That night, Moore's Funeral Home brought the flowers to the house and lined them around the room in the back bedroom. I gave

Tom and Linda my bed, and I slept in the room with the flowers. I lay there on my back, the flowers in my peripheral vision like a wreath, surrounding me. I closed my eyes and breathed in the strong smell of the Stargazer lilies, my hands folded across my chest, as I imagined that I was lying in my own coffin, the people filing by, looking down at me.

The next day Linda and I washed all the dishes in the sink and returned them to the people who had brought food. Along with the dishes, we took people the flower arrangements from the back room. We rode by the historic Memory Hill Cemetery where Mama's new grave beside Daddy's was covered with the pink and white carnation blanket. Beside the cemetery was the large brick First Baptist Church with the tall white steeple rising high into the blue sky. It was the church where I was baptized at age nine, crowned as a queen in Girl's Auxiliary at age eleven, and married Harvill Holsenbeck in 1969. It was the church where Daddy was eulogized on Father's Day in 1966 and the church where Mama's funeral was held two days ago. It is not the church where I will be buried.

Mama had said to Linda and me, "After the settin' up, you girls will pull a U-Haul up to the front door." Mama and Daddy had the large brick house built in 1933. Then Doles Boulevard was a new neighborhood with unpaved streets. Thirteen years later when I was born, the streets were paved, and I had a nice steep hill to ride my bicycle down. A few days after the funeral, Linda and I began cleaning out the house. We began room by room. Tom went back and forth to Wal-mart bringing us good sturdy boxes with handles. We made four sections: (1) keep and divide, (2) give away, (3) throw away, and (4) sell at the estate sale. Mama had not thrown anything away; every drawer, every closet, and every shelf was filled. It took us almost a week to go through everything.

The house had an attic that Daddy had turned into a playhouse for Linda and me. In order to get up there, we had to let down the long heavy ladder in the center of the hallway and then climb up the rungs. I still remember the smell of wood and heat when we stepped up onto the flooring Daddy put there. We could see the back side of the attic fan, as tall as us, covered with dust like gray coral under the sea; the old baby buggy Mama used with both of us; vintage dresses hanging in a side closet; and toys, little stoves and refrigerators, a slinky, dominoes, and jackstones. On a shelf were a stuffed monkey and dolls. Linda's Tiny Tears' arm was stuck to its face. The body of my doll Suzy was melted, and her detached head had fallen to the side. My Alice in Wonderland doll sat on a shelf, her long silky curls cut short and her legs sticking out.

Stacked against the wall were boxes labeled "Sandra" and "Linda." We sat down on the floor, legs akimbo, with the boxes between us. We sat there all afternoon going through what turned out to be old school papers. Math problems were stacked with spelling papers, Weekly Readers, and stories written in our childish handwriting. As I looked through my stack, I found the poem I wrote in third grade that Mrs. Rogers "published" by typing it and running it off on the purple mimeograph machine. I still remember the feeling of awe I had when I held the published poem in my hand and read the words "by Sandra Worsham." I knew then that I wanted to be a writer. In my fourth grade stack, I saw again the handwriting of my favorite teacher, Mrs. Josey. In fourth grade I decided that I wanted my name to be "Sandy." On all my papers from Mrs. Josey's class, I had written

"Sandy Worsham" and, "I love you" beside my name. Next to my words Mrs. Josey had put a red checkmark, which I interpreted as "I love you back." Other teachers wrote messages like, "Sandra, you can do better than this," but not Mrs. Josey. Reading the teacher messages reminded me of the quote often used by teachers, "Kids may not remember what you teach them, but they will always remember how you made them feel."

After Daddy died, Mama had put a heavy lock on his workshop door outside, and no one opened it until after she had died. When the heavy wooden door creaked open, spider webs filled the opening like a silver curtain. Inside were memories of Daddy--his big circular saw where he made sliding door closets and drop-down desktops as I stood beside him, watching the sawdust pile up at my feet, smelling the rich smell of the wood, where he cut a face for my mop friend, and arms to nail across her chest. Lining the shelves were tiny compartments holding nails, screws of various sizes, nuts, and bolts. Hanging to the peg-board paneling were files, hammers, screwdrivers, and wrenches. This was my Daddy's world, the place where he made things. Lined in a corner was a dried dirt dauber nest, long ago abandoned. In the center of the room was a large black heavy thing. It took all three of us to drag it out into the light. When we sprayed it with a heavy layer of Greased Lightning, the black layer slid down like a woman's skirt, revealing shining white porcelain and a brass rim around the bottom. A handle was smooth white porcelain. It was the bottom to a barber chair. It is now in my backyard holding a large planter. Also in the shop were several wooden tool holder/shoe shine boxes that Daddy had made. Some held tools, and others held shoe shine materials, a small round metal tin of black shoe polish and a wooden brush with black bristles. Linda and I divided these and turned them into magazine racks to go beside the toilet in our bathrooms or at the end of the sofa in the living room. Remembering Daddy's shop now, the way it was entombed all those years, I think of that buried side of myself and the way something like white porcelain and a silvery sheen was revealed when I wiped away the black grunge of shame. I wonder now how Daddy would have felt about the way my life has turned out. He was the forgiving one, the one who made excuses for me, the one who spanked me only once. When a report card revealed an A- or a B instead of the expected A, he said, "It's better than I ever did and gave me the customary silver dollar anyway.

In the hall closet we found the old Electrolux vacuum cleaner that Annie used when she cleaned for Mama. I remembered hearing her run the sweeper over the living room floor as I played in my room. One day I discovered inside my Mr. Potato Head box in the back of the closet a sprouted Irish potato that I had played with and put away. Annie said she heard me scream over the noise of the vacuum cleaner all the way to the front of the house. I don't know why I asked to have the vacuum cleaner, for vacuuming was my least favorite housecleaning chore, but Linda said that I could have it. It was in a pasteboard box so old that the corners were crumbling.

One day we got together some of Mama's things to give to Annie. We took a white sweater with pink embroidered roses around the neck, a red Bundt pan, a nice set of knives, and a quilt for her bed. Annie was living with her son and grandchildren in a trailer park. When we got there, we walked up the rickety concrete block steps and pushed the screen door open. Annie's grandchildren were running and playing in the living room. Annie's bedroom was to the right beside the kitchen. We sat on Annie's bed, and faced her, sitting in an armchair. Flies were walking along the shelves behind her head. We gave her the box containing the things we had brought her.

She touched each piece, and then she looked up at us and said, "You know what I really wants? I wants your Mama's vacuum cleaner. I could run it up under my bed and get the dust kitties out. That's what I really wants."

I didn't know what to say, and Linda and I looked at one another. Suddenly I felt sentimental about that old vacuum cleaner, and I couldn't bring myself to give it to her. I feel guilty about that now and think that I must be a terrible, mean, selfish person. And now that Annie is dead, I don't even know where the vacuum cleaner is. That day in the funeral home, I said to Annie, lying there so pretty in her casket, "I'm sorry about the vacuum cleaner. I don't know why I felt so sentimental about Mama's old Electrolux."

After we had finished cleaning out everything, Linda and Tom went back to Kentucky, and I hired somebody to do an estate sale for us. Cars lined the street on Doles Boulevard in both directions; people walked across the yard and streamed in and out all day, carrying away Mama's and Daddy's things in grocery sacks or over their arms. Inside, I stood around the edges like a ghost and watched as they fingered bowls from which I ate my Cheerios, the forks and spoons I used to set the table, counting out four and then three after Daddy died.

On the back porch old men carried away large stacks of Daddy's tools, some of them so black and rusted that they would become wall ornaments or yard art. At the end of the day, I walked through the empty house. The things that were left would go with a flat price to the people who managed the sale. In Mama's bedroom on a table I found the old Christmas tree she had used for years, a small table tree about eighteen inches tall. It was bent and spindly, and I understood why no one had bought it. But suddenly it became filled with sentiment, and I wondered how I could ever have let it be included in the sale. I picked it up and cradled it like a baby, glad that it was still there. Suddenly I heard a voice calling from the front door. It was Mrs. Vincent from down the street. She knew the sale was over and that I would be there, sad. But at that moment she was simply someone who was not my mother.

After the house was empty and the For Sale sign was in the front yard, I went over there and walked through the house. In the privacy of the shiny wooden floors and the sheetrock walls, I called my mother's name loudly, my voice echoing off the empty walls. "Mama! Mama!" I guess I felt that her spirit must still be there, that calling her name would make me feel her presence. I walked through each room, feeling the ghosts of the past. In the dining room, I saw myself riding my tricycle around and around the dining room table. In the living room I saw myself telling Mama about her cancer and hearing her say, "Well, I knew it was something." On the back porch I remembered Annie there, ironing my dresses and refusing to spell a word for me, then years later in that same spot the day of The Telling. I heard her saying those words, "I can't stay here if you do that. I'm going to have to move out of town."

Linda hung Mama's hats on the wall in her house in Kentucky. She made shadow boxes containing razors and scissors from Daddy's barbershop. I made a special spot on two bookshelves, one for Mama and one for Daddy. I put one of the wooden-handled saws from

Daddy's shop up against the back and in front I put a shaving mug and a steel slide and picks from Daddy's guitar. We made shrines, as if to make the grieving easier.

Mama didn't leave right away. She hung around, she lingered, she had to be sure that everything was all right. She came back three times. Not long after Mama died, Maggie had to have surgery on her tail. After the surgery, she had to wear one of those cones around her head. One night when Maggie was sleeping on the bed with me, the phone rang into the darkness in the middle of the night. When I picked it up and said Hello, no one was there, only silence. I turned on the light and looked over at Maggie. She had thrown up in her cone and was struggling to breathe. I was sure that it was Mama on the phone, telling me about Maggie so that I could help her.

The second sign was the card I received from Mama on my birthday, January 15. When I checked the mail after school that day, I had a card saying I love you and signed by Mama. It was sent by one of Mama's friends who didn't know when my birthday was; a note was attached saying, "I was cleaning out a drawer and found this birthday card I got from your mother. I thought you might like to have it." So strange that it arrived on my birthday.

The final sign happened to Linda. One night she and I were talking on the phone, and she was telling me about how badly she needed one more hug from Mama. I remembered the night Mama died and the way that Linda had pulled on her arms. "I feel tormented," Linda told me that night, " I want just one more hug."

When we hung up, I lay in bed in the dark and put my fists up under my chin. I prayed hard, the same way I prayed during Mama's cancer when I asked God for superhuman strength. I asked God and Mama, "Please, go make Linda feel hugged."

It was two weeks later that Linda told me about what happened to her that night. "I was lying in bed, and my heart was beating too fast," she said. "Then suddenly I felt this peace come over me; I felt like I was being hugged."

"How did it feel?" I asked her.

"Like a slight pressure on the covers, from my feet to my shoulders, the way Mama used to pull the quilt up and tuck us in, then smooth the covers around us. That's the way it felt," she said.

CHAPTER SEVEN: PULLING MY FEATHERS IN

"Would you tell me, please, which way I ought to go from here?"
"That depends a good deal on where you want to get to."
— Lewis Carroll, *Alice in Wonderland*

The years went by, and that day in the beginning of Teeny's and my relationship receded far into the past. Teeny's prediction, "But you have so much longer to kick around this old world than I do," began to realize itself. Those words she said then--"This is a galloping horse, but I sure do like its gallop"—she didn't remember at all in the years that followed. If she remembered that she had ever had any physical attraction to me, she had long ago forgotten. I would never forget, but I always honored our promise to one another. We would never be lovers; we would always be friends. But our love for each other went much deeper than simply friendship. We were one another's Number One. I often heard her refer to me as her "partner," but I knew that she did not know the connotation the world had begun to give to that term. As the years went by, the times of ending seemed far away, too distant to be concerned about. I held onto time with as tight a grip as I could muster.

One day Teeny was cleaning out a drawer and found some pictures of herself when she was young. She gave the pictures to me, and I sat and studied them. In her twenties and thirties, Teeny was striking. Her black hair, pulled back into a high wave above her widow's peak, framed her deep, haunting eyes. In one of the photographs, she looked pensive. In another, she was riding a bicycle, the breeze blowing her hair. I longed for time travel, so that I could have known her then, for us to have been together then, and the same age.

When Teeny retired, instead of relaxing or working in the yard after all those years of teaching, she began volunteering. On Monday mornings she drove into town to count the Sunday collection at the rectory with a few other parishioners. She became a Eucharistic Minister, taking Holy Communion to the Catholic veterans at the Georgia War Veterans' Home and the ladies at Green Acres Nursing Home. Every week she took the Eucharist to about sixteen people who couldn't get to Mass. She came home and told me stories about the people she visited. Two Catholic women at the nursing home often got into arguments, and Teeny tried to mediate. One told the other that Catholics didn't add the ending to the Our Father, "For thine is the Kingdom," and that she was saying it wrong and it wasn't going to count. Teeny convinced both of them that the Lord appreciated the prayer, no matter how they said it. Sometimes their arguments became hateful, and Teeny had to ask the priest to go work it out between them.

My favorite stories were the ones she told about the Veterans. Some of them had Alzheimer's and couldn't remember anything. But when she approached them, wearing the pix around her neck in the black leather case, when she said, "Do you want to receive the Lord?" they put their head back and stuck out their tongue. Like my mother remembering the poems she recited, they still remembered the Eucharist, no matter what else they had forgotten. One day I went on her rounds with her, and when we were finished, I felt as if I had been to church and heard an uplifting Homily. She had told me about a man named Mr. Turner who had a stroke. She said that he could say only two things—the Our Father and, as Teeny said, "a bad word." I was looking forward to seeing this for myself.

As we entered the Veterans' Home, I followed close on Teeny's heels. When we got to his room, Teeny introduced me to Mr. Turner. He had a soft black beard, and he took my hand and kissed it, nibbling like a fish, the beard soft as a baby's brush against my hand. Then she went over to the window and picked up a photograph of Mr. Turner's son to show me. When she referred to something she had heard on the radio about the Pope, Mr. Turner wanted to reply but, as usual, he couldn't say the words. He started out with something that sounded like "Dat! Dat! Dat! Dat! Dat," and then he said plainly, "Oh, Shit!" and, giggling, covered his mouth with his hand.

Teeny said, "Now let's show Sandra the other thing you can say." She began, "Our Father..." and Mr. Turner said the whole prayer perfectly without missing a word.

She followed with a short prayer, "Dear Lord, we thank you for coming to us in this beautiful way," and then, "Lord, I am not worthy to receive you, but only say the word and I shall be healed." Mr. Turner stuck out his tongue to receive the Eucharist.

It seemed to me that people took advantage of Teeny's giving nature. When Mr. Elliott at the veterans home got a refrigerator for his room, he started giving her his grocery list. He called up and left it on the answering machine. He was specific in his wants. The list didn't say "Ensure"; it said, "Hazelnut Ensure." It didn't say "Manicotti"; it said, "Stouffer's Manicotti in the red box." If Teeny couldn't find what he wanted at a grocery store in Milledgeville, she drove to Macon to find it there. Each week she climbed the steps to the veterans' home with a grocery sack in each arm, even though she was probably already older than some of the men there. But she could never see when people were taking advantage. All she thought about was their feelings, and she wanted them to have what they wanted. I asked her why that man couldn't get some of the staff at the home to buy his groceries for him, or why he couldn't eat in the cafeteria with the other men. I told her that my job was to keep her feet on the ground; I was the one with feet of clay. Without me, she would sprout wings and float on up.

After Teeny's first hip replacement, I moved into the house with her and never went back to live at my own house. Each day I went around the corner to check the mail and get the newspapers, but mostly, I stayed with Teeny. More and more I brought things over-- summer clothes, then winter, a favorite picture of my mother. Teeny prepared a room for me with a new bedroom suite and some shelves for my books. She worried that I might be grieving for my house. For a while, when I thought of my own house around the corner, I felt guilty, as if a house could feel abandoned or unloved. I called to receive the messages from my answering machine, as if checking to see how the house was getting along without me.

As time went by, I began to drive Teeny to the veterans' home for her rounds. As we approached Mr. Turner's room, she said, "He's gone down a lot since you saw him last." Mr. Turner lay on his side facing us, his eyes closed and his hands gnarled and bent under his chin. His bony white legs were uncovered, the sheet draping off the edge of the bed and dragging the floor. He was wearing a bulky white diaper.

Teeny pulled the sheet up over his bare legs and called his name. "Mr. Turner? Can you hear me? I've brought you the Lord."

He still had his long soft beard, and his lips moved in and out, as if he were sucking them. Without opening his eyes, he moved his legs and arms restlessly under the sheet. I stood at the foot of the bed and watched as Teeny leaned over and touched the wafer to his lips. He opened his mouth, a deep red cavern like an open sore, and the round white host stuck to his tongue. He moved the wet tongue in and out, and Teeny held her hand under his chin in case the Body of Christ should pop loose and fall. As a white string of drool dripped into her hand, Teeny said softly, "Our Father, who art in Heaven..." I was standing at the foot of the bed, my neck and jaw so tense that when Mr. Turner finally began to chew and the Host disappeared down his throat, I thought I would collapse. Teeny leaned down and said softly into to his ear, "You're a strong and brave soldier of Jesus Christ. He knows how willingly you take what he sends you." As Teeny went to the sink to wash her hands, Mr. Turner stuck his tongue out and waved it around as if testing the weather.

Because Teeny and I were different, my living with her meant that she had to put up with a lot. For example, she made her bed perfectly every day. Both sides of the bedspread had to be the exact same distance from the floor and the pillows arranged evenly. I didn't like to have my bed made at all. I liked to get back into it with it scrambled, exactly as I left it. Even when I stayed in a hotel, I told the cleaning women not to make my bed. I thought it was as much trouble to unmake as it was to make. Once when I was giving a teacher's workshop in California, the woman in the white-and-black uniform at the hotel didn't speak English. I told her in my own best Spanish, "No es necesario a lavar mi cuarto." She looked puzzled and nodded, smiling slightly. It wasn't until I got back to Milledgeville and told the Spanish teacher at the high school what I had said that I learned what I had really said: "It is not necessary to wash my room."

Teeny didn't like to have things out lying around. But I was a visual person. If something wasn't out where I could see it, for me it was lost. When I was planning to run errands, I left what I didn't want to forget in front of the door so that I would have to step over it in order to get out. Teeny picked it up and put it in a drawer, and I forgot it; I often accused her of hiding my stuff from me. She was as bad as I was about accumulating paper and old catalogs, but, where I left my piles scattered around the room, in corners and on tabletops, she put hers in dishpans and out of sight on the floor of her closet.

Because I was still teaching, she spoiled and pampered me, doing jobs that I either didn't have time for or didn't want to do. She woke up early and took our dogs to walk. Maggie was over ten years old then and wore diapers when she was indoors. After Itsy Bitsy died, Teeny had bought herself a white toy poodle, Buffy. When Buffy came home with us, the new puppy begged and pleaded every day for Maggie to notice her. But Maggie was old and set in her ways, and for days she pouted and ignored us and the new puppy. But eventually she relented, and the two dogs became friends. On weekend mornings Teeny put leashes on each of them and walked them around the neighborhood while I was still sleeping. Then she walked around the backyard picking up pinecones, throwing miniature tennis balls for Buffy, and bringing in blooming flowers to put in a vase.

On those days when I slept late, she closed my bedroom door and answered the phone quickly, so that I would not be disturbed. When I got up, I played a game with the dogs, whining and scratching the door before I came into the room. Teeny was either sitting in her recliner or in a rocking chair on the back porch reading her *Union-Recorder* and drinking her coffee. She drank coffee all day, often leaving a half-cup somewhere and beginning a new one. Keurig single-cup coffee pots were not invented yet, and she used a percolator, standing at the kitchen sink and assembling the parts. The best smell and sound in the world was her coffeepot perking in the morning. In the evening she cooked supper and filled the dishwasher. Before she went to bed, she had emptied the dishwasher and cleaned up the kitchen.

As Teeny got older, turned seventy, seventy-five, and then eighty, the threat of passing time sat on my shoulder. At night it seemed as if I could hear the threat breathing in the corner of my bedroom. Wordlessly, I prayed, please don't let anything happen. Please don't let anything change. Like the spray we used to keep our charcoal drawings in high school art class from smearing, I wanted to spray our lives and keep them the way they were, to make our time last as long as possible. I saw my life after Teeny stretched out long and empty, a flat straight bridge leading to the end, no more changes, none that would matter anyway. I would try to be a good person like Teeny. I would continue to go to Mass, and each day would be like the other, comfortable that way.

Living in the same house with her was more than I could have ever hoped for. As we sat together in the evening watching television and then praying the Rosary before bed, I looked over at her and felt amazement that we were together, this teacher and the woman I admired accepting me and loving me and making me her important person. That hug and peck on the lips that she gave me in passing was everything to me.

And we continued to have our special moments of closeness. After her second hip replacement, she couldn't reach past her knees; after her shower, I wrapped a big towel around her. I smoothed lotion on her legs and feet. I saw her breasts and her body, and I felt tenderness for them, the way they were a part of her. "I don't want to be a temptation to you," she said. I cut her toenails for her. Her feet were soft and sweet and dear. In the morning when we stood in the kitchen, her in blue satin pajamas with long sleeves, me in a red cotton nightshirt, we hugged good morning. Sometimes in the evening I knelt before her where she sat in her big green recliner and put my head in her lap while she rubbed my back and shoulders. At night I tucked her in her bed, leaned down to her, put my cheek to hers.

Not long after I retired from teaching, Teeny's younger brother Bobby died from pancreatic cancer, and Teeny received a substantial inheritance from his years of working at IBM in Atlanta. Teeny decided that she wanted to use part of that money to send me to Bennington College in Vermont to work on my MFA in creative writing. "You've wanted to do this for a long time," she said, "and I want to make it possible." I was overwhelmed with gratitude.

Teeny had been a long-time friend of Flannery O'Connor's. They both went to Sacred Heart Church, and Teeny often went out to the farm, Andalusia, where Flannery did her writing after she got lupus. Their friendship was not literary, for Teeny didn't quite know what to make of Flannery's writing, but I often heard Teeny use Southern expressions that I knew Flannery had chosen to put into her characters' mouths: "When you get down to brass tacks," for example, or "I'm rubber and you're tar. What you say bounces off me and sticks back on you." Often when I said, "I love you," Teeny responded, "Rubber tar." It was supposed to mean, I love you too, something she found embarrassing to say out loud. She described to me the sound Flannery made as she entered the church and came down the center aisle on her crutches—stump, stump, stump, and then the long thwunk as Flannery made an attempt at genuflecting at the end of the pew. Teeny didn't give Flannery or me much response to our writing, but she valued it just the same. I couldn't believe that she was sending me to Bennington. For my retirement present, she had given me two autographed First Editions of Flannery's books, autographed especially to Teeny. Now she was sending me to Bennington so that I could work on my own writing under the tutelage of the fine writers who taught there.

I began my first residency at Bennington in June of 2004. The first person I met was Ilina Singh. As I was making the bed in my dormitory room, Ilina appeared in my doorway and introduced herself. "Hello, I'm Ilina," she said. "I'm a lesbian." When I think back on that day now, it seems preposterous to me that she could have actually said those words in her introduction, and I wonder if my memory has misconstrued the scene, that I remembered those words as her first because they were so significant to me, lit up in neon.

At Bennington I felt self-conscious as I walked across campus, imagining how I looked to others. A group of lesbians often sat together for drinks before dinner, and sometimes I joined them. One of them asked me, "Are you a lesbian?"

"I don't know," I said, feeling foolish. "I am in a celibate relationship with a woman."

I called Teeny every night from my dormitory room. If she didn't answer, I panicked and imagined her fallen in the backyard with no one to help her up. When she finally answered the phone, my relief was acute.

My second residency was in January, and I had never seen so much snow, even more than we had in Georgia in the seventies when Mary-Louise was abroad. I bought a special coat that I called my Vermont coat, ankle-length, down-filled and denim-colored with a snap front and long zipper, and a blue fur-trimmed hood. When I went out into the waist-high snow, I felt the inside of my nose freeze. I loved the peace of the whiteness, and I still miss it and long for it now. My Vermont coat still hangs in my closet, in hopes that I will someday in my life be where it snows again.

Teeny seemed to get along fine while I was gone for the two-week June and January residencies. When I got back home each time, we settled into a routine, me working on manuscripts to mail to teachers in packets, Teeny doing her own thing.

And then one night, after my third residency, my big fear reared up and struck. I tucked Teeny into her bed as usual, pulled the covers up under her chin, and kissed her lips. At about four a.m., when I was in the middle of a deep sleep, the noise pierced through my consciousness, a long, loud moan, an eerie sound, not like any voice I knew. I threw the covers back, ran into Teeny's room, and turned on the light beside her bed. Her face was pale, round and swollen, a gurgling sound coming from her throat. I thought that I was losing her at that moment, that she must have some terrible invasive cancer that had surreptitiously spread throughout her body. Instinctively, I tried to put my finger into her mouth, but her teeth were clamped shut. She was breathing loudly, her lips going in and out, and when I called 9-1-1, I asked the operator, "Can you hear her, that sound she's making? I'm afraid my friend is dying."

The woman's voice on the phone asked me the address and directions, and with that heightened sense of competence that seems to come in an emergency, I told her the turns that had to be made between the hospital and home. "Go to Dunlap Road, turn right in front of the Fire Station at the top of the hill..." Pink foam began coming from Teeny's clenched teeth, and I laid the receiver on the table and ran to the linen closet for a hand towel that I used to wipe her mouth. The whole time I kept shouting at her, "Stay with me Teeny, Stay with me, Sweetheart, Hail Mary, Full of Grace." Her Rosary was lying on the table beside the bed, and I put the white pearl beads into her hands, but she didn't grasp them; they hung on her fingers as if on a towel rack. I kept picking up the phone receiver, holding it to my ear, and then putting it down again. "Please make them hurry," I said to the woman, watching Teeny's jerking, fearful that it would stop.

"Is there anyone you want me to call?" the woman asked, and I gave her Father McWhorter's name and number. She said she would have him meet us at the emergency room. After Father Drohan at Sacred Heart Church had come Father Marren, then Father Farrelly, and then Father McWhorter. He was stout and resembled my own image of the Friar in the Canterbury Tales. He said his mother named him Michael Landon from Bonanza but that if she had known how he would turn out, she would have named him Hoss. He was a former

Methodist and a former Baptist who knew how to give a sermon like a Pentecostal.

Then the voice on the phone said, "They're out there. Go let them in." I put the phone down, ran to the kitchen, and put the garage door up. The tall square ambulance was beeping loudly and backing down the driveway, the low-hanging Japanese maple limbs dragging across its top with a scraping sound. I ran to the driver's side and yelled, "Just knock them down." Those were Teeny's special trees, beautiful in the autumn in colors of burgundy, red, and bright yellow-orange. They scraped the sides of my car when I came and went, but before now, I would never have suggested that we cut them back.

I led into the house a young man in blue jeans with a white lab shirt and a young woman in a black uniform, her dark straight hair pulled back into a high ponytail which swung from side to side as she hurried to the back of the house. When we got to her, Teeny had become quiet and looked asleep, her hands folded across her chest. Afraid, I touched her shoulder and called her name. Her eyes flew wide open, and she began immediately to thrash about, her arms and legs waving wildly in all directions. When the young man tried to prick her finger, Teeny jerked her hand from him, and blood spurted onto the sheet. She had on her pink flowered satin pajamas that I had bought her because she loved the flannel-brushed inside lining. I saw that she had wet the bed, a dark spot spreading onto the sheet under her.

The next few minutes were filled with confusion. I asked the EMT's if they wanted me to call my cousin Richard who lived down the street to help them hold her, but they said they could get help. The man called on a cell phone attached to his belt, and soon a fire truck arrived in front of the house. Several firemen filled the bedroom, standing around Teeny's bed. I moved back and forth behind them, trying to see between them, standing on my toes to see over them, calling over the chaos, "Teeny, it's okay. I'm right here. Don't be scared. It's going to be all right." I couldn't believe they needed a whole fire truck to control Teeny. They said that she was strong. While the firemen held Teeny's arms and legs, the woman paramedic rolled her over on her side, pulled her pajama bottoms down, and gave her a shot in the hip close to her hip replacement scar. Then the man in the white lab coat felt the pulse in her neck and said softly, "Now."

In the front of the house, several of the firemen had begun to roll a large yellow gurney on wheels into the house. First they tried coming through the family room, moving aside the large mauve Lazy Boy that was my chair, the coffee table, the television set. But the gurney wouldn't go around the corner into the hall. They tried the living room entrance instead. They had to move my mini-trampoline from the middle of the floor and the green-striped sofa from against the wall. Back in Teeny's room, the men had her up on her feet, walking her toward the gurney. They moved slowly, together, as if moving across the stage in a play, Teeny in the middle, surrounded by the big gentle firemen. When they got her on the stretcher, they had to put straps loosely across her because she kept fighting them. Her eyes were wide, and she looked terrified.

I stood behind the ambulance as they put the gurney into the back. I could see Teeny's steel-gray hair and the white sheet pulled up under her chin. I wanted to ride in the ambulance with her, but instead I asked, "Should I come separately in my car?"

"Yes," they said and, with a loud thud, they slammed the doors to the ambulance. I stood in the driveway and watched them drive off.

It was beginning to get light outside, a pink sunrise spreading behind my house around the corner.

I went inside and dressed and got my keys. When I went out into the garage to get in my car, our neighbor Vaness from across the street was standing there in her red flannel housecoat, her graying brown hair brushed straight, her feet in big fluffy bedroom slippers. She had been watering the zinnias around her mailbox when she heard the beeping of the ambulance and the loud motor. "It scared me to death!" she said. "I came right over! What's happened to Teeny?" I told her that I didn't know.

When I got to the hospital, Father McWhorter was sitting in a folding chair in the waiting room. Wearing his black-and-white Roman collar and holding a prayer book, he was officially on duty. I sat down beside him, and immediately the room began to spin around me. A black man and a boy sitting across from us seemed to lean to the side and dissolve into wavy squiggles. I leaned over and put my head in my hands, and Father put his hand on my shoulder.

"You can go back now," a voice said from the registration window. Father held my arm, and the two of us went to the back. Teeny was sitting up, smiling and looking like herself. "I don't know what happened," she said. Father administered the Sacrament of the Sick, and Teeny gave all the responses perfectly, like Mr. Turner at the Veteran's home. Father anointed her forehead and her feet. He forgave her sins, and then he left.

Over the next several hours Teeny was given X-rays, tests, and an IV. The neurologist, Dr. Zialcita, came in. He was a short bald man with a thin black mustache and white skin. When he talked, he moved his hands delicately in the air. He had short fingers and almost no fingernails. When he asked Teeny her name, she said, "Teeny Horne." Then he pointed to me and said to her, "What is her name?"

Looking up at me, Teeny repeated what the doctor said, "Who is she?"

"Yes," said the doctor.

Teeny looked at me and said, "Teeny Horne."

"No, that's you," I said. "Who am I?" I asked, pointing to myself.

"Teeny Horne," she said again, nodding her head and smiling.

Dr. Zialcita made notes on a chart. "Aphasia," he said as he wrote.

"Point to your nose and then to your mouth," the doctor said to her.

Teeny put her finger on her nose and held it there, not moving further.

"One command only," the doctor said, writing on his chart. Then, turning to me, he said, "When you go home, give her only one command at a time." Give Teeny a command? I thought. Why would I give Teeny a command?

"What town do you live in?" the doctor asked her.

Teeny sat pleasantly as if she were enjoying the game. "What town do I live in?" she repeated. She sat for a minute, thinking, and then said, "I don't know."

"What state do you live in?" the doctor asked. Then, "Who is the President of the United States? What is today's date? What is four plus two?"

To each of these questions, Teeny continued to say, "I don't know." She didn't seem upset or frustrated about not knowing. She politely stated the fact: she didn't know.

"Aphasia," the doctor said again. "She doesn't comprehend the questions."

The doctor held his hand up in the air, first on Teeny's left and then on her right. He determined that she had lost some vision on her right side and suggested that I move to the other side so that she could see me better.

Then he told her to close her eyes and hold out her hands, palms upward—violating his own advice about not giving her two commands. She closed her eyes, and he reached down and took her hands by the wrists, turning her palms up. Into her right hand he put what looked like a brass house key. "What do you have in your hand?" he asked Teeny.

She closed her fingers around the object in her hand, feeling it, and then said, "I don't know."

Then the doctor put the key in her left hand and said, "What do you have in your hand now?"

Teeny felt the item in her hand and said immediately, "It feels like a key."

The doctor wrote something on his chart, and as he turned to leave, I felt the room turning around me again. Teeny sat there smiling and seemed to double and become two Teenies, then three. I lay down on another bed in the middle of the room, and a nurse ran in from the main desk in the hall. "Are you all right?" she asked.

"I'm dizzy," I said, the room seeming to blacken in my peripheral vision. Almost immediately the nurse laid a cold wet cloth on my forehead, and I lay there with my eyes closed, waiting. Soon the dizziness passed, and I turned my head to look at Teeny. She was lying there with her head turned, looking at me.

Soon Teeny's doctor came back into the room and told us that Teeny had had a stroke, accompanied by a seizure. He also said that the X-ray had shown a meningioma, which was a benign, slow-growing tumor that was harmless and had nothing to do with the stroke.

In two days, Teeny was moved to the rehabilitation center. It was at this time that her confusion happened and caused the reaction in me that I never expected. To begin with, it felt strange being in the house alone with the dogs, Teeny not there. The house was too quiet and empty.

I could first tell that something was wrong when the following Monday morning, I walked into Teeny's room at the rehabilitation center, and she was sitting in a chair beside her bed, completely focused on the IV tube that was inserted into her arm. The clear tubing hung down from the receptacle behind her chair, and she kept winding the cord into a butterfly, the way she would coil an extension cord to make it neat. This is something that I would never do, wind a cord to make it neat. Around the corner at my house, the hose lay next to the house in a tangled wad, bent and knotted and difficult to straighten. The wires behind my computer looked like a snake nest. Leaning around to look behind her chair to see where the end of the taut cord was, Teeny asked, "What is this thing?"

I explained to her that it was the IV tube, that it was giving her nourishment, but she asked me, "Why don't you have one?" During the visit, I could tell that she thought she was sitting in her chair at home. She tried to get up to go to the kitchen to make us a tomato sandwich. I stood up, blocking her. She tried to go around me, moving to first one side and then another, becoming agitated, wanting me out of her way. Before I left, she said, "I thought I might go to Mass today."

"You know they aren't going to let you leave," I said.

"Why not?" she asked. "There's a twelve o'clock Mass right down there at the church."

"You're in the hospital," I said. "You've had a stroke."

When I told her goodbye and left the room, I hurried down the hospital halls until I found her nurse, a tall woman with short brown hair and a confident manner. "She's not herself," I told her. "She's confused. Could it be the medicine? Is it permanent?"

The nurse waved me off. "This happens all the time with elderly people," she said. "When she gets back in her own surroundings, she'll be fine." When I left that day, Teeny had begun again to re-wind the IV tube.

As I drove home, I had a feeling that I could only describe as fear. For no logical reason that I could think of, I was terrified.

When I called Teeny that night before bed, she said, "I'm glad you called" and then, "What is this place? Who's in charge here?"

Again, my breath caught in my throat, and I felt as if I had been punched in the chest.

When I explained to her again that she had had a stroke and was in the hospital, she said, "Okay, if you say it, it must be so."

I didn't know how to explain, even to myself, what I was feeling. It was a mixture of guilt and fear, and it had me by the neck like a vice. I couldn't get a deep breath. I thought of things it might be, the way you touch a bruise to see if it hurts. Had I done something wrong? Was everything okay? Had I told a lie or stolen something? Had I done something that saying "I'm sorry" wouldn't make all right? I couldn't eat, and I couldn't sleep, even after I had taken two Benedryls. I had diarrhea. My heart was beating fast, and my breath was shallow.

That night after I hung up from Teeny, the whole house looked different to me, gray and frightening. I wasn't afraid of burglars or noises. What I was afraid of was something I couldn't escape from, couldn't call the police or the paramedics about, and couldn't think of a way to explain what I was feeling to any of my cousins or friends. I lay wide-eyed in the dark. I tried to pray, but prayer seemed to intensify the feeling of fear rather than help it. I don't know when I finally fell asleep, but I dreamed that I was standing on a tall concrete building in the middle of dark green water. It was night, and off in the distance was a town with happy blinking lights. Between the lights and me were several miles of black murky water and a steep muddy bank too slick to climb.

When I woke up, it was light outside, and I felt as if the world were a long dark tunnel. I wanted to curl into a ball, pull the covers up, and let the days and weeks go by. I wanted to turn my brain off and sleep deeply for the rest of my life. When I drifted off to sleep again, I dreamed I bought a horse and paid $25,000 for it. But when I got the horse home, it occurred to me that I didn't have a clue how to take care of a horse. I took the horse back to the man I bought it from, and he told me he wouldn't give me ten dollars for that horse.

When I finally got up and walked into the family room, the morning sunlight coming through the patio doors seemed too bright, Maggie and Buffy too cheerful, wanting me to throw the ball. As I started to go to the kitchen to feed them, I felt dizzy and dropped into the recliner, put the bottom up, and closed my eyes. I thought I was having a heart attack. My hands were tingling, and when I opened my eyes, it was as though I was looking through black smoke. I tried to go through the list of people I knew, and none of them seemed right to call--not our across-the-street neighbor (she would think me silly and weak, and she would tell her bridge club), not my cousin (she would think I was over-reacting), and not my friend Jan (she was too busy. She would think I needed more to do.) I imagined myself getting in the car and disappearing down the highway, becoming someone who abandoned the person she loved most in the world. I imagined Teeny in a nursing home and my going to visit her there.

I lay still in the chair and waited for the feeling to pass. After about ten minutes, the feeling lifted, leaving me with the same black feeling I woke up with. Moving in slow motion, I forced myself to feed Maggie and Buffy. I made myself go, robot-like, to the outdoor storehouse to get the birdseed and feed the birds. Both of these were jobs Teeny did. My jobs were to empty the trash and make Teeny's oatmeal in the crockpot the night before. I sat in the chair and waited until nine o'clock when my gynecologist's office opened. Dr. Palmer had helped me find sitters for my mother during her illness, and she was kind. She was the only person I could think of that I could talk to.

The receptionist on the phone asked what my problem was, and I said, "Coping." They scheduled me for eleven a.m.

By the time Dr. Palmer came into her office, I was leaning my head on my arm, face down, at her desk. When she asked me what was wrong, I began to cry huge sobs that felt like they came all the way from my toes.

"I'm terrified," was all I could say.

When she asked, "What are you terrified of?" all I could say was, "I don't know. Teeny is confused. Teeny is gone, and someone else is in her place. I'm at the beginning of a long time."

Dr. Palmer prescribed Zoloft, and I left and stood in line at the drugstore, still crying. My twisted face was there for everyone to see, and I couldn't do anything to hide it.

The doctor had suggested that I go to the crisis center at the hospital, a white wooden building at the edge of the back parking lot. When I got there, a woman met me at the door, as if she were expecting me. She took my hand, her face kind, and she led me into a room where I sat down in a metal folding chair. She left briefly and then came back with a box of tissue and a large red shaggy dog. "This is Clancy," she said. "He's our therapy dog." The dog stood in front of me, his big brown eyes looking right into my face. I patted his head and talked to him, and as soon as I took my hand from his head, he turned and trotted out the partially opened door as if to say, "Time's up!" I pictured him going up to the woman to get the treat that he had earned.

Before I left that day, they had assigned me to Ruth, a therapist. I had never been to therapy before. My sister Linda had, and she asked me once if I ever had. "No," I answered. "I've never needed it."

The next day I saw Ruth for the first time and began to feel better immediately. By the end of the week, Teeny's confusion was gone, she could add four plus two, and she knew who the President was. She even got her sense of humor back: the President was George Washington one day, Abraham Lincoln the next.

One day when I went to see her, I talked to her about what I had learned from Ruth, that what had happened to me was called a panic attack. I told her that I was afraid of losing her, that if anything happened to her, I didn't think I could stand it.

"I know," she said, sitting on the side of the bed in her blue-flowered satin pajamas. "I've known that you feel that way," she said, "But I don't know what to do about it." She held her hands out, palms upward, her shoulders raised in a shrug. "If anything happened to you, I wouldn't like it, but I would go on. I would just pull my feathers in," and she folded her hands together.

"I'm not as strong as you," I told her.

A swallowing test showed that the stroke had caused Teeny to be what was called a silent aspirator, meaning that she was letting liquids slip down her windpipe without knowing it, a condition that could cause pneumonia. In the rehabilitation wing she had to use thickener in her water and other thin liquids. The thickener came in a canister with a plastic lid, and she had to stir the powdery substance into her liquids until they became the consistency of pudding. She let me taste her thickened water, and it was like eating melted plastic. Her meals looked like either something the dog threw up or bright green seaweed. The menu on her tray said "pork chops and green beans," but it was a brown pile and a green pile. Spooning it into her mouth, Teeny said it was seasoned well and tasted good.

Dr. Zialcita smiled when he talked and seemed excited when he tested Teeny, as though hers were a unique case, something he might find in a textbook, something he might talk to his colleagues about.

"How can we keep her from having another stroke?" I asked him one day when I passed him in the hallway.

He said that she would be taking Plavix, one baby aspirin, and Lipitor. He said that the part of her brain that had died would never come back again, but that the other parts around it would fill in and take up the slack. "It's like in an office," he said, moving his hands in the air, gesturing. "When one worker leaves and is not replaced, the others have to pick up and do their part." I imagined an office and how the workers would be disgruntled at having to do the extra work. I wondered if her extra brain cells would be the same way and if they would change Teeny's personality somehow. I was afraid Teeny would be different.

While she was in the hospital, I took Buffy to see her. I stuck the white curly dog down into a large canvas bag and held the top together as I walked down the hall. Buffy kept sticking her head up, and I pushed her back down. When I got into Teeny's room, I lifted Buffy out and put her onto Teeny's bed. Teeny was pleased to see her, but she did not seem surprised that I had brought her. Buffy lay down beside Teeny's outstretched legs, and Teeny read her newspaper, as if she was in her chair at home, which is where she thought she was.

When she came home, Teeny seemed to return to her old self. She went outside to feed the birds, she threw the ball for the puppies in the back yard, and she began to walk them along the street in front of the house. We did brain strengthening exercises with some fourth grade flash cards that had questions that were too hard for both of us. What is the capital of Arkansas? What is the longest river in the world? What does the word *anthropomorphic* mean? Who was the last emperor in China? The questions that seemed hardest for her were the math ones, and on a pad of paper with a pen, she worked on one math problem for a long time. She was having trouble remembering the name of her car, and I tried to help her. There was a song, "Avalon,

Sweet Avalon," and I hummed the tune to help her think of it. "What's the name of my car again?" she asked.

At night when I got into my bed, I remembered the long, loud moan she made when she had the stroke. It seemed to pierce the quietness, and sometimes I was almost asleep when I thought I heard her call my name. I jumped up and went into her room and stood beside her bed, waking her up, then apologized for waking her up. For a while I used a baby monitor so that I wouldn't sleep through her needing me. The monitor had three lights that lit up with the volume of the sound. I learned to distinguish what the different sounds and the lights meant. One steady light meant Teeny was turning over. One blinking light meant Buffy or Maggie were drinking water from their dish in the corner of her bedroom. Two lights and a jumbly-knocking sound meant that Teeny was getting up to go to the bathroom. I could rise up on one elbow and see her in the glow of the nightlight pass through the hall, then back again. Other times I could hear her breathing, a comforting sound, a sound that I would like to record to sleep to sometime in my future.

I couldn't sleep deeply then, but when I did fall asleep I often dreamed of being all alone in a small airplane that was either out of control or being controlled by something remote, something out of my hands. The plane would swoop and glide, and I wouldn't know whether it was going to land safely or slide to the side and crash into flames. Once, it almost hit another plane, and I felt myself shielding my eyes with my hands. One night I dreamed that Teeny had been doing something for years that I didn't know about. Every morning she got on a train that took her deep into the earth, along with some other workers, to do coal mining. In my dream I told her that I wanted to start going with her, that it was dangerous and I didn't want to be left alone or separated from her. I could picture her going down the long dimly-lit tunnels, deeper and deeper into the earth. I was afraid she would be hurt, and if she was, I wanted to be hurt along with her, not left behind. To Ruth I talked about fear, the fear of change, the fear of loss, the fear of the familiar becoming unfamiliar, and the fear of Teeny looking at me one day and not knowing who I was. My fear was a body suit I could not take off.

I wanted Teeny to be able to do the things she did before, not have to give up anything. One day I drove her to do Meals on Wheels while she read off a paper where I should turn. We went to the Hardaway Apartments, a low-income housing complex where we took meals to a white woman with a calico cat named Fluffy, a woman who acted excited to get red Jell-O. She said she hadn't had red Jell-O in a long time. Also in the same complex was a shriveled old black woman who rapped on her window and told us to leave the meal on top of the air-conditioning unit outside her door. She watched us and waited until we got back to the car before leaning out to pick up her Styrofoam container. At the lower end of Liberty Street was a woman whose house looked like a pile of wood stacked on top of concrete blocks. To get to the front door, we had to walk across a narrow bridge that served as a makeshift handicapped ramp. In another neighborhood, an old man came to the door pushing an oxygen canister.

For a while, it seemed that Teeny was almost back to normal. She slept like a baby; I told her it was because she had a clear conscience. But not me; I developed restless legs syndrome. I lay in the bed, my legs pumping and churning like Maggie or Buffy dreaming of chasing a squirrel. When I told Teeny good night, she said, "Don't think bad thoughts. Think about a spring day. Think about the blue sky and the white fluffy clouds."

"Okay," I said, on my way across the hall to my room. But I had another plan. Spring days and fluffy clouds didn't do it for me. I turned off the light, lay down on my bed, and began to imagine water, swimming under water, getting lost in the water. Sometimes I tried to switch to air, but even then I was swimming, swimming through air, my legs kicking, my hands cupped, arms straight in front of me, then out to the side, pushing, propelling me forward, moving ahead. Other times I imagined my backyard at my own house around the corner having been turned into a swimming pool, my whole back yard. I imagined workmen coming in and digging from fence to fence, from back door to property line, scooping out a deep hole, then pouring concrete, and finally filling the hole with clear blue water. I imagined myself going out the back door and stepping straight into the cool blue, the water covering my shoulders and my face, then gliding in and swimming a long way without obstacles. I imagined a large area of water with no sides or walls to bump into, something big like the ocean, only without the tides or the undercurrent. That was my sunny day with bright fluffy clouds, the getting lost in the water.

Time stretched in front of us like a half-eaten sandwich or a bag of coffee, something we were using up every day. I thought of the woman in the Bible who used wheat flour out of a bowl. When she scooped flour off the top of the bowl, more came on the bottom, so that she never ran out. I prayed, Lord please fill up our bowl of time. Please put more on the bottom while we take off the top. I tried to memorize every moment--Teeny sitting on the screened-in back porch in the morning in her pajamas, her scrubbed pink cheeks, and the happy innocent look on her face; Teeny at the end of the street, walking Buffy and Maggie on their leashes; Teeny feeding the birds and watering the garden; the sound of Teeny calling my name.

One day I told Ruth, "I'm afraid something is going to change."

She laughed and said, "I can guarantee you that something is going to change."

"I'm not paying you to tell me that," I said.

Ruth often talked about horses. Horses were the analogy she chose when she wanted to explain something more clearly, to illustrate a point. Horses, when they freak out, she said, will run right over you. They won't look to see if anyone is blocking their path. People, on the other hand, choose fight or flight. Horses know how to react when things happen. When the tiger comes, she said, horses rear, wild-eyed; they flail their hooves in the air; they bolt and run; they yell loudly. Then when the tiger is gone, they don't reflect on when the tiger came, and they don't plan for when the tiger may come again. It's the difference between them and us, she said. It's the cortex.

One day at therapy Ruth asked me if I ever wished that Teeny and I could be lovers. I hadn't thought about that in a long time, but when Ruth asked me that question, I began to think about it.

That night when I tucked Teeny into bed, I asked her, "Do you ever wish that we were more intimate?"

She was lying there with her hands holding the covers on each side of her face like two bear paws. "No!" she said firmly, without hesitation. "And we're not going to either! It's wrong!"

So that was that. I said, "Well, alrighty then!" and went back to my room.

When I look back on those days, it seems to me that I asked her one day, "Will you ever give me a real kiss? Just once?" Now I'm not even sure if I asked the question aloud or if I just thought it. I had so much respect for her, for who she was, and that feeling of humility that she chose me, that little Worsham girl who sat in her class in tenth grade and almost certainly didn't absorb any chemistry.

One day on our way to Wal-mart, Teeny asked me, "What do I do?"

"What do you mean?" I asked, looking over at the side of her face.

"When I get up in the morning? What do I do?"

"You go out in the backyard with the dogs. You pick up pinecones and put them in a pile beside the road. You pick up Buffy's miniature tennis balls and bring them inside. You bring in some of your flowers. You make the coffee, and you read the newspaper."

She was silent for a moment, and then she said, "I think He's getting ready for me."

"He can't have you yet," I said, mentally shielding my eyes.

That fear of change, of Teeny's confusion, of the fear itself returning was always with me. Every day when I got up, it was there; when I went to bed at night, it was there. Praying seemed to make it worse. It was a deep sense of dread. I wanted to live in the present, to enjoy every minute I had with Teeny, but all I could do was shield my eyes against the future. I remembered teaching Keats' "Ode on a Grecian Urn" to my students. In response to the poem, I asked them to write, "Would you rather things stay as they are right now in your life, or would you want them to change?" Of course, young people want things to change. They want to grow older. They don't want adults to tell them what to do. They want to have the profession they imagine. They want to have money. They want to fall in love. But somehow at a point in our lives, we reach the place where we want to just *be*, and then we don't want change anymore. We don't want our parents to die. We don't want our dog to die. We don't want to lose those we love the most. But, like the figures on the Grecian urn, the woman never gets kissed. The trees never lose their leaves. And art is not life.

Every day something new happened. One day I found Teeny's bra lying in the corner of her closet. I picked it up and asked, "Do you know what to do with this?"

"Yes," she said, and she draped it over her shoulder like a scarf.

"No, this is what you do," I said, and I went behind her, eased her breasts inside the cups and pulled the straps up over her shoulders.

"Is everybody inside?" I asked.

"Yep," she said, "everybody's home."

In the middle of the night I saw the light on in her room. When I went to see what was wrong, she was dressing, holding her bra in front of her as if she had forgotten again what to do with it.

"It's the middle of the night," I said to her. "It's not time to get dressed yet. Let's put your pajamas back on." I pulled down her slacks and touched her ankle. "Lift up your foot," I said. She lifted first one foot and then another so that I could remove her pants and put her feet back into her pajama bottoms. Then, like a happy child, she lay back down and I tucked her in. In the morning I found her coffee next to her on the dressing table where she was brushing her hair. But instead of the mug she always used, the coffee was in a cereal bowl. Later when she tried to wash the coffee pot, she held the parts of the percolator in her hand as if she didn't know what they were or how they fit together; they were just a basket and a stick with no relation to one another. I found folded dishtowels in the refrigerator and her toothbrush in the drawer with her combs.

On Christmas, 2004, I had bought my own presents from Teeny and had wrapped them for her. On Christmas morning when we had our traditional exchange, I opened my gifts in front of her and acted surprised. She, of course, was more surprised than I, but I don't think she recognized what she had given me.

I thought she would never finish opening her presents. With each one, she began peeling the paper back from the ends, then the sides, then the middle. In the past she had ripped the paper off hurriedly. When she opened the boxes, she pretended to be pleased, but she didn't seem to know what she had. One of the gifts I gave her was a hummingbird sculpture with fiber-optic lights that changed colors in repeated patterns. I set it up and put it on the shelf in front of her. "Pretty colors," she said.

On Christmas night Maggie went into a seizure that she couldn't come out of. She was lying on her back, stiff, and locked into another world that we couldn't reach. None of our local veterinarians were available, so we put Maggie into the car, Teeny holding her wrapped in a blanket in the passenger's seat beside me. We drove to Macon to the emergency clinic and had to wait in the dark outside the building in an unsavory part of town until the vet arrived. He put Maggie on phenobarbital and said that she should not drink any water until morning. When we got home, Maggie's seizure was gone and we took up her water dishes. All night long she circled the house again and again, looking for her water. The next morning, Monday, I took her to our vet, who recommended that twenty-year-old Maggie be put to sleep. I sat on the sofa in a back room and held Maggie, stroking her and telling her what a good dog she was, and then I handed her to the vet, and I left. In my fragile state, I did not think that I could bear to stay with her. I knew that the vet would be good to her in my place.

After I left the vet's office, I drove into town. Teeny was counting money in the rectory with the other money-counters. I went to the dining room table where they had money laid out in piles. I began to cry and told them what I had had to do. Teeny was sorry, and she was kind. They told me that Teeny had been able to distinguish the dimes from the quarters that morning, something she had not been able to do for several weeks. I had not realized that she was that bad, and that they were allowing her to "help count money" because they loved her.

When we went to see Dr. Zialcita in his office soon after Christmas, he came into the waiting room to see Teeny before asking us back to the examining room. He pointed to a poinsettia sitting on a table beside the window. "What is that?" he asked her.

"It's red," she said. "Some kind of plant. A poinsettia."

Then he pointed to a brightly-lit Christmas tree in the corner of the waiting room. "What is that?" he asked her.

"Colored lights," she said pleasantly, "on a tree. A Christmas tree."

In his office Dr. Zialcita asked Teeny how many ducks were flying in the painting on the wall. There were ten. "One-two-three-four," she said. He then said that Teeny had something called Cortical Blindness. He said that her eyes could see, but her brain couldn't tell her what she saw. When he asked her to look at the clock and tell him what time it was, she simply read the numbers aloud, starting with twelve and going clockwise.

Before we left that day, the doctor asked her to write a sentence on a piece of paper. She wrote, "Please tell me how I can live as long as I possibly can."

He read her words and said, "Good," as if she had written, "See Spot run."

One morning not long after that appointment, I went for breakfast with my friend Sarah, an English teacher at the college. We were sitting at a booth, and the waiter had brought my bowl of oatmeal with fixins' when Sarah asked me, "How is Teeny? Is she still confused?"

"I don't think I can talk about that right now," I said to her, and I felt myself getting dizzy, the room going black. The next thing I knew, I was lying back on the bench and EMT's were standing over me, shining a tiny flashlight into my eyes. I was taken to the hospital in an ambulance, and for two days I was filled with debilitating anxiety. Both my regular physician and Ruth came to see me. I begged each of them. "Please make me better. Can't you give me something to take away this fear?" Andy Griffith came on the television set in the hospital room, and I watched all the happy people and wondered how they could be happy. The doctors upped my Zoloft dosage and added Xanax. As I lay there, I remembered the other times in my life when I had felt that feeling that I didn't know how to name—that extreme anxiety that doctors called panic. I wondered if that was the name for the feeling I had the night of the Telling, the fear that caused me to change my whole life around.

When I returned home from the hospital, Teeny was standing at the kitchen sink. "Where have you been?" she asked. "I've been looking for you everywhere." She sounded slightly annoyed. Again I was hit with the punch in the gut. She was still confused.

At night when she went to bed, I rubbed her dry legs with lotion. "That feels so good," she said. I pulled the covers up under her chin and kissed her forehead. I asked her please to live a long time.

"I don't want to leave you either," she said.

I called Bennington and took the January semester off, postponing my graduation until June of 2006.

Dr. Zialcita said the most recent X-rays showed that Teeny's meningioma was growing faster than expected, and he sent her to a brain surgeon in Augusta. The doctor was a young black man who was a brilliant surgeon. He told us about a procedure called Gamma Knife Radiosurgery that he said would cause her meningioma to stop growing and perhaps even to shrink. He set a date for her to go to Augusta to have the procedure.

The Gamma Knife Radiosurgery was scheduled for January 20, 2005, in Augusta. We had to drive up the night before in order to be ready for the procedure early the next morning. In the hotel room in the middle of the night, I heard Teeny get up. When I opened my eyes, the light was on, and she was standing at the sink, completely dressed and brushing her hair.

I got up and told her again, as I had on many other nights, as if talking to a child. "It's not time to get up yet. It's the middle of the night." I put my hand on the elastic of her pants at her waist and pulled them down around her ankles. As I had many other times, I tapped her ankle and said, "Lift this foot." She steadied herself with her hand against the vanity and lifted her foot. I took off her sandal and her sock and slipped her pants leg off. Then I did the same with the other side. She was obedient and pleasant. She believed me. She knew that I would not tell her wrong. I found her pajama bottoms, which she had folded neatly into her suitcase, and, once again, asked her to lift her foot, slipping her foot into the leg of the pajamas. When her pajamas were back on, she lay back down and went to sleep.

The procedure at the Medical Center took all day. Before they began the procedure, they asked Teeny a question to be sure she was in her right mind. "What is an important event that is happening tomorrow in the United States?" It was the inauguration of George W. Bush. She cupped her hands around her mouth and said, "I don't want to talk about it. I'm a Democrat." They laughed and decided that she was fine.

In order to do the procedure, they had to prepare her head to hold the helmet that they would use to apply the gamma radiation precisely to the meningioma, so that it would not harm any of her other brain tissue. They put screws into each side of her head, above the temple. The screws went all the way to her skull so that the helmet would be completely stationary during the procedure. Throughout the day, she was cheerful and chipper. She was having a good time. During the procedure the doctor came out and told me that he had found another tumor at the back of her head. He wanted to know if it was okay if he zapped that one too. Of course, I told him, Let's get it all. After the procedure the doctor made an appointment for a chest x-ray in two weeks. He wanted to be sure that the second tumor in her brain wasn't a metastasis from a lung cancer, for she had lived many years with her mother's second-hand smoke in the house.

That evening at home was a good one. Teeny was happy, and she went outside and watered the flowers and threw balls for Buffy. We watched television, said a Rosary, and we were content.

But early the next morning, she woke up with a bad headache. She said, "It really hurts bad."

I called 9-1-1, and it seemed to take forever for the ambulance to arrive. I sat in front of her and began the "Hail Mary." She made the sign of the cross and then fell to her side on the bed.

When the EMT's arrived, they took one look at her, shined a flashlight into her eyes, and threw a sheet to the floor, lifting her to it as if to a hammock. One man at each end, they took her on the sheet to the ambulance and were gone immediately, the siren blaring. Unlike the time after her stroke, they didn't bother with the gurney.

I called Father McWhorter, and he said he would meet me at the emergency room. By the time we were allowed into the room where Teeny was, her eyes were glazed over, and she was on a ventilator. The doctor told me in broken English, "She has a bleed at the base of her brain, pressing on the brain stem. Her condition is not compatible with life." I will remember those words forever. Her condition is *not compatible with life.*

I sat down in a folding chair and put my face into my hands. I sobbed in deep retching gasps. Then I stood and leaned over Teeny. I had never seen Teeny cry in her lifetime, in all the years that we had known each other, not even when her mother died. She was not hard-hearted; she just stoically accepted what came with trust in the Lord. But that morning as I was leaning over her, I saw a tear run down her face. I knew that she did not want to leave me. The tear was a gift.

Immediately the word spread throughout Milledgeville. Teeny Horne was dying. She was at the hospital. Everybody go. Within the next hour, her room filled with people from the church. All day in Teeny's hospital room people sang, prayed, and moved aside to let me near her every time I wanted. One of them put a Rosary in her hand. Glassy-eyed, she didn't grasp it. There was never a time all day that there weren't at least ten people in the room. I overheard the people whispering to one another that it was the holy time of a Saint's passing.

All day Teeny's heart beat over 200 beats per minute. At around six o'clock that evening, the heart monitor began to slow down. I went and stood beside her, panicked as I watched and heard the heart monitor continue to slow. The slower Teeny's heart beat, the faster mine. Then, at six o'clock, the solid sound, the straight line.

I put my head across Teeny's chest, listening for the heart that was not beating. I felt the presence of others standing in the dark corners of the room, but the moment was mine and Teeny's alone. I pulled the sheet out from the bottom of the bed and rubbed my hands along her warm legs the way I did when I was putting lotion on her when she went to sleep at night. I wanted to keep feeling her body while it was still warm.

When the nurse came in and removed the tubes, she closed Teeny's eyes and turned off the heart monitor machine. "Can't you close her mouth?" I asked. She tried, but couldn't because it had been open all day for the ventilator. When Mama died, her mouth was open too. How quickly they don't look alive anymore. How quickly they take on another look, a look that makes you draw back, or move closer, to say, Please don't go.

At the funeral home, I was the next of kin who received the people. At the funeral Mass, Father McWhorter spoke of friendship—the friendship of David and Jonathan, of Ruth and Naomi. At home, I sat in the empty room and asked the dog, "What do I do? When I get up in the morning, what do I do?" I asked Teeny how to pull my feathers in, but she didn't answer. She had moved on. Unlike Mama, she wouldn't look back. She had places to go and people to see.

When I went back to Bennington for my final semester and graduation, I chose to drive by myself all the way. Because I was afraid to drive through New Jersey, New York City, or Washington D.C., I planned my route to go up through Ohio and then east across the New York Freeway to Vermont. I had planned to stop for my first night in Mount Airy, North Carolina, the town where "Andy Griffith" was filmed, the town that was "Mayberry." But I got there too early, and the town was as commercial as Milledgeville, so I kept driving until after dark through mountain tunnels to West Virginia, where I spent the night in Charleston. The next day I drove as far as Seneca, New York, and visited the Women's Suffrage Museum. The next day I drove through Albany, New York, and across the state line to Bennington.

My graduation semester was busy with my lecture and my final reading; but still, I was sad because Teeny was not at home for me to call. No Mama, no Teeny, and when you are away from home, their absence seems more pronounced, more dull, more empty. A group of my fellow classmates built a labyrinth out of luminaries, but I didn't participate. I stayed in my room and listened as everyone jovially worked together filling bags with sand and placing them in rows, making pathways. Later after dark through my window shade I saw the yellow glow of the labyrinth as my friends solemly and reverently walked, but I didn't go. Only years later, when I returned for a reunion did I feel strong enough to participate. Without Teeny in my life, I was lost, and I didn't know where my own life path would lead next.

IV.

CHAPTER EIGHT: GOING TO WINGS

"There will come a time when you believe everything is finished. That will be the beginning."--Louis L'Amour

2005

I kept waiting for the Big Grief to hit. But after the day that Teeny died in the hospital room, I entered a period of unknowing numbness. I had always imagined that after Teeny was gone, I would slip into her skin and carry on as she had. Perhaps that's what "pulling my feathers in" meant, to carry on—life wouldn't be as much fun, but I would plow ahead.

Other people also thought that I would fill in for Teeny. They had seen the two of us together so often that it seemed natural that I would jump into her shoes; if not for myself, then for her. But, not only was I not as good as Teeny, I also was not willing to do many of the things that she had done: I didn't want to count money at the church; I didn't want to take communion to the veterans; and, even though I was now a retired teacher, I definitely did not want to attend the Retired Teachers' Meetings, nor the Parish Council of Catholic Women, where it was possible that I would have to iron the altar linens or make a casserole. When asked to do things that Teeny had done, I developed an answer: "I make it my practice never to go anywhere where they read the minutes to the meeting, or you have to carry your own lawn chair."

I had thought that after Teeny died, I would feel even closer to her, since she would be in Heaven where I could talk directly to her and she would intercede for me. But it took years for that to happen. I remembered how, after Mama died, I tended her grave at Memory Hill Cemetery. Years earlier when Daddy died, Mama had hated the mound of red dirt left over his grave before the marble stone arrived. To appease her, the cemetery committee had placed large green magnolia leaves over the mound. Remembering Mama's feelings, Linda and I planted three hibiscus in a row across the top of her grave—red, yellow, and orange. Around the hibiscus we filled in red begonias. After Linda went back to Kentucky, I went to the cemetery several days a week, dragged a hose from the spigot, and watered the mound. As the water ran down the mound in streams between the flowers, I talked to Mama, asking her to make me be more like her. Ten years later, when I went to West View Cemetery across town where Teeny was buried, I asked her the same thing, but I didn't feel that she was listening, and I didn't feel that she was there. Unlike the way that Mama had hung around after she died, to be sure Linda and I were all right, Teeny seemed to disappear to a distant place. What I felt most was her silence. I assumed that she was so glad to see the Holy Family in person that she had forgotten about me, left here to carry on without her.

Once again, it was time for me to clean out the leftovers of a life. I had been through and disposed of Mary-Louise's things, then my mother's, and now Teeny's. Going through a person's belongings after they die is enlightening; you learn things about them that you didn't know before, and it changes you. The seed of my becoming Catholic was the *Prayer-Book* I had found in Mary-Louise's things, from the drawer beside her bed. The book came, not from Mary-Louise who, to my knowledge, had never been Catholic, but from her grandmother, whom she had never mentioned to me. In a person's belongings are the stories they never told you. In Mama's things were photographs of her and Daddy before I was born, pictures of the two of them far younger than I am now. I found old black-and-white pictures of Mama standing beside a mule, riding a horse side-saddle, and kneeling in a dirt yard with her younger brother Herman, whose memory always made her cry. You can hear the stories people tell you, but seeing the pictures of them, the expressions on their faces, and the items lying on the ground nearby tells you much more.

While Teeny was still living, I decided to clean out the house to make it easier for us to find things. I began in the pantry and moved around the house clockwise, cleaning one drawer or one shelf per day. Teeny sat in her chair, and I brought first one thing and then another to her, asking, "Do we want to keep this?" and she answered yes, no, or maybe. When I got to her bedroom, she put her foot down and told me in no uncertain terms not to do her bedroom, that she would handle that.

After Teeny died, I began the process all over again. I saved her room until last, and, once again, I did only one drawer or shelf at the time. Paranoid, I looked over my shoulder, lest she scold me and tell me to stop. I made separate piles for keeping, giving away, or selling at the estate sale. In the drawer beside her bed, I found old prayer books. My favorite was a book of prayers for kneeling before the Blessed Sacrament. It was called *My Sweet Rabboni*, the words that Mary Magdalene may have said when she saw Jesus for the first time after his Crucifixion and Death--"Rabbi!" The prayers in the book were personal, even intimate, talking directly to Jesus, and they made me feel close to him as well as to Teeny. During those days, I often took the book into the church and sat there alone, staring at the tabernacle and the red candle burning nearby and reading from the book in the silence. In the drawer were also many old rosaries, some of them broken, all of them used. I separated those to give to people who were close to Teeny. One of them I gave to a woman who had been one of Teeny's sitters in the hospital. She told me that knowing Teeny had caused her to return to church.

In the weeks after Teeny died, my body ached for touch. Chiropractor, manicure, pedicure, massage—all brought hands to me. I felt the hard smooth furniture in her room, the softness of the clothes in her closet, the smooth porcelain head of the Italian Madonna on her chest of drawers, and the heat of the sun on my skin as I fed the birds in the yard. One night I was outside in the dark with the dog. It was quiet, and I was standing still, waiting for Buffy to go into the grass to potty, when suddenly, I felt a swoop of wings over my head and saw a large white bird in my peripheral vision. It dipped silently near my right shoulder, and I saw the broad white wingspan as it swooped into the black silhouette of woods behind the house. Immediately I heard the sound from the tall pine trees, the whoo-whoo-whoo of an owl. Because the spooky sound frightened me, I hurried back inside and looked on the Internet to find what kind of white owl might be in central Georgia, but I couldn't find one at all. I called it my ghost owl, and I was sure that it was Teeny, giving me a sign, the only sign that I attributed to her after her death.

Soon after Teeny died, I bought a puppy, a black toy poodle that I named "Sandra's Consolation," "Connie" for short. The puppy tried to win Buffy over the way that Buffy had done to Maggie years before. Buffy scolded her, rolling her over on her back where Connie squealed as if she were being tortured, her feet waving straight up in the air. She was only beginning to show the aggressive personality that would later emerge. As she grew, she would look like a miniature Maggie, but as a puppy, she looked like a small black monkey whose ears stuck straight out.

By December of 2005, I was ready for Teeny's estate sale. I hired the same people who did Mama's, and many people came from the church looking for some memento that was Teeny's.

After the sale was over and the leftovers carried off, I wasn't quite sure what to do with myself. One Saturday evening the telephone rang, and it was a former student from the Baldwin High School class of 1976. The student apologized for calling at such late notice, and she asked me to come to a class reunion breakfast at the college cafeteria the next morning. She said that they hadn't thought to invite any teachers to their festivities, but that, at the dance the night before, they had been talking about their teachers and decided to invite a few of us who were still around. It was a spur-of-the-moment request, something I usually chose not to do; but for some reason, that night I accepted.

The next morning I was the only white teacher there, along with a couple of white students. James Hartry, one of the black students I had taught not long after integration, had made my life miserable. Every morning he had danced into my classroom singing from Super Fly, "Git down, git down; git down, git down," and wearing a brown suede jacket with wide lapels and long tails, a big Afro, and shiny black stacked high-heeled shoes. I was practicing Behavior Modification then, trying to ignore the bad behavior and reward the good. I waited all year for James to do something positive that I could reward. James had become a high school teacher and coach, a tall, well-dressed, handsome man. After breakfast, he stood up and said, "I look at my students going down the hall, and I see that nappy-headed boy with his shirt tail hanging out, and I see myself."

Daniel Davis, one of the two white students, was the student I remembered who streaked. Back in the days of the streaking song— "that you, Ethel?"—Daniel had run completely naked from one side of campus to the other. That morning at the reunion breakfast, he stood and said, "I don't know if y'all knew this or not, but when I was in high school, I was an alcoholic. Now I am a veterinarian." He choked up and looked at me. "I wish Miss Horne was here, so that I could tell her. The two of you have no idea how much you did for me."

"She knows," I said to him.

Then Johnny Ross, another black student, stood up. In high school his nickname had been "Pie." He had become a preacher, and he asked us to bow our heads. Then he walked around the room, touching each shoulder and saying in a whisper as his fingers brushed each person. "Thank you, thank you, thank you, thank you, thank you," all the way around the room, that prayer.

One day I received a wedding invitation. My classmate, Ilina Singh, and her partner were getting married at their home in Wendell, Massachusetts, and I decided to go.

Ilina's wedding was the first gay wedding that I had ever attended. It was held on the back steps of their white wooden house. Both sides of the steps were surrounded by wide zinnia beds, every color mixed together and almost blinding in the sun. Ilina's partner stood on the steps in a bright white tuxedo with ruffled shirt and tails. Ilina, dressed in a purple sari, walked slowly down the driveway on her daughter's arm. Earlier in the day I had watched her daughter wind the long purple cloth around and around Ilina in the bedroom of the house. At the wedding I sat in a folding chair along with Ilina's friends—some lesbian couples, some gay male couples, and I looked around at the groups, feeling out of place, still so unsure and confused about who I was and where I fit in.

After the wedding and long into the night, we ate and drank under a large white tent that was erected in the back yard. Same-sex couples danced together. My eyes were especially drawn to a female couple who slow-danced together, no matter what music was playing. They gazed into one another's eyes and seemed completely unaware of their surroundings, so focused were they on one another. Ilina told me that they were a new couple who had just fallen in love. I tried not to stare, but I was drawn to them, their love seeming to bathe them in a soft blue light. I realized that I longed to be in love like that couple.

The next morning we met one of Ilina's friends, a balloonist, at six a.m. for a balloon ride, something else I had never done before. When we got to the field where we were supposed to meet, the balloonist had her balloon lying on its side on the ground. As she turned on a large fan, the balloon filled with air, and its rainbow colors seemed lit up by the sunrise behind it. The basket was small, only big enough for four people. As the balloon filled and began to stand upright, we climbed inside, our butts bumping as the balloon rose slowly into the air, the ground below slipping farther and farther away. Up in the air, the balloonist turned off the fire and the gasses, and we floated in the silence, our arms and back warming one another--a newly-married couple, their daughter, and me, suspended between two worlds.

Back in Milledgeville, throughout the next several weeks, as I sat in my recliner, gripping the arms of the chair; as I fell asleep at night; as I stood in the backyard and stared at the tree line of the woods; as I pushed my cart through the grocery store; as I stared at the sheet music above the organ when I played for Mass, Teeny no longer in the balcony with me; intermittent images passed through my head like the swoop of the ghost owl that night. Inside me was a buried self that was not completely dead: I saw the image of dirt moving, being disturbed from beneath the soil; the image of myself being kissed by a woman, a vision that caused me to swipe the air in front of my face. The image I finally dwelt on, staying with it, encouraging it to return again and again, was of myself being made love to by a woman, as I covered my eyes with my hands and cried with relief and joy. I caught myself standing and staring in public spaces, my face hot, lingering with this image, holding it to me like a lost friend. Then I saw the image of myself looking two ways like the god Janus of my birthday month, the two longings of my Capricorn sign, one foot at home and safe, the other seeking adventure and taking risks. I looked at my cupped hands, one holding excitement and love, the other holding debilitating fear. I saw the image of myself standing between two doors, both open, as I looked back and forth between the two to be sure neither door slammed shut before I could run into it.

Then I saw my therapist, Ruth, for what I thought was the last time. We had covered everything: my inability to separate from my mother, to realize that I had a separate identity, my attempt to find my identity in other people, to attach myself to someone I wanted to become. We were finished, all hidden motives identified and dealt with, and, as I was hugging her good-bye, no new appointment made, I said, "Oh, by the way, I think I might be gay," and we had to start all over again, go back inside her office and get out the appointment book again.

My chiropractor, Sherry, was a gay Reiki Master, and I asked for a special session on a Sunday afternoon. In the dark room, as her hot hands hovered above my different chakras, I said aloud, "I think I might be gay."

She chuckled. "Of course you are," she said. "I've known that for a long time." Her answer made me mad. I should be the one to decide, not her. "You should come to the gay Christmas party this year," she said.

"I can't imagine doing that," I said.

"What are you afraid of?" she asked. "We are all normal people."

My image of myself was of the "good" person I had tried to become and a retired teacher. It seemed to me that I had taught half the people in Milledgeville over the years. Every time I went to the grocery store or the bank or the hospital, I saw former students. I couldn't be a gay woman going to a gay Christmas party and still be the person I thought I was. I had spent too many years convincing myself who I was not. The word *good* to me had come to mean denial.

But that December, I went. It was on a Saturday night, the night that I always played the organ for Mass. The night of the party I dressed up in a green velour pantsuit, and by the time Mass was over, I could tell from moving my feet on the pedal keys that I was going to have electricity in my pants. I could picture myself walking around at the party with my pants clinging to my legs and everybody noticing. Mass ended at 6:30, and the party didn't begin until 7:30. I left the church and drove in the dark to CVS pharmacy. I bought a can of fabric spray and stood in the parking lot outside my car, spraying my pants. Then I drove out to the party, which was being held at Café South, a popular restaurant in town that was run by two gay men. We had the place to ourselves that night. Only at the time I wasn't thinking *we*. I was thinking *me*, and what was I doing, going by myself to a gay Christmas party?

When I drove into the parking lot, only a couple of other cars were there. For a while, I sat in the car and waited. I couldn't imagine being the first one to walk in. I pictured it in my mind, the way I would look, walking in, in my green velour pantsuit, which was now slightly damp and not clinging to my legs, and smiling and speaking to people. Sherry and her partner were supposed to meet me, and I didn't know if they were in there yet. They were the only ones I knew. This was the town I grew up in, and I didn't know who would be there. What if I didn't know anyone? Or worse, what if I did?

A couple pulled up and parked beside me in the parking lot, a man and a woman. In a few minutes, they got out and went in. Finally, I summoned the courage, got out of my car, and walked across the dark parking lot. I felt as if I were pulling an old wagon dragging an empty shroud. Which part of me was doing this? The retired teacher and the good Catholic? Or someone else that I had long ago buried and didn't even know now? And how could I be both, and still be one person? I thought of Robert Frost's poem, "The Road Not Taken" which says, "Sorry I could not travel both and be one traveler, long I stood and looked down one as far as I could." I had taken one road, and now I was stepping out into the darkness, staring down another road, unsure if I would ever travel it. I didn't know myself in this place, and I was afraid of opening the door. Who would be inside? Tattooed people with rings in their noses? Teenagers? People with whom I had nothing in common other than being gay, if I was gay?

When I opened the door, two couples were standing there, four women. They looked about my age, and they looked like normal people.

"I'm sorry I'm early," I said. "I finished playing the organ at church and didn't have time to go home. Plus I didn't want to upset my dogs."

"Oh? Where do you play the organ?" the blonde asked. She introduced herself as Barbara and her partner as Judy. Judy had short gray hair and a charming space between her two front teeth.

"The Catholic," I said. "I play for Saturday nights."

The tall redhead, who introduced herself as Janet, said, motioning to all four of them, "That's where we all go! We go to the nine o'clock on Sunday morning!" Then she introduced her partner as Carmen, a stunning Hispanic blonde.

I couldn't believe it. I felt as if God were putting his hand on my shoulder and saying, "It's okay for you to be here." I learned that Barbara and Judy were chemists, retired from working at CDC in Atlanta, and that they lived up at the lake. Janet and Carmen were both retired as well; Janet was a part-time real estate agent, and Carmen had been a nurse who had cared for AIDS patients, they said, "back in the day." These women had had a history that I had not had, a history that I had avoided and knew nothing about.

I fixed myself a plate of hors d'oeuvres and a glass of wine and stood beside these two couples as other people began to come in. As the night went by, the rooms flooded with couples, men together, women together, many singles; the music and sounds of people talking and laughing became louder and louder. People of all ages were there. I learned that the group of women in my age group met every Tuesday for dinner at The Brick restaurant downtown.

"We call it 'Going to Wings,'" Barbara said.

"Oh, I love that!" I said. "Symbol of freedom, of coming out."

They looked puzzled. "No..." Judy said. "The chicken wings are cheap on Tuesdays."

I laughed.

"Come join us!" they said.

As I mingled through the crowd and met people, suddenly I was standing face to face with a former student. She was a dark-skinned black woman who had been in my English class years before. "Well, Ms. Worsham," she said. "I always thought you were gay." I was floored. How do people think they know if I am gay? How could this student possibly have thought that I was gay long ago? If people thought that I was gay, then who was I fooling all those years? Only myself?

Then I heard a young man who had graduated from Baldwin High yell from across the room, "That's Ms. Worsham! She taught me! And so did her lover, Miss Horne."

Her lover? I pretended not to hear, but inside I was shocked and embarrassed. Why would this young man assume that Teeny and I were lovers? Because we lived together?

I left soon after that, thanking the two couples that I had met first. When I got in the car and started driving home, I began to sob, I'm sorry, Teeny. I'm sorry.

A couple of months after the Christmas party, I finally got up the courage to go to Wings for the first time; it took me that long. What finally caused me to go was an e-mail from Patti, one of the women I met that night, who asked me, "Are you ever going to come to Wings?"

When I got there that Tuesday, several couples were around the table, and I told the two women across from me, who introduced themselves as Mildred and Jo, that I was a widow. "Well, we are all going to get there sometime," Jo said. The two couples I had met from the Christmas party were there—Barbara and Judy, and Janet and Carmen. I was also introduced to Jan and Shirley. Jan had buzz-cut hair and had cleaned houses before she retired. Shirley, blonde and blue-eyed, worked in Human Resources for the Piggly Wiggly. Patti, who played the drums and taught music education at the college, was sitting beside Shirley. Her partner, Leanne, lived in Atlanta and worked for a computer company. She came to Milledgeville, they told me, for the potlucks but not every week for Wings.

I had never eaten wings before, and I watched to see how to order. Jo ordered her wings "naked" with celery and bleu cheese dressing. There were too many choices: plain; with sauce or without—mild, medium, or hot--; with celery or without; with bleu cheese or ranch; flats or drums. Taking my lead from the others, I chose all drums, with mild sauce, celery, and ranch dressing on the side. Everybody ordered side salads first, which came before the wings. When our wing orders were delivered, all in baskets lined up along the arms of the waitresses, who were cute college girls wearing short-shorts, Patti tapped her glass loudly and called out, "Everybody listen!" and the waiters called out each order. Women raised their hands when they recognized their order. They knew the names of the waiters, and they tipped them well.

That first day at Wings, the conversation was about an Alaskan cruise coming up the following October with a company called "Olivia," a cruise line that had been begun by a woman named Judy Dlugacz. It would be a ship filled with all lesbians. It seemed that everyone at Wings that day was going, and I was immediately desperate to be included. I had never heard of such a thing, and I was excited about the idea. I had never been to Alaska or on a cruise, much less an all-women cruise. I took down all the information and immediately went home and registered on-line, putting all the expenses on a credit card.

I had a lot to learn about this new culture that I was becoming a part of, and I often felt on the outside looking in. First, I didn't know how to dress myself. I began to wear my hair short and spiky. I bought sports bras instead of the feminine bras I used to wear because I thought that was probably what the others were wearing. Some of the women were wearing men's cologne, but I continued to wear dangly earrings and lipstick and overheard myself being called a "Lipstick Lesbian" by one of the other women.

I learned that many of the women were retired from Atlanta and lived up at Lake Sinclair. Out on their docks, they put a symbol so that they could recognize one another: a green concrete frog wearing red lipstick. Not long after I went to Wings that first time, Mildred and Jo brought me a concrete frog, which I put on a table in the back yard. It meant that I belonged.

I observed my new friends with a fascinated curiosity. One day two new women showed up at Wings. Their names were Dana and Carole, and they were from Macon. They rode up on motorcycles, which they parked in front of the Brick, and they wore tee shirts with rolled up sleeves, revealing tattoos on their upper arms. They sat with their elbows on the table and their shoulders hunched forward. Dana had a nose ring. They were tough-looking women who worked in a factory in Macon. I noticed that the other women who had become my friends seemed uncomfortable, looking around the restaurant at the other people and appearing to cringe if the two new women used the words *gay* or *lesbian* too loudly or if the conversation became too explicit, the laughter too loud, and the talk too raucous. My friends were members of the garden club and the Pilot club and had many other friends who were married to men and had children. Later I learned that they were nervous about the families with children in the Brick, that they did not want to "put it in people's faces," as they said. I learned that there were certain prejudices within this group. My black students had been prejudiced against students that they deemed "too black." This group seemed to be prejudiced against women who seemed "too gay."

A few weeks after Dana and Carole came for the first time, they broke up and started dating other people. But it didn't last, and they got back together. One night they showed up at Wings and walked in the door at the Brick holding hands. Throughout the evening they were publicly affectionate with one another. For several weeks the older couples, my friends, didn't come to Wings at all. Finally, they told Dana and Carole that they should remember that Milledgeville is a small town, not like Macon, and that they had to be careful, so as not to make the other people in the Brick uncomfortable. The couple never came back to the Brick. I watched these things with interest, and I learned that I was not the only one who had found a hiding place in my past life. I laughed to myself when I considered that maybe the group at Wings wanted to be perceived as a group of church ladies planning a bake sale.

But how could I reconcile being Catholic with being gay? I went on-line and googled "Catholic Lesbians." I found a website where women who were both Catholic and gay spent hours talking with one another on-line. I began to tell my feelings on this site, and I learned that many other Catholic women were struggling with this same issue. I learned on this site about a Catholic Nun, Sister Jeannine Gramick, who started a group called New Ways Ministries in order to support gay Catholics. She was giving an all-day workshop in Milwaukee, and I signed up to go. At that conference I sat in a room with gay people who were struggling with their sexuality and their religion, how to reconcile the two. Sister Jeannine was a kind woman with blue eyes. At the conference she told me to "Go home and tell someone. The more people who know somebody who is gay," she said, "the more tolerant they become."

I came home and did what Sister Jeannine suggested. I told my gynecologist when she was in the midst of checking my breasts for lumps. As soon as I told her, she said, "Guess what? I've known that for a long time." I told my internist, Dr. Roberts, and she hugged me and was pleased that I had told her. When I told my college roommate, who lived in Athens, she told me that she had heard it already. "From whom?" I asked. She said from one of the elementary school principals in Milledgeville. It made me furious. Again I wondered, what was there about me that made people think I was gay? Was it my long relationship with Teeny? Was it something about the way I looked or the way I walked? Had there been a rumor from long ago when I had the clandestine affair with Ellen while I was married to Harvill? I thought that I, not other people, should be the one to decide my own sexual orientation.

I told my cousin Beryl on the phone in the car one day as I was driving somewhere, and before I got the words out, I was sobbing and barely able to talk. She told me that she loved me, no matter what.

When I told my sister Linda, I was standing in the kitchen cooking something, the phone to my ear. "Do you think you are a lesbian?" she asked me.

I was shocked when she used that word, a word that I was not yet comfortable with, a word that I still found shocking and ugly. I told her how afraid I had been to hurt Mama.

"But she accepted you and Teeny," Linda said.

I told her about how other people had told me that they already knew, and how mad it made me.

"But they still picked you for Teacher of the Year," she said.

Linda seemed supportive on the phone, but after we hung up, I didn't hear from her for several days. I learned later that she had to struggle with her own feelings. She told me that she had felt that much of my life, I had not confided in her and that she had felt left out. She had remained a faithful Baptist over the years, and after I told her, she had studied her Bible and had read extensively about the subject. Finally, she came to understand, as well as any straight person can understand, what I was feeling, and she became one of the most outspoken supporters in my life.

Every Monday night after choir practice I went out to eat with two conservative couples who sang in the choir with me. We joked about how liberal and Democratic I was and how conservative and Republican they were. One Monday night I decided to tell them. I began by telling them about going to Milwaukee and about Sister Jeannine. In my explanation I told them that my feelings for a woman were no different from their feelings for their own husbands and wives.

During my time of coming out, I became afraid of losing myself, or at least the self that I knew. I became fiercely protective of my independence and afraid of losing my privacy. I loved those long hours alone with my books and my writing. I went through periods of feeling that smothery panicky feeling that I had when Teeny was confused, and, although I had been off Zoloft for a while since Teeny's death, I asked Ruth to put me back on it. Sometimes the fear of leaving my safe place became terrifying. When I thought of my friends sitting at Wings and hoping that no one in our group was going to say the L word loudly enough for people eating nearby to hear, when my friends feared that two of us might hold hands under the table and someone would see, when they hung their heads or looked away for fear that we would be discovered for who we truly were, I realized that I was not alone, that my friends also felt what I had learned to call internalized homophobia. At our potlucks I asked people about their pasts: "Weren't you scared?" I said, "back then? What was it like?" I wanted to know their coming-out stories, when they knew, how it happened, if they had told their parents. Some of them told me, but others didn't want to talk about it. On the one hand, it had been a long time ago; on the other, it was still as fresh to them as ever.

Then October came, and it was time for the cruise. Four couples went—Barbara and Judy, Janet and Carmen, Patti and Leanne, Mildred and Jo—and me, the only single. They told me that Olivia cruises had a singles group that I could be a part of, but I was skittish.

We caravanned to the airport, something I learned that is common with this group, couples meeting at a gas station to drive to Atlanta, a literal Milledgeville Lesbian parade. I rode with Barbara and Judy.

We arrived in Vancouver, B.C., on Saturday. The ship was to depart on Sunday afternoon. As soon as I got into my room at the hotel, in the phone book I found a Vigil Mass at a Catholic Church nearby. Even though two other couples were Catholic, I was the only one who looked for Mass. The church was within walking distance, and, while the others went shopping along the boardwalk, I walked down the clean shady sidewalks of Vancouver. I passed people walking their dogs, and they smiled and spoke. At a 4:30 Vigil Mass at St. Patrick's Catholic Church, I found the same peace I always felt when attending a church away from my home church. Everything was the same, the readings all over the world, the responses, the handshakes and the smiles of the people at the sign of peace.

When we got to the cruise ship, everything was white—the large tents that covered the port, the ship, the entrance, the gangway. As we walked up the ramp onto the ship, Judy Dlugacz, the owner, stood shaking hands as women entered. She smiled and took my hand and said, "Welcome to the way the world ought to be."

Inside, I was given a pewter dog tag to wear around my neck. In the center was a big red O that meant "single." Slipping the tag inside my sweater, I hurried to catch up with the others. They went to the Lido bar where we ordered drinks and watched as others boarded the ship.

I had never seen that many lesbians in one place before. In fact, I had never seen many lesbians *period*. I saw that there were as many different kinds of lesbians as there are straight people: two women who looked like men, walking and holding hands; couples who looked like male-female couples, one of them with short hair and dressed like a man, the other with long hair and looking feminine. I assumed that the feminine one was the "Lipstick Lesbian" that they had called me. And yet, I did not feel particularly attracted to one "type" more than the other. Many couples looked like our group, in our age bracket and not looking either dominantly male or female. Many couples were young and looked almost like teenagers, with green or pink hair, necklaces tattooed on, and rings in ears and noses.

The ship was Holland America, and young Asian men with small round trays took drink orders. I could smell the chlorine that filled the turquoise indoor pool. The loudspeaker kept repeating, "Welcome, Ladies of Olivia!"

I do not know how to describe the experience of an Olivia cruise, especially through my eyes back then. It began with a sail-away party with loud music and dancing as we watched the lights of the town become smaller and smaller in the distance, the sunset of red and purple turning the rooftops into black pointed silhouettes. Out on the deck a couple danced in front of me, an obese woman in a wheelchair and her partner in front of her, a young Asian woman with long dark hair, twirling and gyrating in front of the seated woman who waved her arms in beat with the music.

At the Ocean Bar each evening we had the drink of the day— Lemon Martinis, Cranberry Margaritas, Lime Mojitos, and Tropical Daiquiris. After a day of excursions—to Juno, to Ketchikan, to Anchorage--we went to our cabin and dressed up, usually in black pants and tops with jewelry. At the Ocean Bar we gathered in big armchairs and snacked on the hors d'oeuvres of the day as Julie Wolf sang slow, sexy jazz piano. Then a band came in and played ballroom dance tunes as the women danced. It was fascinating to watch as the women knew which of them would lead and which would follow. Often, while both looked feminine, one wore pants and a cumberbund while the other wore high pointed heels and a brightly-colored dress with a swirly skirt. Those women could ballroom dance, and I loved watching them.

One couple that were especially fascinating to me were Agatha and Pete. They were an elderly couple that had gone on every Olivia cruise for years. Agatha had wavy brown hair, dangly earrings, and a swirly skirt; Pete had short silver hair and wore a white ruffled tuxedo shirt and black pants. They were experienced ballroom dancers, and I was mesmerized as I watched them, Pete holding Agatha in her arms and leading as Agatha spun and twirled.

With them was a masculine-looking woman with short waxed hair and men's clothing, a necktie and men's shoes. I learned that her name was Virginia and that she was always a single who accompanied Agatha and Pete on cruises. Agatha took turns dancing with both of them. I was hungry to know the history of the women, but I didn't have the courage to ask. Near the end of the cruise, however, I saw that several younger women went over, one at the time, and asked Virginia to dance. She always got up and danced with them. I knew that if I did not go and ask her to dance that I would regret it.

When I saw her sitting alone, I got up, walked over, leaned down to her, and said, "I want to dance with you, but I don't know how to dance. Would you show me?" It took her several tries of rocking back and forth to get up out of the low chair that she was sitting in, but when she stood up, she took the lead. She looked down at her feet and told me how to move. As we danced, she told me that she had turned ninety years old, that she was retired from teaching college English, and that her former students had thrown her a party. When later I went again on an Olivia cruise, Agatha and Pete were there alone, without Virginia. I was glad that I had taken the risk.

The entertainment on an Olivia cruise was diverse. I heard the lesbian comedian, Vicki Shaw, tell stories about her mother: "Why, Vicki, you don't *look* like a lesbian!" to which Vicki said she wanted to respond, "You haven't seen me in bed with Sargent Patch!" her partner who was a cute police officer. The jazz singer Suede took the house down with her rendition of "Sister" from *The Color Purple*. Sweet Baby Jai rocked us with "Meet Me with Your Black Drawers On."

One night they held an "Oldie-Wed, Newly-Wed" game in which couples had to guess what their partner would say in certain situations. Vicki Shaw was the moderator, and she insisted that couples identify themselves by who was the butch and who was the femme. Many of the women there did not like the idea of labeling themselves in this way. But Shaw insisted. In her Texas accent she said, "Y'all might not want to call yourselves one or the other, but, ladies, look around this room!" She was right. In many cases, there was no doubt who was the butch and who was the femme. Sometimes a woman named herself femme when Vicki thought otherwise. She screwed up her face and looked at the audience, rolled her eyes, and said, "Really? If you say so." I was shocked at some of the questions and answers. To a self-identified butch, the question asked was, "What would your femme say is your most prized possession as a couple." The answer the butch gave was "Pinky." Vicki Shaw had fun with that one, for "Pinky" turned out to be a dildo. The audience roared, and so did my friends. I laughed too, but I felt strange. I had never even seen a dildo.

Out by the pool one day, I met a young cop from San Francisco. Her name was Lila, and she patrolled the Castro district. I told her my story, and she took an interest in me. She saw me as the neophyte that I was, and she wanted to educate me. She said that I reminded her of her aunt. She asked me to look around and see which of the women at the pool I might be attracted to. I watched as the women played pool games—volleyball and basketball. Another game was the wet tee shirt competition, where a woman who had had a mastectomy held up her tee shirt and showed a lovely vine-and-flowers tattoo that ran along her scar. Lila encouraged me to get on Match.com to meet someone. One evening I met a couple on the cruise that said they had met on Match.com. They said that it took them forever to finally get together because they were both afraid. This made me feel better; I was not alone in my fear. They said that they had been together for many years and that they had a toddler, a little girl.

The next to the last night was what was called "White Night," and everyone wore all white. The purple lights of the ballroom lit up everyone's clothing in psychedelic glow. I sat and watched as women danced, and I saw how beautiful they were together. The last night was the parade of the Baked Alaskas. Over the loud-speaker the Holland America announcer said, "Ladies and Gentlemen, uh, sorry, Ladies of Olivia, give a hearty welcome to the parade of the Baked Alaskas." Women waved their white napkins in the air as the waiters paraded in, wearing their black and white, holding the beautiful foamy desserts above their heads.

On the way home after the cruise, Barbara and Judy encouraged me to follow through and get on Match.com, as Lila had suggested. "Nobody is going to come knocking on your door in Milledgeville, Georgia," Judy said.

CHAPTER NINE: ON MY WAY TO YOU

"You shall know the truth, and the truth shall make you odd."
--often attributed to Flannery O'Connor

In October, 2008, when I got home from the cruise, I sat down and wrote my profile for Match.com. I made up my mind that I was going to be as honest about myself as possible, and honest about what I wanted in a partner. If someone didn't like who I was and what I wanted, then our relationship wouldn't work. I was no longer going to try to be what I thought someone else wanted me to be. I was no longer going to try to become anyone other than myself. In my profile I wrote that I was a practicing Roman Catholic and that my religion was important to me. I wrote that I didn't smoke and that I didn't want a partner who did. I said that I liked to read and write and that I didn't care for sports. I had learned from my friends that a certain stereotype was often true. My gay friends were good with power tools, and they liked to watch sports on TV. When I read the profiles of others on the site, certain things were red flags for me. I wanted someone who was in my age bracket, not much older and not much younger. It was interesting to see the pictures and read about the women who had posted themselves there, all of them looking for someone to love. It was also easy to be objective. I had to choose photographs of myself to post. I picked one of me holding Connie and Buffy near the Christmas tree. They wore red bandanas, and I wore a Kelly green turtleneck. In one of the excursions on the cruise, I had swum with dolphins in a huge pool. As I clung to the fins, the dolphin swam fast, taking me to the end of the pool where a photographer took my picture. On Match.com I posted the picture of me with the dolphin, as well as another staged, touristy one of me being kissed on the cheek by a sea lion. After I hit the "Post" button that made my profile live, I sat down in my recliner, pushing it back, lying flat. Suddenly, I sat up straight, panicky. What am I doing? I thought. I immediately hurried to take the profile down.

But in that ten-minute block, someone had seen my profile and liked it. She and her sister in Missouri had been looking on line while talking on the phone long distance. In Missouri, her sister had said, "What about that one?"

But in Murphy, North Carolina, when the woman went back to look again, my profile was gone. "Well, crap," she said. Earlier in the year she had left a relationship that had come to an end. She had bought a white West Highland Terrier puppy that she named Sir James Cagney—Cagney, for short. And she spent many nights watching TV with her dog in her lap, alone, wondering where her life was going next. "Will I ever find someone who is right for me?" she asked her sister on the phone. She asked God to send her someone who would love her unconditionally, and to help her to recognize her when she arrived.

The next day I put my profile back up. I prayed to God to send me someone who would be right for me, and to help me to recognize her when she came. In a few hours I had a response from someone who called herself "Black Bear Gal." She listed herself as a Baptist. She didn't smoke. Her interests were singing, reading, and writing in her journal. She was a businesswoman. Her photograph looked like me, big smile, silver hair. She also listed that she always loved the latest gadget, anything to do with technology. This described me, as well. I had a Palm Pilot and a Handspring Visor before anyone else had ever heard of them. At the Milken conference in Los Angeles for the teacher awards, I had a palm-held device with a fold-up keyboard that fit inside my purse. The other teachers had gathered around as if I were the only kid on the block with red Kool-Aid. Across the top of Letha's page was written, "Looking for someone to share my life with. Could it be you?"

I didn't want to talk on the phone right away; I didn't know what to do with the silences. And the idea of talking on the phone to a stranger made me uncomfortable. I wanted to write e-mails instead. I thought we could get to know one another through e-mail, and then we would feel more comfortable on the phone. Black Bear Gal liked to talk on the phone, and she didn't like writing e-mails. When she first wrote me, I responded with questions in an attempt to get to know her better. Did she have any pets? Did she have brothers and sisters? What was her favorite kind of music? What was the last best book she read? What were her hobbies? Where did she go to school?

Instead of answering, she ignored my questions and asked me, "Are your pictures current?" At the time I was aggravated. I didn't know that she had had a bad experience with someone who had posted old photographs and that, after driving a long way to meet her, she found that the woman looked nothing like her pictures and had a painting of a velvet Elvis hanging up in her living room.

I wrote back to Black Bear Gal, "Is two weeks current enough for you? Those photos were taken two weeks ago on an Alaskan cruise." We then began to write back and forth. She answered my questions. She told me about her dog, Cagney. Her father had been a minister who was very strict. She loved all kinds of music, especially Barbra Streisand. She had spent a lot of money going to a Streisand concert, and she didn't regret a dime. Her current favorite books and movies were the Harry Potter series. She had three sisters, and she was the oldest. When she told me their names, she described the way her mother had called all of them to come in for supper, a rhyming song. Later I would ask her to say their names fast because it made me laugh. She had graduated from a college in Oklahoma and then from a school in Texas. Her degrees were in music and elementary education. Her major had been voice, and she loved to sing. She had taught middle school music for several years but had quit to start her own business. When I asked why she called herself Black Bear Gal, she said she ran a cabin rental business by that name in north Georgia. She signed her e-mail "Letha." What a pretty name, I thought.

One day when we were writing, a pop-up message appeared in the upper right corner of my screen. It said, "I see you're on-line now. Would you like to talk on the phone?" She included her phone number. I looked around the room, for it felt as if my privacy had suddenly been invaded by Big Sister. I had felt completely anonymous. I had even listed Macon as my hometown. But when the pop-up said, "I see you're on-line," it scared me. I was afraid of being trapped, of losing my independence, of not knowing how to get out of something if I didn't like it. I turned off the computer, picked up my pocketbook, and left the house. I didn't turn the computer back on for three days. I learned later that Letha had said to herself, "Well, frick! I moved too fast and messed this up!" She was still interested in me.

When I got back on-line three days later, I told her that I had been busy and hadn't gotten her message until then. I told her that I would call her soon. That weekend I went to a pumpkin carving party at Mildred and Jo's house, and I brought my pumpkin home, cut it up, and cooked it down with butter and brown sugar. I was eating it in a bowl in my recliner when I finally called Letha. She said that she was eating dinner but that we could talk. When I asked her what she was eating, she said baked sweet potato with butter and brown sugar, smushed up in a bowl. I found it amusing that, there we were, the two of us—me in Milledgeville and her in Murphy, North Carolina--both of us with short silver hair and eating something orange out of a bowl. We talked for a while and, as soon as a silence came, I told her I had to go and hung up.

One night after midnight I was sitting in my chair watching TV and putting Letha's contact information into my phone, when I accidentally dialed her number. I panicked and, before I could hit the red end-call button, she answered. I was mortified. "I'm sorry!" I said. "I was working on my contacts and accidentally hit your number! I woke you up!"

"It's okay," she said, sleepily, and I could tell that she was smiling.

"Hang up now and go back to sleep," I said. "I'll let you go."

"Well, I'm awake now," she said.

A couple of days later, I was asleep when she called me after midnight. Instead of saying hello, I answered with, "What is this? Payback?" She laughed, and we talked, my phone against the pillow, the lights of cars shining into the window as they turned the corner on my street.

One day when we were e-mailing, she wrote, "We can try this, and if it doesn't work out, we can still be friends. I have a lot of friends that I've met on Match," she said.

Immediately I wrote back, "I'm not on Match.com to make friends. I've got more friends now than I've got time for."

I didn't hear from her for several days after that, but I didn't retract what I had said. I meant it. If something like that caused her to withdraw, my mind was made up that it was okay. But she didn't withdraw. She liked my spunkiness, she said. She told me later on the phone that I sounded like a "tough old broad." I told her that she sounded like a basketball player.

One day I was walking Buffy and Connie around the block in my neighborhood as I was talking to Letha on my cell phone. "When are we going to meet?" I asked her. It had been several months since we first started talking, and it seemed to me that she was continuously putting off our meeting.

"I look exactly like my pictures," she said.

What a ridiculous thing to say, I thought. "Well, I'd like to see the 3-D version," I said. But still, she put me off. I didn't learn until later that she was trying to lose twenty pounds before meeting me.

"I have small hands and feet," she said. "And short nails. I keep them clean and neat. And I hope you like butt, because I have a big one." Later we would laugh about the things we said early in our relationship. We also learned about one another's parallel lives before we met. When Teeny was dying, Letha's mother was also dying in Missouri. We felt that God was leading us to one another.

One night during Thanksgiving weekend when I called, Letha was cooking, making something she called Thanksgiving Dinner casserole. She put me on speaker, and we talked while I heard her scraping pans, running water, and chopping celery, talking to me at the same time and telling me about her recipe. I listened and imagined her, moving around her kitchen.

My friends got together for Thanksgiving dinner at Barbara and Judy's house. Barbara and Judy provided the turkey and dressing, and the rest of us brought sides. I made my mother's candied sweet potatoes recipe. When they asked me about Letha, I said, "We're still talking." When they asked me when we were going to meet, I shrugged and said, "I don't know. She keeps putting me off." During the time there, I went outside and dialed Letha to wish her a Happy Thanksgiving, but she didn't answer. By the time I got back home, I had not been able to reach her, and I didn't hear from her for several days. I was worried and also irritated that she had not wished me a Happy Thanksgiving. I wondered if I should be worried about those gaps in our conversation, if they were the proverbial red flag that I was constantly on alert for. But when she finally called me, she was happy and chatty. I realized that in the beginning of an on-line relationship, both sides are careful, about what they reveal and what they hold back.

One day I sent her a box of long-stemmed yellow roses. She was driving home from work after dark, and we were talking on the phone, when she parked her car in the light of her front porch. She kept talking to me as she got out, locked her car with the beeping sound, and then discovered the box. "What's this?" she said. "I have a package."

"I don't know," I said, smiling. "Open it and see."

She let herself in, and I heard her throw down her keys and begin to tear into the box. She laid the phone down on the counter and put me on speakerphone, and I heard her say, "Oh! Roses in a box! Just like in the movies!" I held the phone and smiled as she repeated, "Just like in the movies!"

For fun I began taking dancing lessons through the continuing education department at Georgia College. Jan decided that she wanted to take classes too and, since her partner Shirley didn't want to participate, Jan and I became partners at the weekly sessions. This was a step toward my coming out in my hometown, for all the other couples in the class were male-female couples. Jan wanted to be the leader, and she wanted me to be the follower. The class was the East Coast Swing, and it was a lot of fun. The gay Christmas party was coming up on December 13, and Jan and I thought that we would practice and get good enough to show off our moves at the party.

I was scheduled to give a writing workshop for teachers in December in Cullowhee, North Carolina, at the North Carolina Center for the Advancement of Teaching. My workshop was entitled, "Making Winners of the No-Win Track," and it was about my work with young black males. I told Letha about my workshop and asked if that would be a convenient time for us to meet, since my route would take me near Murphy. Finally, she agreed.

On Monday, December 8, 2008, Letha and I met for the first time in Murphy, North Carolina. A common joke is, "What do two lesbians carry with them on a first date?" The answer: "U-Hauls." But that wasn't the case for us. We were both nervous about the meeting, ready to turn and run the other way at the first red flag. I was less nervous than Letha; after all my years of looking for myself in other people, coming out gave me a new boldness. As I drove my denim-blue Highlander through the mountains of North Carolina, around the steep curves, one after the other, I tried to imagine how it would be. We were supposed to meet at *Shoebooties* Café in downtown Murphy, but it was closed on Monday, so we decided to meet there and then drive to a Mexican restaurant nearby.

As I stood on the sidewalk outside the restaurant, Letha drove up in a black BMW Z-3 Coupe. I stood there in my purple glasses and purple-flowered chenille top that I had bought at a Crafts Fair, my hair spiked up. I was determined to be completely myself and not try to be what I thought someone else wanted me to be. I had let go of expectations; either it would work out, or it wouldn't. Later, Letha told me that she thought I had on a chenille bedspread.

As she was locking her car across the street, she looked up at me and said, "Hey." Her voice sounded deep. When she reached me, I was entranced. She was pretty—silver hair that glistened in the sun, pink lipstick, a brilliant smile, and a dark sweater, a long matching scarf, and a black leather jacket. She looked younger and cuter than her pictures, and she was shorter than I. So much for sounding like a basketball player on the phone.

At the Mexican restaurant, we both ordered spinach quesadillas, but neither of us ate. We pushed our food around on our plates. I had gotten a second major in Spanish in college, and at the Mexican restaurant, I spoke Spanish to the waiters. Letha told me later that this had embarrassed her and that she wondered if it was a red flag—that, along with the chenille top and purple glasses. We were sitting by the window, and I watched her as she looked out, trying not to look at me.

"Would you consider coming to the gay Christmas party in Milledgeville next week?" I asked her during lunch. It was such short notice that I was sure she would say no, and I was surprised when she said yes.

"Would you like to follow me and come by my townhouse for a little while?" she asked. "I'll introduce you to my dog." She told me later that she had not intended to do that, and she surprised herself when she did.

I followed behind her black sports car as she drove up curvy hills, past a golf course, and into her apartment complex. She parked in front of a gray townhouse with an American flag hanging over a small front porch. Inside was her white Westie. He was excited and jumped up on me while Letha hollered, "Cagney! Stop!" To distract him, I got down on the floor to play with him, but he became even more rambunctious and pulled my hair and tried to bite my head. I got up and sat on the sofa, and Cagney lay down on the floor and stuck his head through the curtain to watch a boy riding a bicycle around and around the parking lot. Every time the boy got in front of Letha's porch, Cagney stood up on his short legs and barked loudly.

As we talked, it seemed to me that Letha had a list in her head of the things she wanted in a partner. I felt as if I were being interviewed, and I expected her to pick up a pad and begin taking notes.

"I want someone who will think I'm the best thing since sliced bread," she said.

"Yes, that would be nice for me as well," I said.

"And I don't mix finances," she said.

"I agree," I said.

"My dog comes with me," she said. "We are a pair."

"Same for me," I said. "Love me, love my dogs."

On a table near her television set was a small Christmas tree with tiny ornaments. She plugged it in and then lit a candle sitting beside it. The candle smelled like cranberry and made a faint sound like a fire in a fireplace. She told me that the realistic wooden wick candles were for sale at a store in downtown Murphy.

When I got up to leave to drive to Cullowhee, Letha walked out to the car with me and watched as I set the GPS, which I called the "Bitch in the Box." She laughed, standing beside the car. When I told her that the GPS lady was polite, that when I got lost, she said, "Recalculating" instead of "Not that way, you dumb shit!" Letha leaned her head into the car and gave me a big hug. She seemed to think that I was funny. I thought that she was funny and adorable. I was drawn to her, and it was hard to leave. I felt silly and giggly, like a school girl.

After my workshop, I considered driving back through Murphy and ringing her doorbell, but I didn't. She told me later that she was hoping I would, but she admitted that it would have probably scared her if I had. We were both afraid of making a mistake. And, after all, she would be in Milledgeville at my house the next weekend.

On Saturday, December 13, 2008, I planned a meal to have ready when she arrived--vegetable beef soup in the crockpot, a salad, and yeast bread. I cleaned up the house and turned on lamps for ambiance. I put slow jazz by Julie Wolf on the CD player. I moved my car over in the garage so that she would have room to park her car.

She called before she arrived because the GPS had sent her to a nearby street, so I walked out to the end of the driveway to flag her down. When she drove into the garage, I stood beside the car, and we looked at one another before she got out, quiet expectant gazes through the glass window. She took out her suitcase, and I took her things to the guest bedroom near the front of the house, a room that had its own bathroom. Cagney, Buffy, and Connie sniffed one another while Letha arranged her things and hung up her clothes in the closet.

I had set the table with the good china, silver, and crystal left over from my marriage to Harvill. I turned the jazz music down low and lit candles. She bragged on my meal as she ate, and we watched one another through the yellow glow of the candlelight.

Then we got into my car, and I took her out to meet Janet and Carmen, Barbara and Judy. She said she felt that it was a test and that I was being sure my friends approved. She was right, of course.

After breakfast the next morning, I sat down at the piano and began to play hymns from my Baptist hymnbook, from the church I grew up in. As a child she had sung solos in church when her father preached, especially, "This little light of mine, I'm gonna let it shine." She came over to the piano and sat down beside me and began to sing the hymns with me. We sang, "It is Well with my Soul," her favorite and "Great is Thy Faithfulness," my favorite. She sang soprano, and I sang alto, the way that Linda and I used to sing.

"I first fell in love with you at that piano," she told me later. "I had looked for love in all the wrong places, but that day, you felt safe and right, and I knew that I was falling in love with you."

That afternoon we drove out to see Darryl and Marsha, a couple of old hippies who ran an Herb Farm in the country. Once again, I was introducing her to my friends, the way I might show off a new puppy. I was proud of her, and I wanted to shout from the rooftops. We bought homemade soaps that were nestled in little baskets, peppermint and green apple. We bought Himalayan pink salt in a grinder, and red bush tea, on which was written, "for that 'coming down with something' feeling." The house smelled of cherry incense and burning wood, and we sat at the table and ate lavender cookies and sipped tea as I watched Letha interact with my friends. Darryl sat in his rocking chair and leaned forward, his coal dark eyes sparking under his shaggy silver bangs and his smile with his floppy silver mustache responding to Letha the way he always responded to everyone who visited their home in the country. Letha was someone who made friends quickly, and I loved watching her, knowing that I didn't have to worry about being sure everyone had something in common. Letha just went off on her own and talked to people, exuberantly and naturally. Marsha, in her long graying ponytail and sweet smile, brought us chili in small bowls. We felt good, holding hands as we walked down the dirt path back to my car.

When we got home and I pulled the car into the garage, letting the door down behind us, Letha said to me, "Do me a favor."

"What?" I asked.

"Give me a kiss," she said.

I leaned over and kissed her, a lingering, simple, non-passionate kiss. Her lips were full and soft. It was the moment I had longed for, my first real kiss from a woman in thirty-five years. Later, for our first anniversary, based on that first date, she gave me a bracelet that spelled out, "Do me a favor." She told me later that the kiss had been a test for me. She said she couldn't be with someone who wasn't a good kisser. I was glad I had passed the test.

That afternoon we played with makeup and dressed for the dance. I wore a black calf-length casual dress with outside seams, an irregular hem and buttons down the front. It was the only dress I had, and it was my dancing dress for the night. Letha wore a red turtleneck and black pants.

I was ecstatically happy. I couldn't stop smiling. I wanted to show Letha off to everybody. "Look what I found!" I wanted to say to my friends. Throughout the night, Letha kept whispering to me, "I'm with my people! I haven't been with my people in a long time!" We had twin smiles, like looking in the mirror. We lost each other often during the night. She was gregarious, moving around the room, talking to everyone. I was dancing the East Coast Swing with Jan. We had practiced the Kansas City moves, and we were showing off. I could feel Letha watching me from the table.

When the disk jockey from Atlanta played songs from the eighties, I didn't know them because, while I was with Teeny, I had not kept up. But everyone in the room, including Letha, sang and made the motions to "Y-M-C-A" and "Play That Funky Music White Boy" and songs by Donna Summer. When the people in the room responded to the disco songs from their pasts, I felt as if I were on the outside looking in. They all had a past that I did not have. I had heard Janet and Carmen, and Barbara and Judy talk about their years of going to Tallullah's in Atlanta. Letha had been there too. But when the disk jockey played Chubby Checker and "Let's Twist Again," I got out on the floor and danced, and Letha danced the twist with me. It was from a generation that I remembered. I also knew the Hokey Pokey from kindergarten and the Electric Slide and the Bunny Hop. During the Electric Slide, Letha sat in a chair at the table and watched me. When the slow dance, "At Last" by Etta James was played, Letha and I danced together. I was dreamy with infatuation, and we looked into each other's eyes with joy. Letha laughed, threw her head back, and said, "I'm in deep Ka-ka." One of our friends made a picture of us that night, and it has always been our favorite picture because of the happiness on our faces. Letha keeps it on the table beside our bed and looks at it every night before turning out the light. Later that evening when we got home, we told each other that we had been watching one another all night, even when we weren't together.

That night, we each slept in our separate rooms. We were still feeling cautious; we were afraid to move too fast; we didn't want to mess it up.

The next day Letha told me that she had asked Janet at the dance, "Do you think she's ready for this?"

Janet had answered, "Are *you* ready?"

Letha was hurting so badly the next morning from dancing the twist that we had to call Sherry, our friend the chiropractor, who had also been at the dance. She arranged to meet Letha at the office that Sunday afternoon, and Letha ended up staying in Milledgeville for several days. But we each stayed in our own bedrooms, although one morning she did stick her head around the corner of my room and wave. Still, when we passed one another in the house, we hugged and kissed, and Letha said to me, "I'm in deep like."

When she got back to Murphy, Letha packed her car and drove to her sister's house in Missouri to spend Christmas and New Year's. I drove to Linda and Tom's in Kentucky to spend Christmas with them. Letha and I stayed on our phones constantly, texting. Letha's sister looked at her, and Linda and Tom looked at me, shaking their heads and rolling their eyes. One night on the phone after I got back home from Linda's, Letha said to me, "You know when we see each other again, we're going to make love, don't you?"

"Oh, we are?" I said, sarcastically. I wasn't so sure.

My friends in Milledgeville had a New Year's Eve party at a couple's house. During the midnight singing of "Auld Lang Syne," when everyone inside was kissing and hugging, I went out on the porch in the dark and called Letha and sang to her, an old McGuire Sisters song called "May You Always." We were so silly. I was in my sixties, but my feelings for Letha, my desire to be in love, had lain dormant for years and was deeper and more mature than I would ever have imagined when I was in my twenties.

One way that I learn is to read books. When I felt panic and fear, both during Teeny's confusion and during my early stages of coming out, I read *Embracing the Fear* by Judith Barrada. During the times of getting to know Letha, I read *If the Buddha Dated*, a book by Charlotte Kasl, an author that I return to again and again. I loved Kasl's Buddist focus on living in the present and getting rid of expectations. I also bought and read books about how lesbians make love. I felt that Letha would be more experienced than I, and I wanted to be prepared. I read a classic called *Lesbian Sex* by JoAnn Loulan and another, *The Whole Lesbian Sex Book* by Felice Newman. Remembering my projects of weight-lifting, yoga, and many others in which I had read every book and bought all accouterments having to do with my current project, Linda said to me, "Sandra, this is not one of your projects." Oh, but it was!

By January 9, 2009, when Letha and I met at *Shoebooties* for lunch, after being apart for so long, we were both in a state of deep lust. I wore a black turtleneck with silver dangly earrings and a silver necklace, tight black jeans, black boots, and a black leather jacket. I wanted to look tough and sexy, and I did; I could see it in Letha's eyes when I met her at the door. She told me later that what she noticed most was my smile. I was looking directly at her, and she was looking away, seeming shy. We asked for a booth in the far back where we would be hidden from the other patrons. With red faces, we looked at each other across the table, and the attraction was almost unbearable. Letha looked beautiful, and I could not wait to put my arms around her, to feel her face against mine, to kiss her passionately. After all the time that we had been apart, it was difficult to see one another for the first time in a public place. Unlike the first meal we had had together in Murphy, we were ravenous this time, not only for one another but for food. We ordered hot artichoke dip, warm chips, and wine, and we ate as if we were starving. When the waitress came back to check on us, we averted our eyes and tried to keep her from detecting the state we were in. When we finally left, we drove fast to Letha's townhouse.

I had imagined the way her apartment would look upstairs. In my fantasies, her bedroom was on the left at the top of the stairs, and we made love to the sexy Suede jazz that I had heard on my first Olivia cruise. I had imagined candles burning around the room and Suede crooning "Teach Me Tonight." Of course, it would not really be that way because Letha had never been on an Olivia cruise and did not know about Suede, but that's the way I had imagined it for weeks in my anticipation.

As soon as we parked and went inside, the door closing behind us, we grabbed each other against the door and began kissing and hugging. Slowly we made our way up the stairs, where her bedroom was on the right, not the left. It is difficult for me to describe the way it felt to feel a woman's naked body next to mine, after all those years. It was warm and nurturing, and, in addition to my desire, I felt comfortable, safe, and loved. I became lost from myself, not thinking, not worrying, not feeling guilty or asking forgiveness. Just letting go, like flying naked over a waterfall, my arms and legs outflung, my body feeling, moving through water, through space. No one needed to tell me what was right. I knew. I saw tears on Letha's face and knew that they were mine.

January 15, 2009, was my sixty-second birthday, and I came back to Murphy where Letha made me a steak on a small grill on her front porch, with baked potatoes, a salad, and caramel cake, which she had learned was my favorite. Throughout the next year, we drove back and forth every couple of weeks. When she was in Milledgeville, she often went to Mass with me and sat upstairs in the balcony as I played the organ. On a few occasions, she sang a solo. When I went to Murphy, we went to St. Williams, a Catholic church, or to Letha's church, Cherry Log Christian Church about forty-five minutes away. It was a church that reminded me of growing up in the Baptist Church, and sometimes I cried with nostalgia for my days in Girls Auxiliary. During this time our friend Jan was diagnosed with breast cancer, and, while our friends helped her in numerous ways, taking her back and forth to chemo and cooking for her, Letha and I didn't help at all because we were driving back and forth to see one another.

I loved watching Letha interact with others. At potlucks with our friends in Milledgeville, she was outgoing, moving around talking to people, making everyone laugh. At the grocery store, she was drawn to children, and she made friends with total strangers in the checkout line. Later, this characteristic would begin to irritate me sometimes, and I would react by saying to myself, "That's my Letha. She has to learn everybody's life story." It is a good quality to have, but sometimes I just want to stay in my introverted little cave and not have to talk to people. But that is part of loving someone. And she had to become accustomed to my grumpiness.

One weekend I brought Cagney home with me so that he wouldn't have to be at home alone in the Murphy townhouse while Letha was at work. Since I was retired, I could stay at home with the dogs. As a terrier, Cagney was filled with more energy than my poodles, who were couch potatoes. One day I decided to take him for a three-mile walk around the neighborhood to tire him out so that he would settle down and sleep well. When we got back home, I let him out into the backyard. He was a digger, but I thought that I had made him tired enough that it wouldn't be a problem. As I was talking to Letha on the phone, I stood up and looked outside. What I saw was Cagney's tail only, wagging in the air as his whole body was buried deep in my raised brick flowerbed, diving for chipmunks.

"Your dog is in big trouble," I told Letha on the phone. My lilies and begonias were out on the ground, roots facing upward. Not long after that, I had the flowerbed dissolved and made into a taller bed in the corner of the yard, too tall for Cagney's reach. The chipmunks, too, relocated.

One day soon after that incident, I went to breakfast with a former teacher colleague of mine. As we were eating, I told her about the incident with Cagney. I said, "You won't believe this dog. He is totally out of control. His name should be Marley."

"What does he look like?" she asked.

When I picked up my phone to show her a picture of Cagney, the phone line looked open. Apparently I had butt-called somebody. I put the phone to my ear and said, "Hello?"

Letha answered. "I've been sitting here for thirty minutes listening to you run down my dog."

I laughed. "Is this going to be a deal breaker?" I asked.

"I guess not," she said, "but just remember, my dog and I are a pair."

Teeny's white poodle, Buffy, got pancreatitis. She was obviously in pain, bending over as she walked, and flopping down on her bed. When she went outside, she had diarrhea and vomiting. Our vet said that she thought it was time. I put Buffy in the car on a blanket and drove to the vet's. When I had Maggie put to sleep that morning after Christmas, I sat in a room with her and loved on her, told her what a good dog she was, and then handed her over to our vet, a kind woman that I knew would be gentle. She had known Maggie for a long time. But with Buffy, I felt that Teeny would want me to stay with her, so I went to the back. The same vet was there, and she had known Buffy for a long time as well. She came into the room and gave Buffy a shot in her back to sedate her; the shot caused Buffy to rear up and squeal loudly, and then she tried to bite me. Soon she slumped down on my arm. I talked to her, put my face into her white curly hair, and told her what a good dog she was, how much Teeny and I had loved her, and that Teeny was waiting for her in Heaven. When the vet came to take her, Buffy's leg moved, and I said, "Wait!" But the vet told me that she was gone, that her movements were just reflex. Perhaps it was because Buffy was all I had left of Teeny, but I had a difficult time getting over Buffy's death. As I drove home from the vet, I kept thinking, "I've killed Buffy! Oh, no, I've killed Buffy!" My heart was broken, and I couldn't stop crying. For months I cringed when I thought of that day and of Buffy's cry when the doctor gave her the shot. I had Buffy cremated and when they gave me the small white box, I took it to the cemetery and buried it at the foot of Teeny's grave.

In January of 2010, it was time for the U-Haul. If there is one thing lesbians know how to do, it is to *move*. Barbara and Judy, and Janet and Carmen drove to Murphy to help us. It rained hard all day that day, making our move a sloppy business. Letha rented a long U-Haul truck and parked it beside the front door of her townhouse. As soon as our friends arrived, Barbara said, "Where are the beds?" Apparently disassembling the beds was her specialty. As Letha and I stood by helplessly, waiting to be told what to do, our four friends went back and forth, packing the truck. They knew how to do it, and they didn't want us interfering. Letha pointed out to them what was going, and she and I wrapped and packed dishes into boxes, driving back and forth to the grocery stores and liquor stores to get more boxes when we ran out.

Then Letha climbed up into the truck cab and drove the large truck out of the subdivision. I followed behind, and our four friends followed behind me in their van. Letha had never driven a truck that big before, and she told us that she would not be able to back up, that we had to go forward all the way. Another lesbian joke is that we don't use the term, "Drive straight" but, rather, "Drive gayly forward." The drive from Murphy to Milledgeville was long and messy, the rain coming down in sheets. At one point Letha had to stop the truck for gasoline. She drove straight in and straight out, never having to back up. When we finally arrived in Milledgeville, it was dark. We parked the truck along the street in front of the house, locked it, and our friends returned the next morning to help us unpack.

In order to make room in the house for Letha, I cleaned off shelves and cleaned out closets. Letha told me later that when she first came to my house, she thought, "This woman has a lot of *stuff!*" She prefers clean and un-cluttered, but my shelves in every room were filled with memorabilia, trinkets from childhood, dolls, and games, things I had brought from Mama's attic, as well as memories of Teeny. Once again, I was going to hire the same people to do a sale for us, and I began collecting the things I would get rid of in boxes in corners. As she unpacked, Letha did the same with her belongings.

In the process of cleaning out, I dropped the Crucifix that Teeny had given me when I became a Catholic. Jesus' hand was broken off, and I knelt on my elbows on the floor and cried. I remembered the day that Mary-Louise was on the floor searching for the scepter and piece of crown off her wooden statue of the Virgin Mary and how I had helped her look for it. Back then, I didn't even know that I would become a Catholic one day.

Letha's cabin-rental business had suffered from the economy, so when she moved to Milledgeville, she got her teaching certificate renewed and began to look for a teaching position. I was worried about her having health insurance, and I lay beside her every night and prayed hard that God would send her a job that would fulfill her and that would also give her health insurance. Instead of renewing her certificate in music, she chose to renew it in technology. Nothing excited her more than the idea of being able to teach technology to young people. She got a job in a nearby county teaching technology in an elementary school, and she was ecstatic. The job would begin the following August and in the meantime, we had time to unpack, have a sale, fix the house the way we wanted, and get married.

We planned our wedding for Valentine's Day, 2010. By then, I would be sixty-three and Letha, fifty-nine. Since I had graduated with my MFA from Bennington College in Vermont, I wanted us to get married there, where same-sex marriage was legal. I loved the little town, and I wanted to show it to Letha. I searched the Internet for an inclusive church in Bennington, and I found the Second Congregational Church, which was in downtown Bennington. In the photograph a rainbow flag flew out front, and the woman pastor was named Reverend Mary Lee-Clark. We wrote a letter to the pastor telling her our wishes for our wedding, and she wrote back. Together through e-mails we planned our service. We made reservations at a bed-and-breakfast in downtown Bennington.

As I had when I was working on my MFA, we flew to Albany, New York, and drove a rental car across the state line into Vermont. I was excited to show Letha the little homes with flower gardens along our route, the Green Mountains in the distance, sharing with her what I called "my Vermont." Every summer when I had arrived at Bennington in June, I stopped and breathed deeply a scent that I attributed only to Vermont in June. But then it was February, and I was disappointed that there wasn't more snow. I had wanted to show Letha Vermont in the snow. In Georgia we almost never got snow, but Vermont, with the green mountains of summer and the white mountains of winter, were like Camelot, and being there gave me a sense of peace. These are the things I was looking forward to sharing with Letha.

As soon as we arrived in Bennington, we went to the Town Center, a white wooden building downtown, to get our marriage license. When we stood at the counter, I said boldly, "We came to get our marriage license." Letha stood quietly beside me, and I knew that she was nervous. A woman led us to a room with a long wooden table. We sat down in straight wooden chairs at the end of the table and waited for the woman to bring us the forms. It felt strange and risky. On the table in front of me were my divorce papers, proving that I was no longer married to Harvill. Letha's eyes were wide, and she kept looking over her shoulder as if someone she knew would come walking in and she would have to explain.

I had even sent our wedding announcement, along with our picture, to the Bennington *Banner*, where it was published. After we had received our license, we walked down the street and into shops. Shopkeepers seemed to know that we were coming, and they came out from behind their counters to hug and congratulate us. It was as if we were in another world, a scene from Harry Potter.

But that night in our room at the bed and breakfast, I got sick. I began to throw up in the bathroom, again and again. Letha thought that I did not want to marry her, that I had changed my mind and didn't know how to get out of it. I threw up all night long. The next morning Letha called my Milledgeville doctor and asked for a prescription for Phenergan, and she went to a drugstore to pick it up for me. She lit a fire in the fireplace in our room and sat in the rocking chair in front of the fire and read while I slept. Every hour I rose up on my elbow and looked to see if she was still there. The fire was golden, and Letha sat in the white rocking chair reading. When I looked up at her, I saw her silver hair and the book in her hands. All day she read and kept wood on the fire. When it came to the vow, "in sickness and in health," Letha had excelled.

The next day when we went to meet the preacher, I felt so bad that I had to lie down on the sofa in the pastor's study. Pastor Lee-Clark was a beautiful young woman, small, like Letha, with straight blonde hair and a warm smile. We liked her immediately. We told her that we would attend the Sunday morning service the next morning.

At the ten o'clock Sunday service the following day, Reverend Clark asked us to stand. "I would like for you to meet Sandra and Letha, who will be married at two o'clock this afternoon." Everyone smiled and clapped for us. "They would be very pleased if you would come and join us," she said.

After the service, a woman came up and asked, "Do you have a reception planned?" We had not even thought about it. It was February in Vermont, and we had told our sisters to wait to come to a reception that we were planning in July in Georgia. When we shook our heads and said no, the woman said, "Well, you do now." She went home and planned a reception for us, coming back later that afternoon with a tiered cake, coffee, and plates, cups, and napkins.

As we drove to the church that afternoon, Letha said, "I never thought this would be possible for me in my life." Because it was Valentine's Day, we wore red and white pantsuits—mine, white with red, Letha's red with white. We were a pair of Hummel bookends. About fifty people from the congregation sat behind us, parishioners who returned to be there for us.

Pastor Lee-Clark's wedding sermon was about time, two kinds of time: Chronos and Kairos. Chronos, she said, was clock time, time that could be measured in seconds, minutes, and hours. Kairos, on the other hand, meant "in the fullness of time." Kairos referred to "the right moment, the perfect moment." It is the blooming of the rose, the ripeness of the peach, the rising of the bread, and it was our Kairos time. The Pastor read the passage from Ecclesiastes: "To everything there is a season, and a time to every purpose under the heaven."

At our request, the pastor read the section on Marriage from Kahlil Gibran's *The Prophet*, which says that, while two people become one, they must also remain separate people:

"Let there be spaces in your togetherness, And let the winds of the heavens dance between you...And stand together yet not too near together: For the pillars of the temple stand apart, And the oak tree and the cypress grow not in each other's shadow."

These were our vows, which we wrote ourselves:

"I, _____, choose you, _____, to be my beloved. As the poet Rumi wrote 2000 years ago, 'Finally a love has come which would cause me more shame were rumor to conceal it rather than to lay it bare for all.' These are the promises I make to you of my own free will and before these people as witnesses. To always be on your side, To see you and love you for who you are—the light and the dark inseparable, to honor our differences as we bring love into each other's hearts and life into each other's souls."

Near the end the pastor played song that Letha and I had begun to call "our song." The song was "On My Way to You" by Nancy Lamott. The lyrics were about all the different roads we travel in our lives, the way we go down different paths and yet, find ourselves in the place we were meant to be all along. Our favorite line was, "If I had changed a single day, What went amiss or went astray, I may have never found my way to you."

We first heard this song at a restaurant one day in Milledgeville, where we were eating lunch. We were talking, and suddenly we both became quiet and listened. We called the waiter over to help us find out what the song was and who was singing it. The words reminded us each of our own histories, as we thought of the many ways the road could have turned differently to cause us never to meet.

At the end of our wedding, the Pastor spread her arms and said the words we had both been waiting for:

"By the power invested in me by the Church and the State of Vermont, I announce that you are legally married; in the name of God, Creator, Redeemer, and Sustainer. Those whom God has joined together, let no one put asunder."

Those words that I had imagined, said by a woman in clergical attire, her arms raised over two women in love, gave me an exhilaration that seemed to lift my feet off the ground. Letha said aloud, "Whoo Hoo!" breaking the sentimental moment and making everyone laugh, including me.

After the wedding, at the reception the woman gave us, we cut the cake and fed each other, just like any other couple at any other wedding.

That night we went on a sleigh ride. When we arrived at the farm, the driver of the sleigh, a young woman, said, "Oh, you must be the ladies that got married today!" We climbed up into the sleigh, and the woman tucked a blanket around our legs. We held hands under the blanket and watched our breath like smoke in the freezing air as the horse pulled us across the snow. The blades made a slicing icy sound, the sky was dark navy blue, and, without artificial light, the stars were brighter than I had ever seen them. When we came to a little cabin, the driver said "Whoa!" and stopped the horse to explain to us about the sugarhouse, where the maple syrup was stored. Now every time I hear the song "Jingle Bells" at Christmas, I remember our own ride in the cold of Vermont in a "one-horse open sleigh."

As we began to pack to go back to Milledgeville, Letha started feeling sick. I tried to get her to let us stay in Vermont until the virus passed—we had decided that we must have picked up a bug on the plane flying up—but she was determined to get back to our home.

When we got to the airport in Albany, snow began to fall. The flight was postponed again and again. As we waited, Letha lay down next to a wall with her head on her pocketbook. Always aware of how she looked, she was too sick to care. Later she asked me if she looked like a beached whale lying there. "A little," I answered.

Finally, beside me on the plane, she kept a barf bag nearby, and when we arrived in Atlanta, we asked for a wheelchair. She asked me later if she looked pitiful riding along in the wheelchair with her barf bag. "Pretty much," I said. "I told people to stay back, that I never knew when you were going to go off."

In the car, she lay down across the back seat all the way home and was sick again and again. When we finally got home, she could hardly walk. I helped her into our bed and looked after her, the way that she had looked after me.

I was able to sell my house around the corner, and for the next several months we cleaned out our belongings and planned a sale. As Mama had suggested, I had framed the Ola dress into a shadow box, but it was big and cumbersome and no longer fit into the house with Letha and me there together.

I chose my second cousin Kathy to give the framed dress to. I thought she was the most sentimental of all the second cousins. I remembered her as a child, her sweet smile, her loving ways. Everyone always said she was the grandchild most like Aunt Alma, my mother's oldest sister. Kathy was the one who sent birthday cards to Mama and pictures of her children in Christmas cards every year. I called her and made plans to meet her at a Mexican Restaurant in Eatonton, Georgia. I took our wedding pictures with me; she was young, and I thought she would be open-minded and non-judgmental.

At the restaurant Kathy looked like a hippy. She had on a soft cotton peasant shirt in colors of purple and green. Her long brownish-graying braid hung like a rope over her left shoulder.

"I'm glad you told me," she said, turning the pages of our album. "Now I can relax. Now I can really hug you." A strange statement, but I thought I understood. It meant, "Now I really know you."

When we went to our cars after lunch, we moved The Ola Dress from my trunk to hers. She seemed pleased to have it.

It wasn't until before the family reunion that I learned that Kathy had told everyone--all my first cousins, her parents, who then told their brothers and sisters. Soon all my first cousins in Atlanta—all of Aunt Alma's children—had been told that I had married a woman. All those cousins, Fundamentalist Baptists, who had surely voted against

Obama. "I didn't even know two women could get married," Kathy said that her mother, my cousin Patsy, had said. Kathy had many excuses for why she had told them: it was an accident; she had let something slip about how happy she was for me, and then Patsy wouldn't let it drop until she told her. Patsy told her husband Buster. Buster called up Larry and Frankie. Larry called up Bertha and Bob. In less than a day, all of Aunt Alma's children and their husbands and wives and offspring knew that I had married a woman.

But I went to the upcoming family reunion anyway. I was determined finally to live my own life. Letha chose not to go, and I didn't blame her.

At the reunion Kathy had an album of her own. She was proud to show me the pictures from hers and her husband Dale's hunting trip to Africa. I sat down and turned the pages. There on every page, one after the other, were pictures of Kathy with her rifle by her side, genuflecting beside the corpse of a dead animal, its feet folded as if in prayer. She was on every page, posed the same way, smiling the same smile, her long braid hanging over her shoulder, proud that she was a real woman who knew how to shoot and kill beautiful animals. She was at the family get-together, but she was not proud of her casserole; she was proud of her album. Zebra, antelope, caribou, wildebeest. Page after page of carnage. Why would you kill a zebra? I was thinking as I turned the pages. I was not thinking, Now I can really hug you.

Before we left, Kathy said, "You and Letha must come and see our house. All the animals have come in, and we have them on the wall. I don't know how you feel about early dead animal." She laughed.

"Well, I'm thinking that The Ola Dress probably doesn't fit in with the décor," I said.

"Not really," she said. "I gave it to Daddy, and he has it on the wall in the basement. It looks good down there."

I pictured it. The Ola dress encased in glass, protected, waiting, ready to be passed down through the generations, the leftover from a dead girl, frozen in place, something that probably wouldn't fit in anywhere.

We planned our wedding reception for July 24, 2010. We prepared invitations that contained a color picture on front of us at the altar with Pastor Lee-Clark on our wedding day. Inside, we asked people to come help us celebrate. We had a book to sign beside the door and in the center of the dining room table, a large tiered wedding cake made by a downtown bakery. Over fifty people came, not only our gay friends but many heterosexual couples throughout town that were friends of ours. I sent invitations to the members of the choir but not to the priest. I didn't want to give him anything that he would have to deal with.

Linda and Tom came from Kentucky, and Letha's youngest sister and her niece. I felt that day that Letha and I had done a good thing by having the reception, for, not only was it fun, but we also increased tolerance in the people who knew and loved us, and probably others as well. A couple of weeks later, when California was overturning the unconstitutional ruling, some people in Milledgeville heard the news, thought of us, and felt differently than before. The choir director at the Catholic Church told me that she used to be judgmental but that since she knew us, she felt differently.

It didn't occur to me what a mistake I had made by sending an invitation to Myrtle Ewers, a friend and fellow choir member and a conservative Catholic. Myrtle and her husband were the friends I went out to eat with after choir practice on Monday nights, and I had already told her that I was gay. I had thought that she was accepting. But when Myrtle received her invitation, she entered a moral dilemma. At the Monday Mass, she showed the invitation to the priest in order to ask his permission to attend. He had only been at our parish a few weeks, and he didn't know me or how long I had attended and played the organ there. But Myrtle had put him in the position of having to deal with me.

On Monday evening, the priest called me at home and asked me to come to the rectory the following morning. When I got there, he asked me to sit down at the dining room table. The room looked much as I remembered it when Teeny used to count money there. I remembered the day I had gone in to tell Teeny that I'd had to put Maggie to sleep, when the church secretary was praising her because she was able to distinguish the quarters from the dimes.

That Tuesday morning the priest sat at the head of the table and told me that the secretary was present as a witness because she "knew the situation," whatever that meant. He held out his cell phone and showed me a photograph he had taken of the outside and inside of the invitation to our reception. "What do you have to say about this?" he asked me.

"What do you want me to say?" I asked him. I should have told him that it was a photo of my friend and me getting installed into the Eastern Star.

"I have struggled with this for a long time," I told him.

Then I looked at the secretary, who had known Teeny for a long time. "I want you to know that this was not mine and Teeny's relationship." I felt that I needed to protect Teeny.

"Oh, I know that!" she said, her eyes wide. "I have no doubt in my mind about that!" I was thinking, how does she know that? The certainty in her voice was insulting. She would expect it of me, but never of Teeny.

"I tried to protect you from this," I said, looking at the priest. "I did not send you an invitation because I did not want you to have to deal with this."

"I, too, wish I was not in this position," he said. "I wish I had not been shown this invitation. What you did wrong here," he said, "is making it public."

"Yes," I said, "it's a 'don't ask, don't tell' policy, isn't it?"

"Well," he said, "you know, the purpose of marriage is procreation, and to my knowledge there is no way two women can have a baby."

His comment sounded so ridiculous to me that I didn't even respond. What I wish I had said is, "I'm a post-menopausal woman. I couldn't have a baby if I was marrying a man."

After a pause, Father continued, "I'm afraid I'm going to have to ask for your resignation from playing the organ."

Boom. Much of that day is a blur to me. I knew that the priest was probably calling me to the rectory to talk to me about things he had heard. But it never occurred to me that he was going to fire me from playing the organ. All I remember for sure is that I tucked my head into my chest and walked out of the office, ashamed. As I walked out the front door, the priest called after me, "You and Letha are welcome to worship with us anytime."

"Can I receive the Eucharist?" I turned and asked.

"Well, no, not that," he answered.

I went home sobbing, hurt to the core. I had played the organ, sung in the choir, served as lector and Eucharistic minister, and attended mass regularly for thirty-five years. It's hard to believe, but, in all those years, I had only missed Mass once in 1982, when I had my hysterectomy. Yet, he easily dismissed me. He couldn't have thought about it or deliberated about it for more than a few hours.

A few days later a card came from the church, signed by the priest, the deacon, and the secretary. "Bless you," said the lavender teddy bear on the front. And on the inside, "For giving of your time, your energy, your self." The priest wrote a note inside the card, "Sandra, you will be missed greatly. Thank you for all your years of service at this church. The doors of this church will always be opened for both of you to join and worship with the community."

I read this, and I thought, Who are you to welcome me to my church? This is my church. What he was also saying was, Welcome to come and sit, but do not join us for the Eucharist. I held the card in my hand and cried in front of Letha. She couldn't believe it, and she was angry. As a few days passed, the more I thought about it, I too became angry. I sat down and wrote a letter to the priest:

Dear Father,

I am not going to be able to have closure, or shake the dust off my feet and move on, until I have expressed to you my feelings about your firing me from my position as cantor and organist at Sacred Heart Church. I feel that what you have done is wrong, and I need to express to you my reasons for feeling this way.

I have been a Catholic convert since 1975. I was twenty-eight years old when I became a Catholic after having grown up Baptist. All those years I was Catholic, I have been faithful and devoted. For thirty years, the only time I missed a Sunday Mass was when I had surgery. I went to Confession regularly. I was a Eucharistic Minister and a Lector, and I sang in the choir.

When Father Marren came to be our priest, he wanted music at all the Masses, so I was recruited to play the organ for the Saturday night Mass. This was at least twenty-five years ago, and from that time until recently, I selected all the hymns for each Sunday Mass and sang the Psalm each Saturday vigil as I played the organ.

When Father McWhorter came, he loved my voice and had me to sing often. In addition to the Christmas and Epiphany Proclamations, he especially loved to hear me sing the "Kyrie" from the "Mass of the Angels."

And why did you fire me? Because I "made public" the fact that I had married my monogamous partner—another woman. "Ah, well, then," you may think…"Then you deserved to be fired. You knew the rules, and you broke them."

First of all, I did not "make public" in any way other than that I sent out invitations to select friends to a reception at my home. I did not send you an invitation because I did not want to put you in that position. One of our parishioners showed you the invitation in confidence, and you took a photograph of it with your cell phone.

You told me in your office the day you fired me, "Where you went wrong was making it public." To me, that is the worst blow of all. Isn't it the secrecy in the Catholic Church that has caused such scandal in recent years? That Bishops hid the fact that they knew priests were abusing children? And were the priests fired, or simply re-located?

The "Don't Ask, Don't Tell" policy that you imply exists in the Catholic Church is highly destructive. By its very nature, it implies that there is something shameful to be hidden about a person. It implies that God must have made a mistake to create such a being as me. It is a destructive policy in the military and, based on the past several years, it is destructive in the Catholic Church as well. This kind of secrecy and fear of scandal is malignant and evil.

Jesus came to teach the Spirit of the Law, not the Letter of the Law. The church website says "To Know, Love, and Serve as Jesus Did." I do not believe that Jesus would have fired me.

In the end, however, it is time for me to thank you. For years I have struggled hard "not to be gay." My becoming Catholic was part of that process. I have, however, in recent years realized that being gay is not a choice. It is not an illness to be cured. I have realized that I am exactly the person that God made me to be, and God doesn't make mistakes. The world is filled with creative, loving, gay people who are contributing a great deal to our society. Some of these gay people have had callings to be nuns and priests, and therefore, they have taken a vow of celibacy. Others do not have a religious vocation and therefore should not be required to take a vow of celibacy.

You told my partner and me that we are welcome to worship with you but not to play the organ and not to come to Communion. How could I do that? Come and hang my head in shame and not be "worthy?" I could go to God's house, but not to his table?

I hope that, as the Catholic Church grows in future years in its understanding of homosexuality, that "Don't Ask, Don't Tell" will cease to exist and that all will be welcomed and loved as the imperfect beings that we are, people who need a loving Savior. And love, not law, is, after all, in the light of eternity, the only thing that matters.

Sincerely,

Sandra Worsham

I sent copies of my letter to the Archbishop in Atlanta and to all previous priests at our parish. I didn't hear back from any of them.

I did not go back to the Catholic Church then. Letha and I tried the Methodist, where we sang in the choir. Then, when the preacher we liked left, we tried the Presbyterian, where there was a woman pastor and a congregation that welcomed us. After a while, when her teaching load became too heavy, Letha began to tell me she wasn't going with me on Sunday mornings, and I began to resent going by myself. As I walked into the Presbyterian Church, I could hear the bells ringing down at the Catholic Church, calling people to mass, and I felt drawn there. I knew that all the people were streaming across the lawn going into the church with the bells. I began to question whether, if I was going to go to church alone, if the Presbyterian was the church I really wanted to go to. I told the Presbyterian pastor that I wanted to learn what Presbyterians believe, and she taught a class on the subject and gave me books to read. I learned about John Calvin and Zwingli and Luther, and I tried to join the Reformation.

One day I received a phone call from one of the parishioners at Sacred Heart. Gerty Fillmore was a former nun who had married a former priest, and she was devout, always arriving early to daily Mass to lead the Rosary. On weekends she attended the vigil Mass where I had played the organ. When I entered Mass on Saturday night to climb the stairs to the organ, the first thing I heard was Gerty's voice saying in her Northern accent, "Hail Mary, Full of Grace..." From the balcony as I knelt there, I saw the back of Gerty's head. She was thin and had beautiful skin, smooth and unwrinkled for her almost eighty years. Her hair was teased and unruly, a mixture of blonde and gray. She did not want to look like a "little old lady." I was surprised to hear her voice on the phone. I assumed that she had heard my story, which was probably circulating throughout the parish. "Sandra Worsham was fired from playing the organ because she got married to a woman. Myrtle Ewers from the choir told the priest." Some would ask, "Why would Myrtle do such a thing? She had to know what would happen." Others would say, "Sandra knows the church laws, and she asked for this." Over the following four years, I would learn from many parishioners, as I ran into them at the grocery store, or the waiting room at the Toyota service department, or at the mall, that they missed me, that they felt that the priest had over-reacted, that firing me from playing the organ was ridiculous and unnecessary.

The day that Gerty called, she asked if she could come to see me. Of course, I said yes. I assumed, knowing Gerty, that she was coming to persuade me to come back, and I knew that I would tell her no. But that was not why she came. When I opened the door, she hugged me. She was wearing a red turtleneck with a black cardigan and black pants. She was elegant, as always, and she smelled good. She walked over and sat down on the sofa. She seemed nervous.

"How are you?" I asked her. "I miss seeing you."

"Oh, Sandra," she said. "I pray for you every day. I am so sorry about what happened." Gerty was breathless, and she waved her delicate hands in the air as she talked. "Every Mass I tell Father that he made a mistake," she said.

"Well, he did what he felt he had to," I said. "I guess he felt that he had no choice."

I had put Connie and Cagney on the porch so that Gerty could get into the door more easily, and I asked her if she minded if I let them in. They were standing side by side, their little faces looking through the glass. She didn't mind. As soon as the dogs came in, they each jumped up on the sofa on both sides of Gerty, and she began to pet them.

"Would you like something to drink?" I asked.

"No," she said. "I need to talk to you. I need to tell you something."

I sat down to listen, giving her my full attention.

"I want to tell you about my son, Paul. He was my adopted son," she said, "and he died ten years ago." She reached into her purse for a handkerchief. "I told everybody that he was hit by a car," she said. "But he really died from AIDS." She looked up at me. "This is the first time I have ever told anyone. What happened to you made me feel that I could tell you what really happened to my Paul."

A few days after Gerty's visit, I wrote to Sister Jeannine Gramick and told her about it. She wrote me back this note:

"Dear Sandra, I was happy to hear how you have helped Gerty to be comfortable enough to talk about her son who died from AIDS. By being yourself, and proud of who God made you to be, you will continue to help countless people—in the South and elsewhere. This is part of your vocation, your mission. Blessings as you continue. Know that the way will not be smooth. 'The disciple is not greater than the master.' If Jesus was rejected, we can expect no less. But you will be participating in Christ's mission of love and service to God's people."

I began to have dreams about playing the organ and about the Catholic Church. One night I dreamed that I went back into Sacred Heart. No one was there but priests and a few lay people. The whole room looked black and white with the priests. The few chairs that were left had people's sweaters and coats and pocketbooks piled on them. There were no seats available for me. The room was loud with the priests' voices talking and laughing. I was aware that I was looking for a quiet place where I could kneel and pray, but there were no empty chairs anywhere, nor quiet places. I was thinking that the Catholic Church had changed and that there was no place for me. I left realizing that the Catholic Church hadn't changed; it was I who had changed.

§

"What will I do when something happens?" asked Janet. "Something happens" always meant death. It was a strange euphemism. It meant, What will I ever do when Carmen, the love of my life, is no longer here with me. We first learned about Carmen's cancer in the Spring of 2012, when Letha saw the two of them together at the doctor's office. She came home and said to me, "Carmen is yellow. As yellow as my shirt."

Later Barbara and Judy came by to tell us the news. "Pancreatic," they said in hushed voices, nodding slowly, looking down. "The death sentence cancer," they said. "This is the worst possible news." After they left our house, they were going to the houses of other friends in our group, to tell them the news.

The following Tuesday Letha and I parked our car as usual in the lot behind the Tourism and Trade office next to the Exchange Bank on our way to Wings. The ginkgo trees that lined the lot were green, the leaves shaped like fans. In the fall the trees were solid yellow. As we locked the car, I told Letha about the short story I had written in college called "The Ginkgo Tree" about the nursing home where my mother used to work as head nurse and about the symbolism I created between old age and death and the way the ginkgo tree suddenly dropped its yellow leaves almost overnight. "That's what will happen to these trees in the fall," I told her. "One day the tree will be covered with the yellow leaves, and the next day the limbs will be bare black skeletons against the blue sky."

When we walked into the Brick, our friends were circled around the table. Janet was there without Carmen, who was home with her parents, who had come from Puerto Rico because of the diagnosis. Judy told everyone that Carmen's pancreatic tumor was inoperable and that Carmen would start chemo soon. Judy took a plastic bag from her purse and passed it around the table, giving each of us a purple bracelet that said, "No one fights alone."

Carmen was an AIDS nurse before she retired. She was blond and beautiful with a colorful Hispanic personality that drew people to her. People who referred to Janet and Carmen called Carmen "the pretty one." Then they followed with, "not that Janet's not pretty, but you know what I mean." Janet was the one who cut the grass and trimmed the shrubbery but could not cook and didn't clean the house. Carmen was fanatical about cleaning, washing the towels every day and mopping the floor with wood soap that made it shine like a mirror. With Carmen's parents there, Janet couldn't set a half-full coffee cup down without one of them picking it up and washing it. And they all spoke Spanish to one another, leaving Janet out. Carmen's mother was constantly patting Carmen's cheek and crying, blubbering in Spanish. Carmen's father was a handsome silver-haired man with dimples, a dignified Hispanic man who looked wistfully at his daughter and sang "Chiquitita" to her. "Chiquitita, tell me what's wrong."

Janet and Carmen had met years ago in a gay bar in Atlanta. Janet was on the prowl. She had a reputation for choosing a different woman every month. Carmen was supposed to be Miss January. Janet saw her from a distance dancing a salsa to a pop eighties song, shaking her bootie and stomping her foot, throwing her blonde hair back and laughing, her white teeth and red lipstick flashing in the strobe lights. Janet went up behind her and put her arms around her. Carmen told everyone later that she thought, "What's this old woman doing talking to me?" But Carmen became the lasting one. They had a commitment ceremony in Florida at a church. Carmen, dressed in a sapphire blue dress with high heels and her hair pulled back with a sparkling barrette, looked like a Spanish princess. Janet wore a black tuxedo with a white ruffled shirt. They told us later that Janet couldn't dance and, during their wedding dance, Janet was thinking, "Is this song ever going to end?" while Carmen was thinking, "Are we ever going to move off this tile?"

Carmen was our "family" nurse. She had been a nun in a Puerto Rican order before she realized that the religious life wasn't her calling. When any of us had to go to the hospital for anything, Carmen went too. When Letha had to have a heart catheterization, Carmen got up at four in the morning to go with us to the hospital.

Janet and Carmen's relationship with Carmen's parents was better than it once had been. When Janet and Carmen first visited them in Puerto Rico, Carmen's mother told them that they couldn't sleep in the same room. "It is against our Catholic faith," she said. She called Janet "that woman."

"That woman has a name," Carmen told her mother. "Her name is Janet, and if we can't have a room together, then we will stay in a hotel." The mother then changed her mind.

During Carmen's illness, the parents gained a new respect for Janet. She was a good caregiver. After Carmen's parents went back to Puerto Rico, Janet and Carmen took a trip to visit them there. They thought it would probably be their last visit. In Puerto Rico, thirty or forty of Carmen's relatives gathered in the house to pray the rosary. A Spanish priest went over and said Mass. Carmen went with her father to the church where she was baptized. Her father had promised God that if Carmen were able to visit Puerto Rico again, he would walk on his knees to the altar. Janet e-mailed pictures to us of the thin, skeletal Carmen walking beside her kneeling, silver-haired father, all the way to the altar.

When they returned from Puerto Rico, Carmen went to the Mayo Clinic in Jacksonville for a round of chemotherapy. While she was there, Jan and Shirley had the potluck at their house. They set up a camera, and we all made a video for Carmen. The introductory music was "Ain't no sunshine when she's gone," and the closing was "Lean on Me." Sandwiched between the music were couples, sitting on the sofa in front of the camera, talking to Carmen, telling her how much we miss her and that our prayers were with her. Letha and I sang a duet, the Irish Blessing, "May the Road Rise to Meet You."

We heard that Carmen was beginning to feel the effects of the chemo. She was sleeping a lot and had dark circles under her eyes. It was a race between her body and the cancer...who would die first. Something was sure to happen. Janet sent an e-mail to everybody, telling us that Carmen did not have good news. The chemo had not shrunk the viability or the size of the tumor.

On May 1, 2012, I had a Mass said at Sacred Heart Church for Carmen's birthday and for her healing. It was the first time I had been back in the Catholic Church in two years. It was not as hard as I imagined it would be. Barbara and Judy picked me up, and Janet and many of our friends were there. We took up two rows, and I wondered how the priest could single me out, how I could not receive the Eucharist, but others could. He regularly took Communion to Janet and Carmen in their home; he did not know about their commitment ceremony. It was wrong that everything was based on what the priest knew or didn't know.

I realized that I had begun to doubt the things that Teeny had believed all her life, and that I had believed for thirty-five years. The Host was in the Monstrance on the altar. How could the Catholic Church believe, I wondered, that the Roman Catholic priests were the only ones who could consecrate the Host and turn it into the true Body and Blood of Christ? How could they make the bread and wine be blessed like magic, to the exclusion of the other clergy in other denominations? And through their secrecy, they were scared to death of losing that power. The words to the liturgy were different in the Mass that day, and I realized that I had gotten so far away that I did not even know the responses.

§

At the end of June in 2012, Letha flew to San Diego to attend the annual convention of the International Society for Technology Educators. We planned that I would fly out at the end of her conference, and we would drive up the Pacific Coast Highway to San Francisco. When I got there, I rented a car and drove to the hotel where Letha was staying. The conference had ended, but many attendees were still there. Letha was still "in conference mode." She had bonded with the other teachers from her school, and she was excited about all the things she had learned. I had the feeling that she was afraid we were going to run into some of her colleagues. She asked me to take off my wedding ring, just in case. I felt distant and left out and that I didn't fit into the world she had been in for the last several days. It felt as if she were having to switch channels, from the workshop with her colleagues, to me and our trip.

That afternoon I called Ethel Moore, a friend I had met in England years ago who lived in San Diego. When I was living in the Carrington Woods Apartments, not long after I became a Catholic, I took a trip to England to improve my ability to teach British Literature. We were on a tour that began in England and then went on to Scotland and Wales. One night in Plymouth, the two of us went for a long walk, during which she told me that for years she had not been able to receive Communion in the Catholic Church. "I got pregnant in high school," she said, as we walked across a bridge. "I married the boy, but he panicked and then disappeared, leaving me high and dry." She looked at me and threw her arms up in the air. "Several years later when I met and married a wonderful man, I couldn't go to Communion. It wasn't easy to get an annulment back then," she said. "We had our children, and for years I sat in the pew while my husband and children went up to receive Communion."

"What happened?" I asked her. "When did you finally get to receive Communion?"

"When my husband died," she said. "And I'll tell you one thing. If that Anglican tour guide tries to prevent us from going to Mass Sunday in Stratford-on-Avon, there's going to be hell to pay."

On Sunday morning in Stratford-on-Avon, Ethel had gathered up all the Catholics on the tour and arranged for us to wait in the hotel lobby for a bus to take us to mass. The tour guide did not let her down, and we received the Eucharist in Shakespeare's hometown.

Years later I had flown to San Diego to give a workshop, when I visited Ethel and stayed a few extra days to be with her. She had begun teaching enameling classes, and she showed me how she did her art and gave me some of her pieces, a small tray containing a purple iris, and a green pendant to wear around my neck. She also told me about a Tour of Madonnas that her parish held every Christmas. People made Madonnas out of papier-mâché and then went from one house to the other to view them. One of her handmade Madonnas was beside my bed in the room I slept in at her house, and when I left, she gave it to me, tied in a cardboard box with a white string. I flew back to Georgia with the Madonna under my feet, and it is now on the end of the piano in our living room.

When I called Ethel that day of Letha's conference in San Diego, I had planned that if it was convenient for her, Letha and I would go to see her and take her out to dinner. She would have been in her nineties by then. But when Ethel answered the phone, she didn't know who I was. She was friendly, but she was confused. "Now who are you again?" she kept asking. "How do I know you?"

I told her about meeting her in England and about visiting her, that she had given me some of her enamels and her Madonna. But she couldn't remember, and I could tell that I was upsetting her. I wished her well and got off the phone. Another loss.

The drive was, as we expected, gorgeous. On our left was the turquoise-blue ocean; on our right, the mountains. Purple flowers were everywhere, big round balls on long stems. In Santa Barbara, we stayed at the Lavender Inn, a bed-and-breakfast with wine and cheese, cookies and milk, and pretty furniture. At the beach where we had dinner, people were walking their dogs. A man in a wetsuit tried to surf on small waves as the tide came in, his daughter in a tiny identical wetsuit riding the waves on her stomach. We watched a couple taking selfies on the beach as the sun set; they made a black silhouette against the orange and red, their feet standing on the shiny wet sand reflecting in the pink light.

As we drove the next day, the grape orchards began to appear, miles and miles of them. We ate dinner at Nepenthe, a restaurant on top of the mountain at Big Sur. Near us was a gay male couple who kept looking over at our table. Letha began talking with them, and I joined in. They were from Seattle and were on their way to San Diego, driving the Pacific Coast Highway going in the opposite direction from us.

"So what do you do?" Letha asked.

The younger blond, darkly tanned and handsome, answered that he worked in construction, building houses on the sides of mountains in San Diego. The other man had bushy black hair with gray streaks and was a history teacher in a high school. Letha told them about the Lavender Inn where we had stayed in Santa Barbara, and they said they would check it out on their way. Then we learned that they had stayed in Cannery Row in Monterey where we were headed. To my surprise, Letha told them that we were married.

"Cool!" said the blond. "In what state?"

"Vermont," Letha said.

The blonde nudged his partner with his elbow. "See?" he said. Then he looked at us and said, "We'll get there!" Pointing to the gray-haired man, he said, "He's nervous. He thinks I'm too young."

Back on the highway, we stopped at a roadside stand and found fruit for sale that was freshly picked from a nearby farm. The strawberries were huge and bright red, and we bought a couple of baskets. On Saturday, June 30, we arrived in Monterey. Our hotel was the Spindrift Inn in Cannery Row. I bought Steinbeck's novel of that name and began reading it in that location. It was fascinating to read stories about the buildings up and down the street and the imaginary people who could have lived and worked there. For dinner that night we ate at a restaurant beside the water and watched out the window at the sea lions stretched out on the rocks below. After dinner we went to a dark bar with loud music and had drinks. Many couples were dancing, and I kept nudging Letha, trying to get her to dance with me, but she was hesitant. She was afraid the people in the bar would become angry if we did, and she could have been right.

Driving the next day, we saw the lettuce growing in the fields in Carmel and artichokes in Castroville, the artichoke capital of the world. The globe artichokes in the market were huge and piled on top of one another. We had no way to bring them back to Georgia, but we wanted to. Nearby, they grew tall in the fields. Further along, migrants worked their way across fields of strawberries.

On Sunday, July 1, we arrived in San Francisco, where we stayed at Fisherman's Wharf. On Monday, July 2, we visited a French Restaurant outside the gates of China Town. We drank wonderful coffee, ate Madeleines, and I remembered Marcel Proust's scene in which one taste of the sweet pastry took him back to another time and place. In China Town people were waiting for something to happen. Strings of paper fireworks were hanging over the street, and people stood around as if a parade was coming.

"When does it start?" Letha asked a stout Chinese woman wearing yellow and red.

"When the important people get here," the woman answered. Soon a long black limousine pulled up in the street and six Chinese men dressed in black suits got out. A man in blue jeans nearby lit the string of fireworks, and they went off, loud popping and hissing and shooting fire from one side of the street to the other, finally stopping and leaving the street filled with smoke. The audience applauded.

We had heard that sometimes San Francisco was foggy and that tourists couldn't see the Golden Gate Bridge, that there was even a large billboard for people to stand in front of to take a picture, if necessary. But that wasn't the case with us. The sky was clear, and we drove back and forth across that incredible bridge, amazed that we were really there.

Soon we called Lila, the young cop that I had met on the cruise. She came to our hotel in her patrol car and wearing her black police uniform. I introduced her to Letha, and she gave me a high-five. "Way to go, Girl," she said to me, grinning. After sitting beside the pool with her on the cruise, it was strange to see her there in her uniform.

"You're the reason we're together," I said. "I did what you said and got on Match.com."

She put us into the back of her patrol car and took our picture. I had no idea how uncomfortable the backseat of a police car was; it was made of hard plastic with no upholstery and almost no room for our feet. Then Lila took us on a personal tour of the Castro District, which used to be her beat. The first thing we saw were naked old men sitting at tables outside a restaurant. All day we passed people that Lila knew.

Lila was determined that I was going to go to my first gay bar. Since I had first gone to Wings, I had heard my friends talking about the gay bars they had been to in Atlanta, but I had never been to one. We walked up and down the street as she looked for one she could take me to, but none of them seemed to be what she wanted. Finally, she led us into a dark bar that had only one patron, an older man sitting at the bar. We sat at a table and ordered drinks, but it was nothing special, and Lila was disappointed.

Then we went to the Gay and Lesbian Museum and saw the Harvey Milk Memorial. We also saw the pantsuits of Del Martin and her partner, Phyllis Lyon, who were married on June 16, 2008. Theirs was the first same-sex marriage to take place in San Francisco. They were eighty-four and eighty-seven on their wedding day. A Catholic Church in the Castro district stated on a sign out front that it was inclusive and that it was "in the Catholic tradition," words that meant that it was probably not sanctioned by Rome. I wanted to see inside, but the doors were locked.

On July 4, we went on a fireworks cruise in the San Francisco bay. Milledgeville was having the hottest summer ever, but in California we were freezing, even in hoodies and jackets. Mark Twain wrote that the coldest winter he ever spent was July in San Francisco. Letha and I looked like two little old ladies with our heads wrapped up in hoodies, strings pulled tight under our chins. The boat was full, and we were sitting on a bench being jostled by others on all sides. We could see the lights of the Gharidelli chocolate shop on the shore. Then I saw a full moon that sat right under the Bay Bridge while the fireworks went off around it. Looking at it, I felt a still center grow in me and a sense of awe that the still moon was settled there in the midst of all the man-made bluster and flashing lights. The full yellow moon, resting there in the arch between the two peaks of the bridge. I reached over and squeezed Letha's hand.

§

Back in Milledgeville, I picked up Carmen and took her to chemo. Her hair had thinned and was cut short. The blonde had grown out, and her hair had become silver like her mother's. Her eyes looked big and brown in her thin face. She told me that she and Janet had been talking about which was worse, what Carmen was going through or what Janet was going through. She told me that, if it were up to her, she would ask the Lord to take her then, but she kept holding on for Janet and her family. She said she prayed for Janet every day. She was trying to teach Janet how to cook and how to wash and stack the towels, that she should put the fresh towels on the bottom of the stack and take the new ones off the top. I didn't tell her that Letha and I repeatedly washed the same ones and hung them back up. Carmen had her way of doing things, and she wanted Janet to learn. She weighed eighty-five pounds then, but she wore clothes that fit her and dressed up in makeup and earrings. She did not want to look sick, and, despite the way her body was ravaged, she was still a beautiful woman.

We had all begun talking about death. Letha and I had been writing our own obituaries. We had gone down to my family's plot in Memory Hill Cemetery to see if there would be room for us to be buried there. We decided that if we were cremated, we could both be buried under one slab, my name at one end and hers at the other. There would be room for us beside my daddy.

§

In mid-January, 2013, a group of us went on the Olivia Fortieth Anniversary Cruise to the Caribbean. Janet and Carmen had planned to go with us, as a way for them to have some rest; but as the time neared for us to go, they cancelled because they were afraid to be away from Carmen's doctors. "There is no rest from this cancer," Janet said.

The book I took to read on the cruise was *Alice in Wonderland* by Lewis Carroll. As I read, I saw the metaphors that connected Alice's journey to my own. I thought of my childhood "Alice in Wonderland" doll sitting at home on the shelf, legs sticking out, no shoes on her feet, and her long shiny locks cut short. I remembered sitting on my bed at home, the scissors in my hand slicing through her hair, the strands lying neatly in a pile on my pillow like the men's hair Daddy used to let fall to the floor in his barbershop. I read about the journey

Alice took through the mazes underground, the people and animals she met, each of whom taught her something she needed to know, the looking glass which told her the truth about herself, and her journey home, where she rose into the light, surprising everyone with her new-found understanding of herself and who she was.

In Curacao, we went into the caves and saw bats. We saw a rock formation that was supposed to be the Virgin Mary. I stood in front of that image, and I felt drawn to it. I realized that I could not turn away from Mary. She was so close to me that, as I left the cave and walked into the light, I was speaking to the Mary I carried in my mind, No matter what else happens, I will not turn away from you.

The last night of the cruise was the most special. It focused on the beginning of Olivia Records forty years ago that recorded the music of Meg Christian and Cris Williamson, two lesbian singers. It was also the beginning of the fight for Gay Civil Rights, something I knew nothing about. One speaker said, "I knew that I was a lesbian, but I was the only lesbian in the world, as most of us were." Remembering myself in the early seventies, I knew exactly what she was talking about, and we were sitting in a full auditorium of women who also knew. Another speaker said that there were 2400 women on our ship. "The world has no idea how many of us there are," she said.

Back in the time when Judy Dlugacz was starting Olivia Records, I was angry at always being the one to cook for Harvill, standing up at NOW meetings saying that I was tired of being a maid. Everybody, the speaker said, was fighting her own internalized homophobia in her own way. Wow. I was not alone. Letha was not alone, as she led her public and her private life. Years ago, I had discovered Cris Williamson's music. She was my age, and I listened to her songs in secret and felt guilty for doing so. I had books hidden on my shelf behind other books, books that I was so afraid someone would find that I eventually wrapped them up in brown paper and threw them into the trash. At the time I was marrying Harvill in Milledgeville, the Stonewall Rebellions were happening in New York City. While I was confessing my sins in the priest's dark closet, my friends were living two lives, the open one at work and the secret one at home. One speaker asked from the stage, "How many of you are Catholic?" I didn't raise my hand. If I had wanted to, it wouldn't have been the popular thing to do. The next question from the stage was, "How many of you are reformed Catholics?" There was lots of laughter and hands raised. But I didn't raise my hand then either. I could not laugh at or make fun of what had meant so much to me.

That night I sobbed, as 2400 women swayed from side to side, their arms in the air, singing along with Cris Williamson and Meg Christian on stage. Billy Jean King was there, and all of those courageous women were fighting for us while I was having the affair with Ellen and thinking that she and I were aberrations. I pulled Letha close to me, and we stood arm in arm and swayed, singing the lyrics to Cris Williamson's "Song of the Soul" in unison with all the women on the ship. Over the years this song had become a lesbian anthem: "Love of my life I am crying; I am not dying, I am dancing; Dancing along in the madness, There is no sadness, Only the song of the soul."

One evening Letha wanted us to go to a disco on the ship. When we got to the door, it was dark and crowded inside, and the music was very loud. Letha felt excited because it reminded her of the gay bars she had gone to. But it felt frightening to me, and I couldn't make myself go in. I knew that I had disappointed her.

§

All my life I have seen symbols. As a student at Georgia Southern University, I passed a small dogwood tree each morning on my way to class. For several days the tree held two blooms, side by side. I had been reading *Wuthering Heights* in my English class. One morning as I passed, one of the blooms was gone, leaving a single bloom. I stopped a moment, and, remembering the deceased Catherine tapping on the window of Heathcliff's room in an attempt to be re-united with Heathcliff in that space between the living and the dead, I pulled off the single bloom that was left alone on the tree. I remembered that time, as we all feared for the day when Janet would be alone.

One month we held the potluck at Janet and Carmen's house. I took my sweet potato casserole with the brown sugar and pecan topping because Carmen liked it. I also took my cranberry congealed salad with the nuts and celery and the sour cream topping. Barbara and Judy brought several desserts and cornbread dressing. Jan and Shirley brought green bean casserole. It was good for us all to be together again.

§

February 14, 2013, was Letha's and my fourth wedding anniversary. Letha told me that Valentine's Day was something she always hated as a child because she never got any Valentines in her box. I made her a Valentines Box and filled it with notes of all the things I loved about her. The covered shoebox was full. When she got home from work that day, I told her that I had a program planned. I typed out the words to Meg Christian's "Valentine Song." Then I gave it to Letha and asked her to follow along while I played it on my phone. "With happiness here for our taking, Resting easy, feeling strong, As I delight in this life that we're making, I sing you this Valentine Song." Then we read our wedding vows to each other again.

§

One day when I took my walk beside the Oliver Hardy Lake near our house, I saw that the white duck I usually saw swimming with the geese was alone. The geese that stayed there all summer had left for the winter. Then, waddling from under a bush, was one remaining goose. As I watched, the goose went into the water, flapped its wings, and then went back to the shore and walked up to the duck. The two appeared to have become a couple. Geese, I had heard, mated for life. The goose was saying to the duck, I stayed to be with you.

§

One Tuesday when I got home from Wings, I noticed that my purple bracelet was not on my arm. I panicked, afraid that it was a sign. Then I found it on the floor of the closet and put it back around my wrist. I was relieved.

Carmen was getting worse. Death hung over our heads and sat on our shoulders. Time went by. It was summer. The yellow angel trumpet was blooming, the blossoms bowing their heads towards the ground as if praying. One day I came home to find a branch broken, and again I thought it was a sign. I tried to prop the branch up, to make it live, but the next morning the leaves and the blooms had shriveled on that one fallen branch.

Carmen had begun to gain weight, all fluid build-up around her abdomen. It was affecting her the way that Mama's ovarian cancer had affected her. The fluid increased every day and made Carmen so heavy that she couldn't stand up by herself but had to be pushed around in a wheelchair. Finally the fluid seeped from her pores and ran down her legs and puddled on the floor around her feet. Janet tried taping together Kotex pads to lay across Carmen's stomach to collect the fluid. I set up my sewing machine and began cutting baby diapers into long strips and sewing them together again the way I had for Mama. Janet told me that they worked much better than the Kotex pads.

§

I went out one evening to the back yard with the dogs and found a dead bird lying on the step. Sometimes when that happened, the bird had flown into the window and was stunned. When I picked it up, the bird would wake up and fly away. But this one was dead. It was a purple finch, the bird Teeny had described as a sparrow dipped in cranberry juice. Its head and neck were a soft red. Its eyes were closed, and it was beautiful in death. I smoothed the soft feathers with my fingers. Its stillness gave me that sad feeling of awe and silence that came with death. Each death was new, and one never prepared you for the next. I buried the finch in the front flowerbed underneath a small stone angel, my favorite piece of yard art.

The next morning as I made my coffee, I looked out the window and saw another purple finch exactly like the other one sitting on the rim of the birdbath. It was sitting still and staring, looking stunned. Its feathers were wet and ragged because it had just bathed. It kept tilting its head to one side. Something in me wanted to go and try to wake up the dead bird that I had buried and say, "Come on! Your partner is missing you! You can't go yet!" Then the finch flew into the weeping cherry tree and perched there among the leaves. Almost immediately several other finches flew into the branches, surrounding the bird.

§

One day Janet asked me to come stay with Carmen in the hospital so that she could run some errands. Carmen slept the whole time Janet was gone, and I watched her. All her hair was gone, her head was as round and white as an onion, and her chest was hollow. Her fingers on top of the sheet looked like bones. Her mouth was open, and her breathing was labored. Her swollen stomach rose under the sheet as if she were pregnant.

When Janet came back, she leaned over Carmen and said, "How are you, Hon?" Instead of looking at Janet, Carmen looked at me and asked, "You'll tell me when it's time, won't you? When it's time for me to let go?"

"You'll know when it's time," I said, "and you'll tell Janet, and she'll tell you it's okay."

But in truth, it wasn't okay with Janet. It would never be okay. Janet was in denial and was praying for a miracle, which she was still sure would come. "You can't go tomorrow," said Janet. "You've got a doctor's appointment."

At their next appointment, the doctor told Carmen and Janet that there was nothing else to be done, that she could have no more chemo. He recommended hospice. "But she'll die if we go with hospice," said Janet. Serenity Hospice came and signed Carmen into their program.

They brought a hospital bed and a bedside potty chair and many pads to collect the seeping fluids. They gave Janet instructions for Carmen's around-the-clock pain medicine. Carmen's parents came back from Puerto Rico to stay the duration. Her father was quiet, and her mother cried non-stop and wouldn't leave Carmen's side. Janet never had any time alone with Carmen.

One night Letha woke me up at 3:00 a.m. She had dreamed that I was cold and dead beside her. We decided that we had been talking about death too much. I comforted her and convinced her that I was alive.

One Tuesday Janet asked us all to come to their house for Wings. Someone went to the Brick and brought a big basket of wings, flats and drums, and celery with containers of bleu cheese and ranch dressing. When we arrived, Carmen was lying in the hospital bed and was only partially aware that we were there. We were in the kitchen laughing and talking, and the door was open to Carmen's room. We took turns going in and out, standing beside her bed, quiet and still. We leaned over and kissed Carmen's forehead and whispered that we loved her. Her lips moved as she tried to whisper back.

A few days later Janet called and told us that it wouldn't be long. She wanted us to come out. We stood around Carmen's bed and sang songs, "Amazing Grace," "How Great Thou Art," and a Spanish song that Carmen's parents knew, something that translated into someone walking beside the seashore and leaving all their belongings in the boat. It was a song that I used to play on the organ for Carmen at Mass, and we always sang the last verse in Spanish.

Remembering that Carmen used to tell her dying AIDS patients to follow the light, Janet turned on the lamp on the dresser. Carmen opened her eyes and looked up at all of us standing around her bed. "I'm ready to go!" she said, her voice momentarily strong, "and you are all holding me back!"

When we left, Janet was crying. "I knew this would happen if we went with hospice," she said. No one tried to reason with her.

On July 16, 2014, at four a.m. our phone rang beside the bed. I answered, and Janet's voice said, "Carmen has gone to be with Jesus." She wanted us to come out.

When we got there, Carmen's body was lying on the bed, covered in a sheet up to her chin. Her mother was sitting beside the bed with her hand on Carmen's forehead, which was still warm. Janet paced back and forth between the kitchen and the death room. The funeral home people were on their way. Janet had made them promise that they wouldn't put Carmen in a black plastic bag. "We don't do that," the man assured her.

While we waited, Janet and Carmen's mother bathed Carmen's body. The door was closed, and when they invited us back in, Carmen was lying on the bed wearing a red-flowered dress. Powder and lipstick were on her face, and she looked pretty, as if she were about to jump up and put on her dancing shoes.

The memorial service was held at Sacred Heart Catholic Church. The priest said that Carmen had taught him a lot about what it meant to be a Christian and a good person. He looked out at the mourners in the church, most of them gay women, and he said, "Don't let anyone, *anyone*, keep you from your faith." On the second *anyone*, he looked directly at me.

One night several days later I dreamed that Carmen had come back. We were all sitting outside around a barbeque, and she came and sat beside me. I was happy to see her, and I asked, "What is it like?"

"Heaven is dark," she said, "and there are a lot of old people there."

I thought in my dream that maybe each person's Heaven was personal, and that maybe Carmen's Heaven seemed dark to her because we weren't there with her.

§

I didn't dream about Teeny for several years, not until Letha came into my life. Then the dreams came, one after the other. I dreamed that she was alive, and we were together. She was really here. I could touch her and smell her, the way her neck smelled under her ear. We were in the parish hall of the Catholic Church, and people kept coming in and interrupting her. She was trying to tell me something important, that something had changed, but I couldn't understand what she was saying. I told her how much I missed the Catholic Church, and she was puzzled. "Miss it?" she asked. "Why would you miss it?"

"I was fired," I told her, and she seemed puzzled about that, as if she wanted me to explain more. I did, however, feel that she was on my side and still loving me. She was still trying to tell me something, and I was straining to hear, but we kept getting interrupted, and her voice was so soft that I couldn't make out the words. It seemed to me that she was going to say that things could be different now, that she had changed her mind and that we could be intimate in all the ways a couple could be, but I wasn't sure that's what she was going to say, and it seemed that she was saying it because she saw that I was with Letha. I was jumping ahead in my mind thinking about the position that would put me in, that I would be expected to choose. I felt loyal to Letha, and what I was most inclined to say to Teeny was that it was too late, that I was already with Letha now, and that if she had made this decision sooner, we could have been together. I felt comfortable with her, and she seemed more open with me, as if she were showing me how she really felt about me. She was looking at me, and when we hugged and people walked in, she didn't jump and pull back or act embarrassed. I hated to wake up because it felt good being with her, but it was also a relief when I realized that she wasn't really back alive and I wasn't really having to choose between Letha and her.

§

In the Presbyterian Church I tried to make myself believe. It was almost like trying to change myself again, not from gay to straight, but from Catholic to Presbyterian. I cannot be a Catholic, I said to myself. I do not believe any longer what you have to believe to be a Catholic. I do not believe that the Pope is infallible. I do not believe in the apostolic succession. I do not believe that the only host that is real must be consecrated by a direct descendant of Peter. I do not believe that I have to confess my sins to a priest for them to be forgiven. I no longer believe that being as good as I can possibly be is the path to my salvation. I do believe, however, as John Calvin taught, that it is not possible for me to be good enough for salvation. Salvation is God's gift freely given and God's grace. It cannot be earned, and there is nothing, absolutely nothing, that I can do to deserve it.

One night I dreamed again that I was back at the Catholic Church. Letha was with me, and I had gone to say Goodbye. I was standing in front of the priest, and he put his hands up, palms facing me and asked me to put my palms against his and to lean forward toward him. As I did so, he said the words, "Blacks, Vietnamese, Chinese." He thought that I was going to draw back when he said those words.

I said to him, "If you think that, then you don't know me very well." Then I asked that he lean towards me with our palms touching. As he did so, I said the word "Gay." He looked startled, and that was the end of my dream.

While Letha was at work, I found myself lost in daydreams, sitting in my chair and staring into space. I could not clear my mind of my longing and my dilemma:

I am banished. I want to be who God made me to be. I want to bring Letha, my wife, and stand before God and feel his blessing. Why can't mine and Letha's love be blessed the way men's and women's love is blessed? I feel shut out, want in, want it to change, it wants me to change, we cannot fit together like hand and glove, we are mismatched, how can it be that Letha and I are accused? The church and I are looking at one another...you must change. You cannot bring that dark part of you inside. No, you must change. I cannot accept your dark parts. How can I want and not want the same thing? I want this church that I am banished from and some of whose practices repulse me.

It is ironic that I was a half person walking around with something inside me that I could not bring out into the open. Now I love a church that also has big things inside that are dark, that should be changed. I guess that's why the light and the dark are inseparable. How can I be a lesbian and a good person at the same time? How can I be a Catholic and not a Catholic at the same time? It seems that there is truly no place for me. I know no way to have what I love and deny what I don't believe or feel is evil. In the Catholic Church, does the darkness outweigh the light. Or vice versa?

I am in a dilemma. How can I reconcile these things? What I love is what I love, and it is big. What I hate is what I hate, and it, too, is big. And yet, nothing else is the same for me. I go to the Methodist Church, and I can pray. I hear a good sermon, I sing. I take away something to think about. I am in community with other people. I go to the Presbyterian Church, and I can pray. I hear a good sermon by a woman pastor. I have study groups to go to where we discuss interesting topics, I take away something to think about. But it isn't the same. It feels as though I am missing Jesus as I grieve the Catholic Church. Inside me are still the Liturgical seasons, the rosary, the Sacred Heart of Jesus, and Mary. Inside me is still Jesus, Mary, and Joseph, the holy family. It is the Mass I miss. It is the Mystery I miss. I am trying to make the other churches be the same for me, but something important is missing.

On March 4, 2013, I told Letha, sobbing, "I miss the Catholic Church." I thought she would be angry or think I had lost my mind, but she was kind. She was understanding. She wanted me to be happy.

When I have a dilemma, I make a list of pros and cons:

The things I love about the Catholic Church:

- The Blessed Mother
- The Sacred Heart of Jesus
- All the Angels and Saints
- The Holy Eucharist
- The Rosary
- The Real Presence
- Benediction
- The Mass, especially the Mass
- The personal relationship with Jesus in the Blessed Sacrament
- The Gregorian Chant
- Cantoring the Psalm
- Playing the organ, the way it feels like praying
- The Holy Water, the Sacramentals, the Incense
- The Tantum Ergo
- The Stations of the Cross
- The Daily Mass
- The Liturgical Seasons
- The people I know who miss me, whom I miss

The things I don't like, or no longer believe, about the Catholic Church:

- The Pope, the big boss of all things
- Confession, I can talk to God directly, I don't have to go through a priest
- The belief in the Infallibility of the Pope
- The Apostolic Succession

- The All-Male Hierarchy
- The exclusivity, that only a Roman Catholic priest can change the host into the body of Christ
- The rigidity of being out of touch with real people in the real world
- No women priests
- No married priests
- No gay people receiving the Eucharist or even playing the organ
- Priest sex abuse
- Secrecy, Fear of Scandal
- So far away from the Gospel, from the teachings of Jesus

The dreams about Teeny continued. At first the dreams were of me trying to get to her and not being able to. In one dream I climbed up several flights of stairs to where she was supposed to be, and when I got there, two glass doors were locked between her and me. Behind the second glass door, Teeny was sitting in a chair. I knocked and knocked and called her name, but she couldn't hear me. Then I had a couple of dreams in which Teeny was alive and living here in Milledgeville, but I had left her for Letha. I was feeling bad about that and was trying to get the three of us together, trying to convince both Letha and Teeny how much they would like each other and trying to persuade Letha to let Teeny come live with us. In one dream, we were all together. Teeny and I were more intimate than we ever were during her life on earth, and at the end I persuaded her and Letha both to join me in a group hug. I could feel and smell both of them, all of our faces so close that I could feel their breath on my face and their skin against my cheeks.

On March 12, 2013, Letha left for school at 6:30. I always got up with her and after she left, I often went back to bed and had long imaginative dreams that I looked forward to. I never knew what would be there when I climbed back into the covers and settled in. But that morning I sat in my chair with a heavy heart. I had been watching the Roman Catholic Cardinals on TV going into the Conclave to elect a new Pope. Letha had been watching with me, and she knew how drawn I was to the whole proceeding. The night before, Letha had said something to me that I thought was important. She said that I should go to the priest and tell him that he had wronged me and that I needed to forgive him.

After she left, I sat in the chair and cried and thought and prayed until I had made up my mind. Daily mass was at twelve. At ten until twelve I dressed and drove in to mass. At the front of the church I made the sign of the cross, bowed, and went in and sat next to Gerty, who was saying the rosary. The sun was coming through the long windows, and it was too bright and too hot, reflecting off the shiny wooden pews. I wanted to move into a shadow, but I didn't want to hurt Gerty's feelings. I knew that she would think my being there was an answer to her prayer.

Everybody I remembered was there, about ten people, and they told me they were glad to see me. I was the Prodigal Daughter. Rose Smith was there and John and Mary Hargaden and Mary Thomas and her son George and the Phillipino man who delivered Meals on Wheels and lived down the street. He hugged me tightly for a long time. I didn't know that my absence had mattered that much to him. It seemed that many people had been grieving for me, or for something to do with me. Were they feeling sorry for me? As the priest was preparing the altar, Gerty called out, "Father! Father! Look who's here!"

Father said from the altar, "Sandra, we are glad to see you. Welcome."

Communion was difficult for me, to be the only one not going. I felt sad and could not stop crying in front of everyone. The responses had changed over the four years I had been away, and I said them wrong. In the small group, others could hear that I said the old responses. I had forgotten about not singing the Alleluia during Lent.

Afterwards Deacon John came up and asked if I wanted to talk. I said, "I need to talk to him," pointing to Father in his purple vestments standing on the porch.

Deacon John said, "Let's catch him. He has a way of sneaking out."

The priest took me into his office in the rectory—the same place where he fired me—and gave me a box of Kleenex. He said it was a new box. Funny that I remember that. He had aged a lot; he had flecks of gray in his hair.

I looked out the window as I began, but then I looked directly at him, into his eyes. I said to him, "I want you to let me talk and not say anything until I am finished." He nodded in agreement. I waited a minute until I could talk, and then I said, "I am a Catholic. I am not a Methodist. I am not a Presbyterian. I am a Catholic. From the time I felt a calling in 1975, I have been a Catholic. I have played the organ for twenty-five years, and I have sung the Psalm. It has meant so much to me. I am angry at you, and I need to forgive you. I have been hurt by you. When you told me I couldn't play the organ and cantor the Psalm anymore, you ripped my heart out. That was my way of praying."

Out the window a teenager was riding a bicycle down the sidewalk. I blew my nose. The priest sat quietly. Then I looked back up at him and continued. "Father McWhorter liked hearing me sing. He loved my voice, and he told me so all the time. You took away my voice in more ways than one. You took away my way of praying—singing—you put shame on me. You hurt me to the core. You took away everything that meant anything to me, and I need to forgive you. I miss the Catholic Church."

He was still listening to me, and he did not interrupt.

I continued, "You told me, 'You and Letha are welcome to worship with us.' But you can't tell me that. This is my church. You had just come here. I had been here for thirty-five years. Letha and I were no different from Janet and Carmen, and yet you took them Communion regularly. You let Janet take communion to Carmen, and I'm glad that you did. It seems wrong to me that whether or not I can receive Communion depends on what the priest knows or doesn't know. What am I guilty of? Of finding love. Did you even think about it? It seemed as if it was easy for you. I want to come back, and I want to go to Communion." There, I said it. I sat quietly, spent, waiting for him to speak.

He waited for a little while, to be sure that I was finished, and then he said, "I prayed and prayed. I couldn't sleep at night. I kept wondering if there was another way. The problem was that it was public. When Myrtle Ewers showed the invitation to me, there was the picture and the date, and I had no choice but to ask the Bishop what I should do." He told me that because it was public and I was an employee of the church that he had no choice but to address it. The bishop told him to have a witness. "I hated having to do it," he said. "You played the organ with such passion and sang with such feeling, and I loved hearing you. But I felt I had no choice."

"I want to come back, and I want to go to Communion," I told him.

At that point, he looked out the window and asked me, "How far are you from St. Joseph's in Macon, or Christ our King and Savior in Greensboro?"

He was suggesting that I could receive Communion in one of those other churches, where I am not known.

"For four years," I told him, "People that I don't even know have come up and told me how much they miss me. One of the things I have always loved about the Catholic Church is that people don't worry about one another's sins; they only worry about their own."

"People tell me all the time how much they miss you," he said.

"Don't you see how confusing this is for lay people?" I asked. "When they see scandal in the Catholic Church and Priests abusing children?"

"Yes," he said. "I do see. Out of my class of nine priests, only four are still priests." Then he told me that if I came to him in the Communion line, he could not deny me, that priests are not supposed to make a scene at the altar, that they are not supposed to "presume."

"I can guarantee you," I said, "that I would never even get in the Communion line unless I believed I was worthy to receive the Lord."

After we talked, I asked him if he felt better.

"Jesus always hates to lose a sheep," he said. "Any time I hear of one of our parishioners going somewhere else, I always blame myself."

"Are you sorry that Myrtle Ewers showed you the invitation?" I asked him.

"Oh, yes," he said. "I wish she never had."

"Why did she?" I asked.

He said he didn't know. But I think I know. Myrtle was one of the adult Catholics who depend on the church to tell them everything. She was afraid it would be wrong to come to our reception. So she asked the priest's permission, the way she might ask if it was ok to read a book, or watch a movie, or attend a family member's wedding at a non-Catholic church. I understood the kind of Catholic that Myrtle was. Because I used to be one.

My sister Linda asked me if I regretted having the reception. "The only thing I regret," I said, "is sending Myrtle Ewers an invitation."

I wrote a letter to Sister Jeannine and told her about my conversation with the priest. This was her response:

"Dear Sandra,

I am glad you spoke to the priest. What he did was not what Jesus would do. I believe that if you went to your church and went to Communion, you would actually be helping him, as well as your being nourished by the Body and Blood of Christ. According to canon law, a priest must give the Eucharist to anyone who comes to Communion because no one can judge the conscience of another. Yes, he may feel uncomfortable at first, but conversions entail being uncomfortable. St. Paul was somewhat uncomfortable when he was knocked off his horse!

"The people in the parish (which is the real Church) want you at church. To me, this is a sign. It's as though you are being called. Of course you need to decide what is best for you, where you feel God is calling you to be. I will pray for you, for the priest, and for the parishioners."

Peace and blessings,

Sister Jeanine

On March 13, 2013, Pope Francis was chosen. Letha and I watched the proceedings on TV all day.

It took me a year and six months to make up my mind. Pope Francis had given me hope. On September 4, 2014, I called the church and asked the priest if I could come in to talk with him. We sat in the church on a pew near the back. I went to a casual face-to-face confession. I confessed being angry with him and with the church. I confessed missing Mass for four years. I told Father that I didn't agree with what he did but that I knew he did what he believed was right. I confessed trying to join the Reformation. I did not mention Letha and me at all. At the end, Father put out his hand and said, "Welcome home! And for your penance, you can go home and celebrate." Later that evening I sent him a text and told him that for my penance, Letha and I were having brie and pate.

On June 26, 2015, the Supreme Court overturned DOMA and ruled that same sex marriage is legal throughout the United States. It is the law of the land. We were ecstatic. The White House was lit up in rainbow lights, as was Disneyland, Niagara Falls, and the Empire

State Building. Facebook streaming was covered with colorful rainbows. Saturday night, June 27, 2015, I went to Mass, still feeling happy. I parked behind a white truck and then looked up to see written in big red letters on the back windshield, "The Supreme Court has no Christian values." I knew that the truck belonged to someone who had just walked into Mass.

The priest's sermon was all about the Supreme Court decision, how sad it was, how the priest feared that the Catholic Church would be persecuted, how he, as a Vietnamese immigrant, knew what persecution was. I wanted to stand and say, "Let me tell you about persecution!" He began by saying that the church teaches love and acceptance for gays, and I could tell that he was leading up to the big *but* that would negate everything that he had said. Then he said that what the Supreme Court did was wrong and that he would not be able to perform such marriages.

I stared straight at him the whole time. Briefly, briefly, I doubted myself. Had I made the wrong decision to come back? Then I corrected myself. The priest is not God. The priest is not Jesus. He is simply a man, and many other priests feel and act differently. Then I remembered what Sister Jeannine had said, that the hierarchy is not the church; the lay people are the church, and I knew that, never mind the owner of the white truck, the majority of the people at Mass are happy for Letha and me. I decided that my life is a sermon, as Sister Jeannine had said, and that I would not let him make me feel that he speaks for the whole church, because he doesn't. I was in good voice that night, and I sang loudly, louder than the others in the congregation. We sang all five verses of "Amazing Grace," and it was as though I was leading the singing with my voice. Amazing Grace. When it was time for the Eucharist, when I put out my hands for

Father to give me the host, when he said, "The Body of Christ," I all but shouted AMEN! I left after Communion because I did not want to speak to the priest that night, but I continued to think to myself, My life is a sermon, and this is my church.

The next time I went to Mass, I sat beside the aisle, and Father put his arm around my shoulders both as he entered and as he exited. He said in his homily that he has to say what he believes, because that is who he is. My sister Linda told me that I have to allow him to have his feelings and beliefs, the same as I have mine. After Mass when I went to speak to him, he threw his arms out and gave me a big hug and told me to tell Letha hello.

One Saturday night before Mass began, Mavis Trueblood, a woman whose children I had taught, turned around and said to me, "I am so glad you have come back. You know, we all have ways in which we fall short, and sometimes, the priest (she pointed towards the altar) falls short too."

I am a different Catholic from the one who left in 2010. I am watching to see where the church will go. I am watching to see what changes Pope Francis will make. When I go to Mass, I pray directly to Jesus, and I ask him to show me the way. I thank him daily for sending Letha into my life and for helping me to accept myself as he made me.

When Pope Francis came to America, Letha and I watched him together on television. As we watched him at the bottom of Ground Zero, we couldn't talk. We could hardly breathe as we watched the massive crowd, the people holding their hands up, seeking something that the Pope wanted to give. The Pope's message was love and peace. And yet, when I went to Mass at Sacred Heart that weekend, the priest didn't even mention the Pope's visit or his message but instead focused on the gospel for the evening: If your eye offends you, pluck it out. If your right hand offends you, cut it off. It is better to go to Heaven with one hand than to go to Gehenna with both.

I ate of the tree of knowledge, and now I know that which I did not know. Teeny was a scientist, and yet she believed everything with no contradictions. When I think now of believing all I once believed, I sense a squirrely doubter on my shoulder, laughing in my ear. At Mass the figure of the priest rises up, a black shadow with arms out like webbed bat wings, obscuring my view of Jesus and the altar.

Recently when I went to the Vigil Mass on a Saturday night, I sat all the way at the front on the left side, in front of the statue of the Blessed Mother. In all my years of going to that church, I had never sat at the front. Up close to the altar that way, I began to feel what I once felt. I could see around the priest to the altar, and I could pray, the way I once could. The ending lines of Gerard Manley Hopkins' "God's Grandeur" came to me: "Because the Holy Ghost over the bent world broods with warm breast and with ah! bright wings." My life is a sermon, I thought again. My life is a sermon.

In September, 2015, a couple in our group, Amy and Jeanette, got legally married in Georgia. They are younger than most of us and work in law enforcement. Genie, a single in our group, is a preacher at a little white wooden church out in the country, Beulah Baptist Church. Her father and grandfather were preachers at the church before her, and she is the first woman pastor there. I am a substitute pianist for Genie. Amy and Jeanette chose to get married at their home when they had their potluck, and all of us went.

Wearing her rainbow stole, Genie stood with her wedding service book in the corner of the room in front of the fireplace. Amy and Jeanette stood in front of her. Letha and I, Barbara and Judy, Janet, and about six other couples stood in a group. I had my arm around Letha. When Genie began, "We are gathered here today to join Amy and Jeanette in Holy Matrimony," she choked up and said, "This is something we never thought we would be able to do in Georgia." We were all aware that we were involved in a moment in time.

And then we heard those glorious words from Genie that Letha and I had heard from our own pastor in Vermont on February 14, 2010: "By the authority invested in me by the state of Georgia and as a minister of the gospel of Christ, I pronounce that you can finally say to the world, We are married...spouses for life. What God has joined together, let no one put asunder."

Letha and I are happy. At the beginning we thought that we were just alike, and we noticed our similarities more than our differences. The longer we are together, however, the more we appreciate our differences. She still prefers to have cleaned off shelves, and clutter bothers her. I still like to have things out where I can see them. She prefers fantasy movies, and I prefer reality. But we have learned to compromise. We often do things for one another, things that make us both feel loved. She fixes the computer and helps me with technology, and I proofread and spell for her. She tightens the sheets and fluffs the pillows before we go to bed at night. I snuggle down and say, "I love the way you fix the bed."

"I love to hear you say that," she says.

I do the cooking, and she washes the dishes. Because she still works and I am retired, I get up with her, fix her lunch, and make her coffee in the morning. Because we found each other so late in life, we have become Vegan, hoping to have as many years together as we can. We eat lots of colorful fruits and vegetables, and we ask our bodies to be kind to us.

CHAPTER TEN: THE PRESENT

"When she transformed into a butterfly, the caterpillars spoke not of her beauty, but of her weirdness. They wanted her to change back into what she had always been.

But she had wings." --Dean Jackson

My African violets made my life a sandwich. In 1975, they grew in the sunny morning window in my Carrington Woods Apartment. I collected them into a nosegay and took them as an offering to Teeny. Forty-five years later I again have a sunny morning window filled with blooming violets, and Letha to love.

Letha has taken up drawing. Sitting beside me with a thin black art pen, she draws on a pad, intricate lines and shapes that come together to make a whole. She is good; she won best in drawing at our local visual arts competition. I have a photograph of her standing beside her framed drawing and smiling. When she is drawing, she is as lost in her drawing as I am in my writing. We go hours not speaking and yet, we say more than either of us has ever said to anyone else.

I have taken up swimming again. As a child I went to the city pool. Wearing a yellow tank suit, I took a deep breath and slowly let it out as I drifted to the bottom of the pool, the bubbles traveling in a row in front of my eyes, my hair waving like Medusa's, letting all the air out and sitting on the concrete bottom as long as I could, still, quiet, not needing breath. I almost got my Senior Lifeguard certification but for one thing: I was not able to swim to the bottom of the pool and bring the heavy drain cover to the surface. I tried and tried. Each time that

I got within three feet of the surface, I had to make a choice: drop the drain cover or drown.

Because returning to swimming is my new project, of course I have a swimsuit for every day of the week, swim caps to match, goggles, and a new waterproof iPod that I clip to my swimsuit. As I ease my way into the clear blue water, the feeling I have is peace, like moving through peace. I look forward to my swim every day, and I find that my body longs for the water in a primal way, like the water of the womb, of birth, of baptism, of rising to new life. As I go to sleep at night, I imagine myself gliding through the light blue of water, of sky, my arms moving like swimming, like flying.

Sandra Worsham

ACKNOWLEDGEMENTS

I would like to thank my family, Linda and Tom Waller, and the many cousins on both the Worsham and Fordham sides for loving and supporting me. Thank you also to Letha's sisters and brother-in-law for welcoming me into the family.

Thank you to my friends and family and to the "Wing Nuts" who read this book in its many drafts and gave me feedback. Thank you to Nancy Arnold Campbell and Audrey Roach for seeing the things that I didn't see.

Thank you to my writing teachers: Sarah Gordon, Jill McCorkle, Alice Mattison, Sheila Kohler, Betsy Cox, Peter Selgin, and Allen Gee. Each of you brought something different to my work, and together, you helped me to find my own voice.

Thank you to Frank and Pat at the Brick for your support in planning the cover photo, to photographer Joe DeGrandis, and to Letha Hawkins for the cover design.

Thank you to Robert Canipe at Third Lung Press for believing in my book enough to want to see it published. You are a wonderful new friend and a joy to work with.

Finally, thank you to Letha for designing my beautiful cover. I love our hours, sitting in our recliners, side-by-side, designing and proofing. I look forward to future times of being creative together. Thank you for putting up with my crazy moods during the times when I was procrastinating and for constant encouragement to keep writing. Thank you for believing in my ability and for the joy you bring to my life. I look forward to growing old with you.

ABOUT THE AUTHOR

Sandra Worsham's stories have been published in *Memphis Magazine, Carolina Quarterly, Western Humanities Review, Ascent,* and *Chattahoochee Review,* among others. She won "First in Fiction" in the *Red Hen Press* competition, and her story "Pinnacle" was published in the 2008 *Los Angeles Review.* Two of her stories were Finalists at *Glimmer Train.* After she retired from teaching writing to high school students for thirty years, her book on teaching writing, *Essential Ingredients: Recipes for Teaching Writing* was published by ASCD in 2001. She was Georgia's 1982 *Teacher of the Year* and a 1992 *Milken Award* winner. In 2000, she was inducted into the *National Teachers Hall of Fame.* In June, 2006, she received her MFA in Fiction from Bennington College. She lives in Milledgeville, Georgia, with her spouse and their two dogs.